Constructing identities in online communities of practice

Constructing identities in online communities of practice

A case study of online learning

Leila Kajee

PETER LANG
Oxford · Bern · Berlin · Bruxelles · Frankfurt am Main · New York · Wien

Bibliographic information published by Die Deutsche Bibliothek
Die Deutsche Bibliothek lists this publication in the Deutsche Nationalbibliografie; detailed bibliographic data is available on the Internet at <http://dnb.ddb.de>.

British Library and Library of Congress Cataloguing-in-Publication Data:
A catalogue record for this book is available from The British Library, Great Britain, and from The Library of Congress, USA

ISBN 978-3-03911-105-3

Cover Design: Kara Trapani, Peter Lang Ltd

Hochfeldstrasse 32, Postfach 746, CH-3000 Bern 9, Switzerland
info@peterlang.com, www.peterlang.com, www.peterlang.net

Printed in Germany

For my family, Farad, Alia and Jahaan, as always. Without you none of this would have been possible or worthwhile.

Contents

Preface

Having been involved in the educational sphere for many, many years as an English Language and Communication lecturer, I suppose it was inevitable that I became interested in the use of ICTs in the teaching and learning of English. So the journey began: I read voraciously, attended several conferences, and experimented in the field over the years. It didn't stop there, the thought of a PhD evolved, then the journey led to this publication. And all because I shared the anxieties felt by my students, and because I really didn't have a choice.

This book is located at the interface of online learning within a context of English language studies and academic literacy and is underpinned, from a critical theoretical perspective, by an understanding of the implications of the digital divide for developing countries worldwide. The work includes an exploration of online learning in an undergraduate English language and academic literacy classroom at a university in South Africa. The study draws on research and theorising that argues for the need for technology in developing countries as a means of social inclusion. The aim is to explore the extent to which communities of practice are enabled in an online environment, among English non-mother tongue speakers from technologically under-resourced backgrounds. To achieve the aim the study examines the extent to which the students participate, negotiate meaning, and construct identities in online spaces.

From a sociocultural perspective, and recognising that learning does not occur in isolation, the work of Lave and Wenger and others, who locate learning as a form of interaction and co-participation, and argue that learning occurs within specific contexts or communities of practice, is used to frame the study. Thus the focus on how individuals become members of 'communities of practice'. The study suggests that practice and participation are underpinned, and to some extent determined, by the identities constructed by participants in the online communities.

From observations, participant-interviews, questionnaires, written data, and the analysis of messages posted to discussion threads over the duration of a year, the study demonstrates that the online environment facilitates the construction of communities of practice, by enabling participants to develop and sustain local and global relationships, and to construct identities in the medium. The findings suggest that online environments be considered, not merely as alternative modes of delivery in the language classroom, but for social inclusion, provided that facilitators and learners are adequately prepared for the use of digital technology.

Acknowledgements

An endeavour as rigorous as getting a manuscript ready for publication is never a solitary one. In this case, I acknowledge the students who participated so enthusiastically in the project reported on in this work, and who still ask 'Are you done yet?' Now I can answer quite truthfully.

I also acknowledge the invaluable input of Professor Robert Balfour when this was still part of a PhD thesis in preparation, and possibilities of publication were just a glimmer in the author's eyes. Thank you for your support Robert.

Thank you too to Helena Sedgwick for her rigorous editing and constructive feedback.

List of figures

Introduction: A context for online communities of practice

An area of research

I observe as my students enter the computer laboratory for the first time, some excited at the prospect, others more apprehensive. Why are these students excited, yet afraid of switching on their computers, which many worldwide take for granted? Such ambivalence might be explained through the anxieties surrounding broader areas such as politics, the economy, and education in developing countries. In the educational sphere, for instance, policies are vigorously debated and planned, but sometimes only sporadically implemented and evaluated. Such is the case with information and communication technologies (ICTs) in educational environments in a newly democratic South Africa.[1] Current South African higher education policy documents[2] recommend the implementation of ICTs[3] and resource-based education. However, there is often a mismatch between what is articulated in policy and in its implementation, and the emergence of ICTs in social, political, and educational spheres has been met with some ambivalence in South Africa. On one hand, the use of ICTs is perceived as enabling developing countries to acquire the status of global players, while on the other hand, the lack of infrastructure and resources has a detrimental effect on global participation and devel-

1 South Africa attained its democracy in 1994.

2 Such as the *Green Paper on Higher Education* (1996), the *White Paper on Education and Training* (1994) and the *Higher Education Act* (1997). At primary and secondary school level, the *Draft White Paper on e-Education* (2004) is relevant.

3 Definitions of ICTs are varied, although it is generally understood by most to encompass electronics and computers. In this book I adopt Gunton's (1993) view of ICTs to include electronic technologies that are used to collect, store, process, and communicate information.

opment. However, South African researchers and stakeholders in education[4] imply that to withhold new technologies is to marginalise developing countries even further.

Shifts in language teaching and learning pedagogies to incorporate multimedia ICT modes of delivery have introduced change to the South African educational landscape (Kajee, 2005a, 2005b). It is inevitable that teachers, to accommodate such shifts and changes, seek new strategies to manage and understand the new modes of delivery. It is also inevitable that teachers sometimes resist change and consider themselves inadequate and under-prepared to use the new modes in their teaching. This gives rise to questions around how ICT modes of delivery are used in the classroom, as well as how students, particularly those with minimal previous access to technology, position themselves in relation to its use, and make meaning in new online spaces. To address such concerns I provide in this introductory chapter the aim of this book on online communities of practice, the key questions that framed my methodological approach, as well as the underlying rationale for the study. I situate this work within perspectives of the digital divide, and the English language debates in South Africa. I further locate the work within the African and South African contexts, by focusing on ICT policy, practice and initiatives, with emphasis on higher education.

This book is an exploration of online learning, as mediated by ICTs, in an undergraduate English classroom at a university in Johannesburg, South Africa. Although the work is located in South Africa, it has implications for other developing countries[5] as well. The main aim of this work is to explore the extent to which communities of practice are enabled in an online environment, among English non-mother tongue speakers, who have had minimal previous access to ICTs. I use the case study which I find appropriate because of its ability to provide an intensive view of the participants as they unravel the complexities of their technological and digital engagement. In this case study I make reference to asynchronous ICT practices such as the use of the Internet

4 For example, Czerniewicz (2004), Czerniewicz and Carr (2005), Czerniewicz and Brown (2005), and Lelliot, Pendlebury and Enslin (2000).

5 I use the term 'developing', acknowledging the debates surrounding its use.

(Net), e-mail, and discussion forums on online Web course management systems. From a sociocultural perspective, and recognising that learning does not occur in isolation, this text draws on the work of Lave and Wenger (1991, 2002) who, rather than merely define learning as the acquisition of knowledge, situate it as forms of interaction and co-participation. Wenger (1998), for instance, considers learning to be interactive relationships among people and their environments. Lave and Wenger (1991, 1996, 2002) and Wenger (1998) therefore advocate learning in a specific context, and focus on how individuals become members of 'communities of practice' (COPs). COPs are viewed as sets of relations among people, activities and the world, over time, and in relation to other overlapping COPs (Lave and Wenger, 1991, 1996, 2002; Rogoff, 2003). The emphasis, therefore, is the interconnectedness of people, learning, practice, participation, and the social world. Development occurs as a process where a person gradually increases his/her participation and belonging to society's various communities of practice.

I argue in this work that practice and participation are underpinned, and to some extent determined, by the identities constructed by participants in the online communities. I examine participants' ICT-practices through the lens of literacy, in this case electronic literacy, as a social practice and New Literacy Studies, where I draw on the work of Gee (1996, 1997, 2000), Street (1984, 1993, 1998, 2003) and Barton, Hamilton and Ivanic (2000). I also refer to Lankshear and Knobel (1997, 2004) and Knobel and Lankshear (2002) to examine technological, or electronic literacies.

Finally, I explore constructions of identity from Hall's (1992) post-structural view that old identities, which stabilised the social world as we knew it, are in decline, giving rise to new identities and fragmenting the modern individual as a unified subject. With new technologies networking the world, computer-mediated communication (CMC) produces a vast array of virtual communities, which give rise to the construction of virtual identities (Castells, 1996). Thus, technological change should be located in the social context in which it is taking place, and by which it is being shaped.

My main aim then, is to establish the extent to which COPs are enabled in an online environment, among participants from under-resourced backgrounds, to whom the use of ICTs in the teaching-learning context is still a novel practice.

For the purpose of this book, I refer to Kearsley's (1998) interpretation of online learning, which he views as any form of learning and teaching that takes place *via* a computer network, bulletin board, the Net, World Wide Web (WWW), local area network (LAN), or intranet. I examine this definition, and others more critically later in Chapter 1. In particular, I examine issues relating to how participants interact, develop relationships, and construct identities in online spaces.

In order to conceptualise, design and initiate a project that explores online communities of practice in the English classroom, questions need to be posed about the use of online technology, as well as the emerging communities of practice, and it is these questions that I attempt to address in the study and present in the section to follow.

Questions for research on online communities of practice

Although ICT-based applications in English language teaching are currently being used sporadically at South African higher education institutions, international studies, such as those by Warschauer (1996a, 1997a, 2000c, 2001, 2004), Mak (1995a, 1995b), Peyton (1990), Marcos (1994), Langston and Batson (1990), and others indicate that the use of ICTs and WWW technology, including the Internet, in English teaching opens doors to enhanced teaching and learning experiences. Knobel and Lankshear (2002) for instance suggest that personal computing, the Net, and digital communications media have changed what it means to learn, know and do things. My work focuses more specifically on the extent to which the use of online practices such as the Net, e-mail, and discussion forums on web course management systems facilitate online communities of practice. In order to address the main aim of my research, I ask: to what extent do English non-mother tongue speakers in a university English classroom engage in communities of practice in online spaces?

Recognising that communities of practice encompass negotiation of meaning, participation and the establishment of relationships, all of which are facilitated by the construction of participant-identities, I find it necessary to pose further related questions in this work:

- What are the electronic (ICT)-literacy practices of higher education English non-mother tongue speakers, and how do these practices shape their perceptions of ICT-use in an English language classroom?
- What relationships do the participants develop and sustain in online environments?
- How do the participants construct identities in online environments?

In order to address the first question, I examine participants' 'in- and out-of-school' electronic literacy practices, with specific focus on ICTs, by looking at issues of ICT access, proficiency and their perceptions of the use of technology for the teaching and learning of English. I use the notion 'literacy as social practice' as a lens through which to focus on their home, high school, and university ICT-literacy practices. I draw on the work of Gee (1996, 1997, 2000), Street (1984, 1993, 1998, 2003), Barton et al. (2000), and Lankshear and Knobel (1997, 2004) who suggest that the conventional meaning of 'literacy' is narrow, and that literacy is a social practice. I expand their views on literacy to include electronic literacy, with specific focus on ICTs. To answer the second question, I adopt Rogoff's (2003) and Lave and Wenger's (1991, 2002) concepts of relationships and legitimate peripheral participation, which relate to collaboration and interaction. I employ Hall's (1992) and Norton (Pierce's) (1995, 1997, 2000)[6] interpretation of identity, self and subjectivity from a post-structural position to examine how participants' construct online identities. I then examine in Chapter 5 how participants construct their identities by critically analysing their discussion forum messages. Finally, I apply a

6 Earlier work is attributed to Norton-Pierce (1995), while later works are attributed to Norton (1997, 2000). In her work on language and identity, Norton (1995, 1997, 2000) uses 'identity' to refer to how people understand their relationship to the world, how that relationship is constructed across time and space, and how people understand their possibilities for the future. I found such constructions relevant to participants' online textual presence. Lam's (2000) work on the construction of textual identity on the Net is also referred to.

critical sociocultural framework to examine how their postings position them in relation to themes found in key course readings.

Providing the rationale for this work

Current trends in South Africa demonstrate a sporadic, though increasing interest in the use of ICTs in teaching and learning. This phenomenon has to do with the lack of resources and insufficient teacher-development in the area of ICT education. This is compounded by the entry of students into the higher education sector who have neither had previous access to ICTs, nor share the medium of instruction of the institution, English. Thus I provide the underlying rationale for my study as being juxtaposed with power struggles around issues of ICT access and access to English.

ICT inconsistencies in higher education: Demystifying the digital divide

Concerns relating to the use of ICTs have been examined primarily against the backdrop of the binary view of developing and developed nations. It is usually assumed that what is appropriate in first world countries cannot be adopted in its present condition in developing countries such as South Africa. Warschauer (2002a, 2002b, 2003a, 2003b, 2004b), for instance, cautions against replicating common weaknesses in introducing ICTs to developing countries, from an instrumentalist perspective, such using overly-sophisticated technology, and not training teachers and key participants sufficiently in its use. Lelliott, Pendlebury and Enslin (2000) further caution against locating Africa with developed nations when they say 'In Africa and the rest of the developing world, patterns of inclusion and exclusion, empowerment and disempowerment have differed from those of Europe and North America' (2000: 42).

It is inevitable that limited access to, and lack of proficiency in ICTs hampers the use of technology. Thus, the digital divide, or distinction between 'haves' and 'have nots' is particularly evident in developing countries. However, the notion is somewhat inaccurate because the stratification that exists in relation to access to online information has little to do with ICTs, but rather more to do with political, economic, institutional, cultural, and linguistic contexts that shape meaning in people's lives (Warschauer, 2002a, 2002b, 2004b, 2005, in press). Warschauer therefore considers the notion of the divide 'oversimplified' (2003b: Foreword). He emphasises 'A consideration of how people can use computers and the Internet to further the process of *social inclusion* is paramount in any effort to install new technology into an environment lacking in it' (my italics, 2003a: 44). Thus he perceives the divide, or inequality, as social rather than digital. His approach concurs with Feenberg's (1991) more critical stance that the shaping of technology is related strongly to issues of class and power, and not just to issues of access.

The use of ICTs is both a threat and an opportunity to higher education. The threat appears in the form of widening the digital divide to those who lack power and access to the dominant technological requirements. Its opportunities take on the form of its implications for material and commercial empowerment, where higher-paid jobs and skilled employment will demand its use. Kennard (2001) for instance argues that the issue of access to new technology will also determine workers' progress up the socio-economic ladder, and adds that those who are literate in computer languages and familiar with new technologies will succeed, while those who are not, will not (2001:196).

The issue of power and access to technology mirrors Bourdieu's (1991) views on the English language debate, where those with access to the English language are in a position of power: they attain material and commercial power because of the access it creates to jobs and eventual economic gain. This results in an access paradox in that the more the English language is used, the greater its symbolic power, while those who do not acquire the language are denied such power (Janks, 2004). The consequence is a twofold divide.

I suggest that the ICTs debate follows similar reasoning to Bourdieu's (1991) argument around the role of English as a gate-keeping language. In the ICT access debate, those with access to, and proficiency in the use of ICTs, attain material and commercial power, as we are reminded by Kennard (2001). The use of ICTs perpetuates the power of technology, and those who do not have access and proficiency find themselves marginalised, especially in the higher education sector. Thus, South Africa, like other developing countries, has to position itself in the debate by making conscious choices regarding the use of technology, given that resources and availability are not widespread, nor can be taken for granted.

Conflict surrounding the digital divide in South Africa and Africa at large is evident when one considers the possibilities of *not* implementing technology in educational contexts. Included among the opportunities promised by ICTs is that they transcend discrepancies in location, distance and time. ICTs also offer the possibility of lower costs and wider choices, thus providing a lucrative opportunity for empowering stakeholders and making teaching and learning more equitable. With appropriate use emerging ICTs can therefore help developing countries by enabling educational reform.

However, current inconsistencies in the use of ICTs in higher education in South Africa can conflict with the goals of attaining quality education. There are the two key gaps or 'silences' in current ICT endeavours in South African higher education institutions at undergraduate level. First, many students enter higher education institutions from schools that may not have access to ICTs, therefore the students cannot cope with the demands of the technological requirements of higher education, where basic computer literacy is taken for granted. Thus students might feel excluded, or denied membership to the broader university community that privileges those with ICT proficiency. The second gap is that current research in the field of ICTs in South Africa is relatively new and its impact on learning still has to be explored.

The first 'gap': limited access and proficiency in ICTs, is particularly relevant to students from under-resourced schools in rural or township areas in South Africa, despite recommendations of ICT access for all teachers and learners in government policy documents. Most higher education institutions provide students with access to computer laboratories, however, many of these institutions do not assume responsibility for students' computer literacy. The students therefore acquire computer literacy skills in an *ad hoc* manner, where they may learn by observing others, by 'trial and error' (Kajee, 2002, 2003), or by attending computer literacy courses at their own expense.

The second gap, relevant to students and teachers, is whether the use of technology in education necessarily equates with learning. Many researchers (such as Clark, 1994 and Cummins, 2000) are adamant that it is not the technology, but the pedagogy that impacts on learning, and that there is no justifiable evidence that the investment in ICTs has improved student achievement levels. Technology might increase the time spent on tasks such as reading, but it is the increased time expended, not the technology, that might improve achievement, they argue.

Against the backdrop of the digital divide in South Africa this book explores the use of ICTs in the teaching and learning of English. My rationale for focusing on English in the university context is justifiable because first, it is an accredited course of study, and second, the language is dominant in the university environment because it is the medium of instruction, as well as the language in which most of the materials are available. The third reason is that the language is often perceived by non-mother tongue speakers as a route to success in their studies as well as their careers.

The English language and learning debates

Locating my research in a higher education English course is appropriate because of current debates concerning the language's flexibility and its status as a 'world language' (Graddol, 1997: 6).

It is not uncommon in South Africa that English non-mother tongue speakers enter university under-prepared for the academic and linguistic demands and discourses where English is the medium of instruction. Thus, this work examines not just how participants construct their identities in the online medium, but how participants construct their identities through the medium of *English*.

Historically too, English has played a controversial role in South Africa, and has been central to debates about English usage and hegemony (refer, for instance to Lemmer, 1996; Silva, 1997; Chick,

1998; du Pre, 2002; Kajee, 2000, 2001; Kamwangamalu, 2000; Kamwangamalu, 2003). Key concerns regarding the role played by, and the use of English, particularly in the higher education context, are therefore given attention in this book. My decision to focus on English is also justifiable because it is a subject of choice and current medium of instruction at the majority of higher education institutions in South Africa. My background of over twenty years in the teaching of English, attendance at, and implementation of training courses in the use of ICTs to teach English, and the changing role played by the language in South Africa's history has motivated me further to explore more fully the teaching and learning of the language in online environments. Although policy documents[7] in South Africa describe the need for technology and resource-based learning, they do not elaborate on the implications for the teaching and learning of English. However, I am of the view that local and international studies[8] on the use of ICT practices in the English classroom unlock a world of pedagogical possibilities.

There have been many changes in the political, cultural and educational spheres in South Africa since the first democratic elections held in 1994. In particular, the issue of increased access to education has become a primary concern. With the formation of a single educational body, the National Department of Education, higher education became the responsibility of one Department. The primary task of the Department was to provide access to all South Africans to all institutions of education. Thus access, or what has commonly come to be perceived as massification, ensued.

The years of disadvantage that characterised the apartheid era (1948–1994) were especially apparent in black students' under-preparedness for higher education, and many of these inequities were attributed directly to language injustices associated with the marginalisation of African languages (du Pre, 2002). For instance, non-mother tongue English speakers were expected to compete with English mother tongue speakers in an English medium of instruction environment. The lack of suitable preparation also emanated from the remnants of the

7 Refer, for instance, to the *Green Paper on Higher Education* (1996) and the *Higher Education Act* (1997).

8 These studies are discussed in Chapter 1.

Bantu education system of the apartheid era, in which black schools were deliberately under-resourced and teachers were inadequately trained and prepared for their roles (Hartshorne, 1987). This became apparent when students from such environments entered their first year at higher education institutions in South Africa (see for example, Hartshorne, 1987; Dreyer, 1995).

In relation to language rights, use, and development, the *Constitution of South Africa* specifies eleven official languages,[9] however, the distribution of speakers of these languages is diverse. Mother tongue speakers of English were reported to number about 39.5% (Statistics South Africa, 2001 Census), however, English still assumes a dominant role in primary domains: education, commerce, science and technology, and as the language of internal and international communication. Among the reasons provided for its dominance, as alluded to in the previous section, is that English has linguistic capital (Bourdieu, 1991). Aligned with Graddol's (1997) argument that the language is a world language, Bourdieu (1991) says it has symbolic power. That is, it has commercial, cultural and material value: it ensures career success, opens doors to trade and it uplifts the economy (Lazenby, 1996; Mesthrie in Chick, 1998). Consequently, mother-tongue education was perceived to play an exclusionary role in apartheid South Africa, and black parents began to see English as a route to upward mobility and empowerment (Kamwangamalu, 2000; Kamwangamalu, 2003; Setati et al., 2002; Kajee, 2000, 2001; Titlestad, 1998; Silva, 1997). The view of parents, learners, and teachers was that English has an almost mystical power: 'If you know English well, desired things will follow' (Lemmer, 1996: 84).

English therefore appears to be a pragmatic choice at the level of higher education. However, the arguments do not articulate the need for the use of ICTs in the English classroom context. Cummins' comment is apt:

9 Act No 108 of 1996. The languages are IsiZulu, IsiXhosa, English, Afrikaans, SeSotho, Northern Sotho, Setswana, Xitsonga, Siswati, Tshivenda and IsiNdebele, as well as Sign Language as an unofficial twelfth language.

> Our task as educators in general, and as language educators in particular, should be to access the potential of IT to improve the human condition. As educators we are committed to drawing out the potential of students we teach; as language educators, we strive to increase students' capacity to use language to fulfil their personal goals and contribute to their societies (2000: 539).

This void prompted me to query how ICTs are being used in the English language classroom. In particular, I am interested in answering questions from a sociocultural perspective, around the extent to which participants collaborate and negotiate meaning, as well as construct identities in online spaces where these exist.

Contextualising the work

In contextualising this work, I first provide an overview of the use of ICTs on the African continent, primarily as a means of social inclusion. I then narrow the field by presenting an overview of the South African context, where I examine key policy documents and initiatives relevant to the use of ICTs in schools, industry, and the higher education context.

Describing the African context

Much of the argument cautioning against the use of ICTs in Africa, as explained by Lelliott et al. (2000), is made around the continent's more pressing concerns: war, famine, poverty and lack of basic education. Particularly apt are views such as the following:

> How can a woman be interested in Information and Communication Technologies (ICTs) on a hungry stomach with a child crying on her back for food and another she is carrying in her arms dying because of lack of medical care? (Ochieng and Radloff, 1996).[10]

10 Cited in Lelliott et al. (2000: 43).

Although the writers are vocal about such critical issues, which are relevant to any developing nation, they do support the use of ICTs in promoting new opportunities for democracy in Africa, such as extending its use to women, providing education to geographically distant areas, and in disseminating health information. The view is supported by Chapman (1996), who argues that society should exploit technology to provide education for democratic, socially inclusive, economically advanced communities. Warschauer's (2002a, 2002b, 2003a, 2003b, 2004, 2005, in press) studies in Egypt support this stance, while simultaneously demonstrating the difficulties encountered with bureaucracy in developing countries.

The need for inclusion across the African continent is further articulated by current South African President Mbeki, who speaks about the need to improve connectivity among people in Africa. He also draws links between connectivity as a strategy for poverty reduction in NEPAD[11] (Chisholm, 2003). This view is important in identifying not only the possibility of ICT skills being taught, but in providing a time frame for *when* they are taught.

In relation to connectivity, issues of infrastructure cannot be ignored. The SADC[12] e-readiness study (SADC, 2002), aligned with NEPAD, considers regional cooperation, the development of infrastructure and education essential for ICT development. In order to maximise benefits to communities the study recommends the following, in no particular order, across the African continent: basic infrastructure, electrification, education, integration of ICT by government, increased telegeography, growth of teledensity and mobile penetration, increased PC penetration, increased Internet population, growth of banking infrastructure, policy and regulation, liberalisation of communications infrastructure, affordability, and multipurpose community centres (SADC 2002; Chisholm et al., 2004).

In relation to practice, initiatives such as SchoolNet Africa are underway, connecting schools across Africa. The aim of the initiative is to provide improved education access, quality and efficiency through

11 NEPAD – New Partnership for Africa's Development.

12 SADC – Southern African Development Community.

the use of ICTs in African schools.[13] The organisation supports the right of all African youth to education and lifelong learning, by providing affordable and sustainable access to information, African education content on the Net, and online content in local languages. Currently, thirty-one African countries form part of the SchoolNet network, including South Africa.[14]

Describing the South African context

In locating my study in the South African context, I examine government's call for ICT-based initiatives in the country, ICT initiatives introduced at the level of school and industry, and then examine policy issues that underpin learning principles and the use of ICTs.

Over the past four years (2002–2005) current South African President Mbeki has reminded South Africans (in his State of the Nation Addresses) of the vital role played by ICTs in creating global economic networks for South Africa.[15] Bearing in mind the words of its current president, South Africa is considered the most technologically

13 www.schoolnetafrica.net Last accessed 5 October 2005.

14 The countries are: Angola, Benin, Botswana, Cameroon, Cape Verde, Cote D'Ivoire, Egypt, Ethiopia, The Gambia, Ghana, Kenya, Lesotho, Liberia, Madagascar, Malawi, Mauritius, Morocco, Mozambique, Namibia, Nigeria, Rwanda, Senegal, Malawi, Mauritius, Morocco, Mozambique, Namibia, Nigeria, Rwanda, Senegal, Sierra Leone, South Africa, Swaziland, Tanzania, Tunisia, Uganda, Zambia, Zimbabwe.

15 For example, in his Address in 2002, he said 'a critical and pervasive element in economic development in the current age is the optimum utilisation of information and communication technology' (Mbeki, 2002, online). In 2003 he promised that greater attention would be paid to the development of ICT capabilities among the youth (Mbeki, 2003, online). In 2004 he urged South Africans to ensure that the country and people are properly positioned within the global community of nations, fully understanding and responding to the diverse political, economic, social and technological challenges of the process of globalisation (Mbeki, 2004, online). And in 2005 he said that government would focus more on ICT and telecommunications systems. President Mbeki's State of the Nation Addresses (2002, 2003, 2004, 2005) www.info.gov.za/ speeches/ Accessed on 5 October 2005.

advanced country in Africa. At the end of 2003, 3.23 million South Africans, or one in thirteen of a population of 47.5 million were reported to have access to the Internet (Internet World Statistics), this of course considering that not all circumstances are equitable. South Africa was also rated as having the highest number of domains and websites of the SADC countries: 187 649 domains and 3002 websites, compared with Angola, for instance, with eight domains and 136 websites (in Chisholm et al., 2004).

The country has also made several initiatives into the field of ICTs at school level, largely as a result of documents such as the *Draft White Paper on e-Education* (2004), which is aimed at promoting the use of ICTs in schools. The document calls for all teachers and learners to have access to ICTs in order to promote socio-economic growth in the country, and to narrow the digital divide by 2013. Discussion around the document led to initiatives such as the Thutong Project,[16] which is the Department of Education's Web portal designed to support teaching and learning in South Africa. The portal aims to help teachers technologically by providing high quality materials, and enabling them to communicate and work together. However, the project is still in its introductory phase.

Another initiative, located in the Gauteng region to promote ICT access and use among the youth is the GautengOnline Project.[17] The Project hopes to bridge the digital divide in Gauteng by positioning the province at the centre of technological change and innovation. The Project was launched with the South African information technology (IT) industry designing IT solutions for Gauteng schools, and computers were introduced to selected classrooms. Other technological initiatives are being made in industry with the newly drafted ICT Empowerment Charter (2005).[18] The Charter arose as a result of apartheid policies that denied black people and women access to economic resources in South Africa on the basis of race and gender. The document aims to bridge the digital divide by promoting access to ICTs, in particular to black South Africans and women, as an equity initiative. It is viewed as a route to

16 Please refer to www.thutong.org.za for more detail. Accessed 20 August 2005.

17 Please refer to www.gautengonline.com Accessed 5 October 2005.

18 Please refer to www.ictcharter.org.za/ Accessed 29 August 2005.

reducing unemployment and poverty in the country. Further initiatives in commerce and industry include the development of organisations such as the Meraka Institute,[19] which is designed to facilitate socio-economic development through technology, once again, in an attempt to narrow the digital divide.

Thus, South Africa is making inroads into technological redress at the levels of policy, school and industry. At the level of policy, key recommendations are being made in relation to ICTs and a resource-based approach. While endeavours such as the *Draft White Paper on e-Education* (2004) are currently not emulated in higher education, policies such as the *Higher Education National Plan* and the *Green Paper on Higher Education*, highlight the need for an ICT approach.[20]

Like at school and industry levels, the overarching recommendation for the use of ICTs is joining the competitive global economic market, and the borderless world of ICTs is proposed as a route to global participation. Thus higher education is seen as playing a pivotal role in preparing the youth for the knowledge and information society. The *Green Paper* suggests further that one of the measures that can be introduced to improve the efficiency of the higher education system, reduce unit costs and increase productivity, is by introducing new teaching and learning strategies such as open and resource-based learning which are less labour-intensive. The document proposes that this would lead to significant changes in traditional modes of programme delivery and staff-student ratios.[21]

Despite the call for an ICT-based approach to global participation, the role played by ICTs in higher education teaching and learning spheres is fairly uncharted territory in South Africa. Recommendations made in discussion documents have yet to filter extensively into

19 Please refer to www.meraka.org.za for further details. Accessed 29 August 2005.

20 'As South Africa locates itself in this network of global exchanges and interactions, higher education will have to produce the skills and technological innovations necessary for successful economic participation in the global market. It must also socialise a new generation with the requisite cultural values and communication competencies to become citizens of an international global community' (Section 3.1, Chapter 2, *Green Paper on Higher Education*, 1996).

21 Section 5.3, Chapter 2, *Green Paper on Higher Education* (1996).

teaching-learning paradigms. However, studies such as those conducted by van der Merwe (2004); SAIDE[22] (2000a, 2000b, 2003); Czerniewicz (2004), Czerniewicz and Brown (2005); Czerniewicz and Carr (2005); Spurrett (2005); Hodgkinson-Williams and Mostert (2005); Turkington and Frank (2005); Carr, Cox, Eden and Hanslo (2004); and Lundall and Howell (2000), indicate a growing awareness of the value of the use of ICTs. Although the studies focus on the higher education, as well as school sectors, I have included them because they demonstrate similar concerns.

Van der Merwe (2004) evaluates the use of *WebCT* at the university of Stellenbosch, and the SAIDE (2000a, 2000b, 2003) projects examine ICT-use in schools and higher education. Czerniewicz (2004) frames a discussion of the articulation of computers in teaching and learning in higher education, with a focus on the University of Cape Town, while Czerniewicz and Carr (2005) call for a community of practice of researchers in the field of ICTs. Spurrett (2005) conducts research into an online critical thinking component of a Philosophy course at the University of KwaZulu-Natal, and Hodgkinson-Williams and Mostert (2005) examine staff and student perceptions of the use online debate in encouraging online learning communities among B.Ed students. Turkington and Frank (2005) narrate their Journalism students' experiences with the creation of an online newspaper, while Carr et al. (2004) examine online student participation from a community of practice perspective in an Economics course at the University of Cape Town. Finally, Lundall and Howell (2000) survey the use of computers in schools. The studies cumulatively indicate that ICTs is a growing area of research in South Africa though many of the studies also demonstrate that teachers and learners are not yet sufficiently prepared for, or trained in its use. Although studies are being undertaken in the field of ICTs within an educational context, applied research into ICT teaching-learning paradigms and pedagogies, particularly in higher education, is still in need of further consolidation.

Higher education institutions are currently in a phase of transition and transformation, and face challenges such as open learning, lifelong

22 SAIDE – South African Institute of Distance Education.

learning, commercialisation and quality requirements.[23] Such challenges could be answered by an ICT-based approach. For instance, the concept 'open learning' encapsulates many of the features of learning in higher education, and may be defined as:

> a flexible, learner-centred approach to education, seeking to increase access to educational opportunities by removing all unnecessary barriers to learning. This involves using the full spectrum of available resources to ensure quality and cost-effectiveness in meeting diverse educational needs, including preparation of the widest possible range of learners for the process of lifelong learning (in SAIDE, 1997: 4).

The key features of open learning are relevant to this text because they concur with the theoretical concepts underpinning communities of practice. The features of open learning may be summarised thus (in SAIDE, 1997):

- *Learner-centeredness*: Key to learner-centeredness is that the learner should be the focus of the educational process and an active decision-maker. Education should build on learners' experiences and encourage independent and critical thinking.
- *Lifelong learning*: The concept entails that learners should continue their learning throughout their lives, and that learning should be relevant to learners' needs and life experiences.
- *Flexibility*: Learning should be flexible in order to cater for learners' needs regarding what they want to learn, how they want to learn, when they want to learn, and the pace they want to learn at.
- *Removal of access barriers*: Open learning allows for the removal of barriers such as geographical constraints, race, gender, age and physical disability.
- *Recognition of prior learning*: Learners should be able to accumulate credits for other learning experiences and contexts.
- *Learner support*: Learners should receive adequate support within the learning environment, such as counselling, tutoring, interaction and access to facilities and resources.
- *Expectations of success*: Learners should be afforded opportunities to complete learning programmes, and the qualifications they receive are marketable.

23 White Paper on Education and Training, 1994; Green Paper on Higher Education, 1996.

- *Quality learning*: Learning should be of the highest quality and should be evaluated and adapted regularly.
- *Cost-effectiveness*: Learning opportunities should be cost-effective, which does not mean cheap, rather, quality learning which utilises a range of resources for its success.

Thus in this book I suggest that it is precisely the basic tenets of documents such as the *Green* and *White Papers on Higher Education*, as shown above, that need to be implemented, or else they remain confined to policy.

However, my position is also that some caution in relation to the use of ICTs is necessary. As is spelt out in the documents, additional budgetary outlays are required in the form of investment in hardware, software, and the development of online materials. Further concerns are expressed about the utilisation of ICTs and their sustainability. Also, if such an approach were to be adopted extensively in South Africa and elsewhere, it would have serious implications for teacher-training and professional development, as improvement in the quality of teaching-learning pedagogies involving the use of ICTs is essential.

Therefore, although South Africa is considered a prominent player in the field of ICTs in the SADC region, the country is a relatively minor player globally, and research in the field of ICTs at macro- and micro-levels in the country is valuable within its context as a developing country. As was stated earlier, in the higher education context, researchers have begun to examine ICT-based issues. However, such studies are minimal, particularly in the area of English language education, and I hope that books such as this can help provide insight into ICT-implementation at the level of classroom pedagogy, as well as into learners and how they construct and position themselves in relation to its use.

Bearing in mind the challenges surrounding the implementation of ICT-based teaching and learning practices, the issue of ICT use is not restricted to issues of policy, access, training and budget. The use of ICTs also impinges on power struggles created by inconsistent access to technology, for its potential users. Broadly, this book contributes to the following ten key issues, and these in turn provide the scope and focus of the research.

While the focus of this book is ICTs, I consider the Internet (Net) and the World Wide Web (WWW) as an integral component of ICTs, and in providing its scope and contribution, include reference to the Net and WWW as ICT practices at specific points. Thus, this book hopes to contribute in the following ten overlapping areas:

First, *educational reform, equity and empowerment*: the South African government has set out to build a solid foundation for the development of its people after the first democratic elections that were held in 1994. Reforms such as those in the educational system have improved the lives of millions of South Africans by making learning more accessible through the implementation of the *National Qualifications Framework* (NQF) and the *Higher Education Act* of 1997 (van Buren-Schele and Odendaal, 2001). Conversely, it is evident that higher education systems in many other sub-Saharan African countries have deteriorated. According to the African Virtual University[24] statistics in 2003, for instance, higher education is provided to only 3.5% of the population, compared to 60% in industrialised countries. ICTs have great potential implications for the education sector. Theoretically, using Internet technology, for instance, has the capacity to make higher education more accessible, by delivering materials to remote areas and by providing multiple access routes. This has implications for issues of equity and empowerment by providing education to those who have not had equitable access in the past. The *Green Paper on Higher Education* (South Africa, 1996) and the subsequent *Higher Education Act* (South Africa, 1997) endorse this development.

Second, *the development of ICTs as an innovative teaching tool*: the Net, for example has been referred to as an innovative teaching tool that enhances learning (Gordin, Gomez, Pea and Fishman, 1996; Johnson and Huff, 2000), however contrasting views that it may contribute to the marginalisation of those who cannot afford technology

24 African Virtual University (AVU) is a World Bank initiative established to provide quality education to African countries utilising telecommunications. AVU is based in Nairobi, Kenya, and has over fifty-seven Learning Centres in twenty-seven African countries. Please refer to http://www.avu.org.

or access to it, exist (Asmal, 2000; Lelliott et al., 2000). Although initially, much of the growth of ICT-use was attributed to technologists and researchers, it was when educators and learners were introduced to e-mail, newsgroups and listservs that utilisation grew (*Wall Street Journal*, 4 February 2002). The use of the Net in the educational context has therefore grown tremendously. However, there are conflicting views regarding its value.

Third, *building diversity awareness and providing opportunities for growth*: on one hand, the Net may be seen as a medium for providing lessons to vast numbers of people from diverse cultural and geographic backgrounds, bringing people closer and facilitating communication (Moote, 2002). On the other hand, it may be considered a lucrative business opportunity. Moote (2002) points out that global expenditure on education was estimated at between US$ 1 trillion and US$ 2.1 trillion, making one consider the potential of courses targeted at a market that has access to telecommunications systems. This book examines how a web course impacts on learners in relation to creating local and global opportunities for communication. Although such courses have implications for income-generation in the educational sphere, I do not explore this possibility at this stage.

Fourth, *the development of new, more integrative strategies for teaching and learning*: as provided in the research context of this chapter, in South Africa, the use of computers in education and online learning is a relatively new phenomenon. The lack of electronic and digital resources is not alleviated in any way by the fact that many schools, especially those in under-resourced rural areas, do not even have electricity, let alone computers. However, there are initiatives in place that are starting to introduce computers to schools more concertedly, the GautengOnline Project being one of them. The project aims to introduce computers to schools in a more structured manner, as well as to train teachers in the use of computer strategies in their teaching. The Thutong Portal, as discussed earlier in this chapter, is another initiative. The SchoolNet Project is a further initiative that aims to open doors to communication among teachers across Africa.

While technological approaches to teaching and learning were initially limited to behaviourist-like approaches, there is a shift to more integrative, participative approaches which include multimedia in the form of visual and audio texts. This book explores the introduction of a web course that runs parallel to a face-to-face English course, as a teaching intervention to promote interaction and participation among all participants.

Fifth, *mobilisation of higher education and industry to meet the needs of the country*: there are increasing demands from industry that traditional education provided by higher education institutions are falling short of the needs of industry (Zafeiriou, Nunes and Ford, 2001). Because of changing circumstances, higher education institutions, in particular, are being encouraged to develop web-based curricula in order to meet these needs. Therefore the benefits of the use of technology in educational environments need to be considered carefully within learning environments in higher education, where my project is located.

Sixth, *potential as a learning resource*: the WWW has great potential as a learning resource, by providing teachers and learners with unlimited access to information, previously only available in libraries. The learning opportunities should therefore be more profound, with access being available in the classroom and at home, at any time. The implications for the teaching and learning of English and English second language in particular, are important. The Net has the ability to expose students of English to other English speakers worldwide at the 'click of a mouse'. Authentic learning experiences, a requirement for optimal learning, as spelt out by many researchers and theorists (for instance, Vygotsky, 1978; Krashen, 1981; Lave and Wenger, 1991) are therefore enabled.

Seventh, *possible links between ICTs, learning and cognition*: one of the key issues surrounding the use of ICTs in education concerns its contribution to learning. Does their use equate neatly with learning and cognition, and if so, how? On an affective level it may be motivating for students to use new technology, but until it can be established whether learning occurs, the use of ICTs will remain a novelty. Obstacles, as listed by van Buren-Schele and Odendaal (2001) and Lelliott et al. (2000) earlier in this chapter, include the lack of a communication infrastructure for online teaching and learning, the high costs of telecommunications in South Africa compared to other developed countries, illiteracy and lack of computer skills, limitations on the availability of bandwidth which influences the speed of data processing, and access to basic computers. Obstacles notwithstanding, the implications for learning and cognition need to be considered, because higher education institutions are being encouraged to take on the challenge by introducing the utilisation of information and communication technology in the curriculum. A more extensive examination of learning models is provided in Chapter 2.

Eighth, *reaching large numbers of students*: web-based distance and flexible learning environments enable higher education institutions, in particular, to reach an increasing number of students. Zafeiriou et al. (2001) refer to online environments and the use of the WWW as an educational panacea, which provides students with skills such as online communication, discussion, problem analysis, problem solving, critical thinking, and negotiation of meaning. This issue may be debated as online learning becomes more fully integrated in educational institutions and its impact on learning is established. Although online learning was initially used to supplement classroom instruction, online classes are increasingly providing a popular form of interaction for participants. Online learning has also changed the social dynamics of education by placing learners and educators on equal footing – a move away from the traditional dominant role of the educator. In the project described in this text I examine the role of the participants (learners and facilitator) in the online environment.

Ninth, *preparation for e-learning*: online strategies and courses provide students with a powerful medium for peer learning and prepares them for e-learning.[25] With regard to the learning environment, for instance, English might be taught face-to-face or online, or using a blend of both methods. In the latter case, students might be able to apply what they have learnt in face-to-face classrooms to the online context and vice versa (Kannan and MackNish, 2000). Online courses and course components therefore contribute to an additional learning environment. According to Kannan and MackNish's (2000) experience,

25 e-learning comprises a variety of multimedia modes, including the Net, while online learning utilises the Net. Also refer to Holms and Gardner (2006). The concept is discussed in more detail in the section where I define online learning.

online course components influence learner motivation and self-directed learning, which I explore in some depth in my study.

Tenth, *positioning learners as global players*: South African higher education institutions are in a period of transition and transformation. To ensure a more democratic teaching-learning environment that is underpinned by equity and empowerment, as encapsulated in the *Higher Education Act* (1997), one way forward is the introduction of technology into higher education curricula, ensuring that South Africa becomes a more global player in the field.

Having presented the key aim and research questions framing this book, as well as the rationale and context, I now provide an overview of its structure.

An outline of chapters

In order to address my main research query 'To what extent do English non-mother tongue speakers in a university English classroom engage in communities of practice in online spaces?' I have organised the book into four parts, which consist of seven chapters:

In the Introduction, I present the aim, research questions, rationale, and context of the study and the impetus for my work, by locating ICTs and the digital era in the African and South African contexts. This chapter also provides an introduction to my research project by describing the context of higher education and recognising the role played by English at the university.

Part I: Beyond the digital divide: context, theory, access comprises Chapters 1 and 2. Chapter 1 reviews literature in the field of online learning. I examine international and local studies in the field, then examine the following key issues: the concept of online learning; the paradigm shift from face-to-face classrooms to virtual classrooms; computer-mediated communication and the emergence of computer-assisted language learning in the English classroom; the use of specific Internet-based strategies that are appropriate for the teaching and learning of English; and the changing role of the teacher as a result of the introduction of technology in the classroom.

Chapter 2 provides a theoretical framework for the work by theorising the following broad concepts: online learning, communities of practice, literacy as a social practice, New Literacy Studies, and identity. I explore literature related to learning theories that are based on the assertion that learning is an active, learner-centred process. These assertions are discussed within the framework of Vygotsky's (1978) Sociocultural Theory of Learning, and Rogoff's (2003) and Lave and Wenger's (1991, 1996, 2002) Situated Learning Theory and communities of practice theories. The concepts of literacy as a social practice and New Literacy Studies is theorised around the work of Gee (1996, 1997, 2000), Street (1984, 1993, 1998, 2003), Barton et al. (2000), Lankshear and Knobel (1997, 2004), and Knobel and Lankshear (2002). The construction of participant identities is examined in relation to the work of Hall (1992) and Norton (Pierce) (1995, 1997, 2000).

In Part II, I present Chapter 3, the design, methodology and implications of my study. The case study as an approach to research is presented, and the project is described in terms of planning, time frames, implementation and review. The participant sample and research methodology is presented. The research methodology includes survey questionnaires to establish participants' access to, and proficiency with ICTs, participants' electronic literacy histories, observations of participants, questionnaires issued to school managers, semi-structured interviews with students, linguistic analyses of messages posted to discussion threads, and facilitator diaries and journalistic notes. All the data collection methods are discussed and the strengths and limitations of each are explored.

The data emanating from the project are presented in two chapters: Chapters 4 and 5, which constitute Part III of the book: Electronic literacy and identity. In the first of these, Chapter 4, I present and analyse data relating to participants' electronic and digital literacy practices within and outside of the university community. I explore issues of ICT access, proficiency, and use, both of the Net, and the *Nicenet* online course. The broad context is also described in terms of the university where the study is based, lecturer use of ICTs, and the English courses selected for this study.

In Chapter 5, I present data from observations, participants' electronic literacy histories, interviews and data elicited from discussion threads to illustrate how participants make meaning through participation, the relationships they establish, how their identities are constructed in online communities of practice, and how they position themselves in relation to an ICT-mode of delivery, and social issues in key course readings.

Finally, in Part IV: Implications for teaching and learning: towards a model for online learning, I present Chapter 6 which is a summary of the findings of my project on online communities of practice. The implications of my research, as based on findings from survey questionnaires, personal observations, student electronic literacy histories, interviews with students, facilitator journals and the analyses of discussion thread postings, are presented. I contend that online communities of practice are facilitated by instructors among students who have not had extensive previous exposure to the use of ICTs. This is achieved by enabling participants to develop and sustain relationships locally and globally, as well as by facilitating their identity-construction. I suggest that the roles played by facilitators and learners are changing with the introduction of ICTs in the teaching-learning environment, and recommend changes in policy, practice, curriculum design, and in the role of teachers and learners. Possible limitations of my research, as well as a potential model of online learning are offered.

Conclusion

This introductory chapter has overviewed the aims, rationale, key research questions and the context of this work on online communities of practice in South Africa. The motivation for this book is that the introduction of ICTs to curricula ensures a more democratic teaching-learning environment that is underscored by equity, empowerment, and social inclusion. Issues within the African and South African context, presented from the perspective of ICT-use in developing countries, illustrate the need for this assumption to become the lived experience of learners if they are to succeed as autonomous, lifelong learners who are able to participate and interact successfully, not just within the university environment, but in a globally competitive world. In Chapter 1, I explore the terrain of online learning, where the concept of 'online learning' is defined and the notion 'computer-mediated communication' is deconstructed.

Part I

Beyond the digital divide: Context, theory, access

Chapter 1
The terrain of online learning: A local and global perspective

The use of ICTs in South Africa is worth consideration, given the context of development, and because issues of power arise concerning access to, and the use of, ICTs. Chapter 1 provides international and local research findings in the field of online learning, and explores the terrain of online learning in greater detail, by problematising six specific areas which I consider central to this text. I define online learning and discuss the paradigm shift from face-to-face teaching and learning to teaching and learning in a virtual environment. The notion 'computer-mediated communication' and its role in the teaching and learning of English are discussed. The concept 'computer-assisted language learning' is presented within a framework that describes the transition from behaviourist, to communicative, and integrative approaches, as well as network-based language teaching. Specific online practices such as e-mail, e-journals and weblogs, the WWW, audio and video streaming, and web course managers that are appropriate for the teaching and learning of English are presented and discussed. Finally, I consider the changing role of the teacher in an online environment. I demonstrate in this chapter that the use of ICTs in online teaching and learning of English mirrors the historical shifts in face-to-face approaches to teaching the language.

The debates concerning ICTs in teaching and learning

The use of ICTs in teaching and learning is not a new phenomenon as teachers and learners find themselves more involved in, or influenced by, the digital era. There is, however, some debate regarding whether the use of ICTs has the potential to transform the teaching-learning process by influencing student achievement, or whether it is a tool in the process of learning. On one hand there is recognition that ICTs have the potential to enhance the quality of teaching and learning (Greyling and Pete, 2001), while on the other hand there is debate that ICTs are the vehicle to deliver instruction, and that they do not influence student achievement (Clark, 1983, 1994, 2001). Clark explains that students benefit when learning from the use of multimedia, but that the benefits derive, not from the media *per se*, but from the learning strategies that are incorporated with the media.

Studies of the influence of ICTs are not limited to its impact on achievement. Other key areas in which the possible influence of ICTs in the English classroom have been studied, include international and local studies on its influence on teaching and learning, the teaching-learning context, teacher and learner perceptions of ICT-use, online collaboration and participation, and finally the impact of ICTs in educational contexts. In sections to follow, I present the results of studies in these key areas, both internationally and locally, which are relevant to this work. The international studies focus on issues from the context of developed countries, while the local studies focus on the developing country context.

International studies in ICT-use

ICT-use, influence on teaching and learning, and the teaching-learning context

Internationally, the use of ICTs has been found to influence English language teaching and learning significantly. For example, in his study of thirty-eight higher education institutions offering English foreign language courses in the United Kingdom, Jarvis (2003, 2004) finds that ICTs are a significant feature in courses and recommends that teachers and learners be effectively trained to use ICTs in teaching and learning.

In their examination of how the Net is influencing teaching and learning in higher education institutions, Shaw and Polovina (1999) found that the construction of courses placed heavy demands on tutors' time, and that tutors and teachers had to be prepared professionally for computer and Net literacy in the classroom before they could be involved with students.[1]

In relation to the teaching-learning context, proponents of online learning claim that it can transform education by promoting student-centred communication, collaboration and inquiry.[2] However, Warschauer's (1996a) study of ICT-based writing at Miller College (Hawai'i) demonstrates that while this might be so, sociocultural factors also shape online courses. He finds that discipline and order prevailed in the English class studied, as was consistent with the ethos of the Christian nature of the College, as well as the teacher's teaching philosophy.

1 Shaw and Polovina's (1999) study was conducted at London's South Bank University.

2 Such as Shaw and Polovina (1999).

Extensive international studies, such as those by Cunningham (2000), Karyan and Crowe (1997), Koszalka (2001), Zafeiriou, Nunes and Ford (2001), and Hara and Kling (1999), have been conducted to establish teacher and learner-perceptions of the use of ICTs.

The studies collectively demonstrate that students perceive ICTs to have both positive and negative influences on the teaching and learning of English: on one hand, Cunningham (2000), for example, finds that students felt the use of ICTs was non-threatening and challenging, that it benefited their writing, and that their grades had improved as a result of its use. On the other hand, Karyan and Crowe (1997) found that students were equally divided between those who felt there was a change in their behaviour and those who felt there was not, as a result of online interventions. Some of the students objected to being forced to participate in discussion groups, while others felt that they did not have sufficient access to technology and that they did not enjoy participating in online group discussions.

In their study of student perceptions of conditions affecting participation in online group work, Zafeiriou et al. (2001) studied the perceptions of about fifty students at the University of Sheffield. Six intervening factors were found to facilitate or constrain online group participation: familiarity with computers (students who were more familiar with computers participated more comfortably and confidently); familiarity with the subject (participants reported that prior knowledge of the subject influenced participation positively); typing skills (this was found to be important especially in synchronous communication, as students who could participate successfully synchronously and in several discussion threads could type relatively well); group size and attendance (students preferred smaller groups and students who did not attend regularly were frowned upon); level of interest; and technical problems (students felt they lost time and were frustrated by technical problems).

Hara and Kling (1999) highlight some of the student frustrations in their case study of a Web-based distance education course at a North American university. They determined that students felt frustrated at having to e-mail their responses, even if it was only to respond 'I agree', whereas in a face-to-face class they would simply nod. Some of them also experienced difficulty that they did not get immediate feedback from the instructor. They also experienced difficulty in accessing information from the Net. A further frustration was technological problems and the absence of technical support personnel. The instructor also felt frustrated at times that she could not help students with technical problems. Students also felt frustrated that the instructor's instructions were ambiguous or vague, leaving them uncertain of what to do, while the instructor felt she was giving them options. Hara and Kling (1999) therefore conclude that instructors must develop new pedagogies as well as different approaches to managing online courses.

In relation to teacher perceptions, teachers who use ICTs are said to have a more positive attitude towards its use in the classroom. In her study of forty K-12 teachers across six states in the United States, Koszalka (2001) confirmed her hypothesis that teachers who communicated *via* listservs about the use of Web-based resources in the classroom have a more positive attitude towards them. They also had stronger beliefs and feelings towards the use of other WWW resources. She therefore feels that knowledge about an innovation and a positive attitude is a prerequisite to using it. In their study of teacher-perceptions, Karyan and Crowe (1997) also found that teachers were positive about the use of discussion boards for various reasons, including: it facilitates discussion outside class, encourages group interaction, facilitates after-hours student interaction, and encourages ESL students to become more fluent in English.

Participation, collaboration and social presence

The computer-mediated communication environment is believed to promote participation, and encourage social presence. Warschauer (1996a), for example, examines whether second language students participate more equally in face-to-face or electronic discussions. In his study students were given two questions to discuss, the first face-to-face, and the second, electronically. He found that electronic exchanges were longer, and that there was more equal participation in the electronic discussion than the face-to-face discussion. However, collaboration is not always positive in online environments, as found by Davey (2001), whose students experienced difficulty collaborating on Web page projects.

In relation to social presence, Abdullah's (2001) study of twelve students (from Japan, Turkey, Sweden and parts of the United States, who were studying *via* an online course), demonstrated that the medium stimulated the use of social presence cues. Most social presence cues used included interactional prompts (invitations to respond, requests for support, addressing others by name, greetings), self-disclosure cues (reflections on personal perspectives, emotions), demonstrating courtesy (capitalising names, discussing interests), and tonal indicators (playful remarks and asides).

Although some studies indicate feelings of isolation in online environments (for example, a study by Shaw and Polovina, 1999), the use of computer-mediated communication is also said to have a positive impact on feelings of isolation. Johnson and Huff (2000) found that the use of a class listserv, which was used to post lecture outlines and questions, helped students feel connected to their classmates and overcome isolation.

The impact of ICTs on schools

To summarise, ICTs are said to have a positive impact on teaching and learning in schools.[3] According to Reeves (1998) there is considerable evidence that learners develop critical thinking skills as authors, designers and constructors of multimedia or as active participants in constructivist learning environments. Further research on whether media and technology are as effective as teachers and other methods is no longer needed (Reeves, 1998: online, 38 of 48).

Reeves (1998) celebrates the positive impact of ICTs in schools. The findings of his survey of the impact of the use of media and

3 Although this book does not focus on the school context, I draw on pertinent studies conducted in the school context in cases where the issues studied are similar to my work in the higher education context.

technology in schools in Australia, Canada, United Kingdom and the United States, may be summarised as follows: first, computers as tutors have positive effects on learning as measured by standardised assessment tests, and are more motivating to students. Second, computers are accepted more readily by teachers than other technologies, and are supported more by administrators, parents, teachers, politicians and the public. Third, students are able to complete a given set of educational objectives in less time with computer-based instruction than in the time needed in traditional approaches.

In essence, international studies demonstrate that ICTs influence teaching and learning significantly. In particular the studies point out that students communicate and collaborate more extensively in an online environment, and that the online environment also appears to encourage learner autonomy. Internationally, teachers and learners have positive attitudes towards online learning, although technological problems have been noted to cause frustration. Having provided a cross-section of international studies in some of the key areas of focus in my study, studies located in South Africa follow.

Studies on ICT-use in South Africa

Current studies located in South Africa on the use of ICTs in English language education are minimal. Thus I make general reference to a variety of South African studies in which ICTs, rather than English, is the focus in order to illustrate some of the current areas of interest in the country: the possibilities and limitations of online learning environments (Cronje, 1997), learning, motivation and student preferences (Sanders and Ayayee, 1997), lecturer preferences (Cronje and Murdoch, 2001), distance learning (van Buren Schele and Odendaal, 2001), and the use of the Net as an outreach tool (Keats, Collins, Peterson, 2001). Further studies conducted by the Multimedia Education Group at the Technology Unit at the University of Cape Town are also mentioned. Although some of the studies are school-based, rather than focused on the higher education context, I believe that the issues examined are equally relevant to the higher education context, given the scarcity of studies in the latter instance.

First, in order to work successfully in an online environment, students must be familiar with the basics of technology (Cronje, 1997). In his study Cronje (1997) determined that co-operative learning works well in online environments, as does online discussion. In relation to student achievement and learning, it was found by Clarke and Cronje (1998) that the medium of ICTs does not overly influence learning when student results in online and face-to-face classes were compared. However, the online medium can influence students effectively, in relation to interest and motivation.

Students were also generally positive about using computers in South Africa, although in relation to student preferences and individual differences, Sanders and Ayayee (1997) found that race and gender demographics influence computer use. Female students, they argue, are more cautious about using ICTs, and black South African students feel less capable than white students, having little prior experience with computers. Given that their study is almost ten years old, the situation of access remains one that is evident along racial divides. The under-resourced schools tend to be located in black rural and township areas, while the better-equipped schools are located in urban areas, and although the latter are currently attended by students from all race groups, they are still strongly populated by white students. Therefore, it is quite possible that black students from under-resourced backgrounds feel less proficient with ICTs. I explore the issue further when I examine access and proficiency among the students selected for this study.

Lecturer preferences also indicate that lecturers who are positive about using ICTs tend to use it in their teaching, according to Cronje and Murdoch (2001), who examined the use of *WebCT* at Rand Afrikaans University (renamed the University of Johannesburg). Lecturers indicated that ICTs also offered benefits such as increasing the opportunity for interaction, developing students' computer skills, and decreasing the administrative burden. Problems identified included that it took up too much time, it provided little academic interaction with students, it is not considered for promotion, there is not enough support available, technology is intimidating, and that there is too little knowledge about *WebCT* to utilise it optimally.

South Africa also experiences specific problems in its context as a developing country. Van Buren-Schele and Odendaal (2001) examine some of the problems of introducing online courses at Technikon South Africa, a distance education institution. The obstacles they identify include the lack of communication infrastructure for online teaching and learning, high costs of telecommunications, lack of coverage in rural areas, illiteracy and lack of computer skills, limitations on the availability of bandwidth (which affects the speed of data processing) and limited access to computers.

Odendaal's (2001) case study examines the use of technology in the design, development and delivery of a distance education online course at Technikon South Africa. One of the objectives of her study was to examine the responses of participants to determine the effect of interactive online learning on learners, their changing roles, participation patterns, and the problems they experience. She found that learners experienced communication anxiety, particularly about communicating online, which was a new experience for most of them. The role of the instructor changed from lecturer to facilitator and from provider to participator, and needed training to adapt to the new role. Odendaal (2001) found, however, that learner participation was not spread out equitably through the year. There was more participation around assignment due dates and examinations. Peer interaction was low, with the facilitator using most of the online time. With regard to problems experienced, learners indicated that access to, and knowledge of computers, technical problems, and slow network times were challenging. In relation to language use, Odendaal (2001) also found that texts should also cater for the needs of English second and third language speakers.

South African studies also explore the use of ICTs as an outreach tool. Keats et al. (2001) investigated the Net, in their case, as an outreach tool at the University of the Western Cape in order to address three challenges facing the university: declining student enrolment; attracting and servicing adult learners; and competing in the global marketplace. Outreach projects in the form of Biology projects were produced for their website, and guest-book comments were analysed.

In the period 1997–1999, however, they found that the site was being used primarily by North American, and to a lesser extent, South African teachers, learners and parents, which off course could be attributed to South African teachers', learners' and parents' limited ICT-access.

Research in the field of ICTs has also emanated from Technology Units at universities such as the one located at the University of Cape Town in South Africa. The Multimedia Education Group located at the Technology Unit conducts research into ICT-related issues such as policy, access, and pedagogy across South Africa. Studies include those by Czerniewicz (2004), Czerniewicz and Carr (2005), and Czerniewicz and Brown (2005). Their work covers a range of issues relevant to the South African context, including the possibilities and challenges of implementing computers for teaching and learning at the University of Cape Town (Czerniewicz, 2004); creating communities of practice among educational technology researchers and practitioners in developing contexts (Czerniewicz and Carr, 2005); and issues of access and the digital divide, where the researchers describe a model of technological access and practices (Czerniewicz and Brown, 2005). The studies are relevant to my work, concerned as it is with the use of technology in a developing context, from the perspective of a communities of practice framework in the higher education context.

Given the scarcity of research in ICTs and English language and education in South Africa, this book focuses on online learning from the perspective of English Language Studies and its educational implications. I am concerned with how ICTs are being utilised from a sociocultural perspective, in particular the extent to which they facilitate communities of practice, and the extent to which participants engage with and interact in the medium in the English classroom. To this end I explore how participants make meaning of the social issues raised in the English course readings in their written postings, while Chapter 2 examines theories relevant to my interests in more depth. In order to deconstruct the concept 'online learning' as used in this book, some definition and clarification of the term is necessary at this point.

Defining online learning

Terminology such as e-learning, Internet learning, distributed learning, networked learning, tele-learning, virtual learning, computer-assisted learning, web-based learning, and distance learning have been commonly used to refer to online learning in the international context (Ally, 2004; Kearsley, 1998). In his use of the term 'online learning' Ally (2004) cites Carliner (1999), who defines the concept as educational material presented on a computer, and Khan (1997), who defines it as an approach that delivers instruction to a remote audience, using the Web as a medium. However, online learning involves more than the presentation and delivery of materials. Ally (2004) argues that the learner and the learning process should be the focus, and therefore defines online learning as:

> The use of the Internet to access learning materials; to interact with the content, instructor, and other learners, and to obtain support during the learning process, in order to acquire knowledge, to construct personal meaning, and to grow from personal experience (Ally, 2004: 5).

As opposed to Kearsley (1998) referred to in the Introduction, who also regards online learning as learning via a computer, Ally (2004) expands the notion to take into account how students make meaning and interact with other participants in the online environment. The latter interpretation appears more appropriate for my study because it transcends the notion of online learning as merely an ICT-based resource or tool.

The term e-learning is actually an overarching concept because it involves the use of a greater variety of multimedia modes of delivery such as computers, DVDs, CDs, as well as electronic devices such as mobile phones (refer to Stockley, 2005). Online learning is restricted to the use of the Net. In my project I utilise e-mail and the Net to support my web course, and I also refer students to additional websites. Because I do not utilise other multimedia devices such as CD-Roms or DVDs, I use the term 'online learning', rather than e-learning, drawing on the key concepts of computer-assisted language learning (CALL), which is developed later in this chapter.

The emergence of online applications in the teaching-learning context has undoubtedly introduced a paradigm shift from the conventional face-to-face classroom to electronic applications in teaching and learning. The shift has highlighted similarities and differences between the two modes of delivery.

Distinctions between face-to-face and electronic online classrooms

Distinctions can be made between the traditional face-to-face classroom and the electronic classroom in terms of resources (also refer to Burgstahler, 1997). The primary instructional tools of the conventional classroom include texts, slides, lectures, printed handouts, products to demonstrate, and the classroom. The primary learning vehicles of electronic classrooms include texts, electronic mail, electronic distribution lists, and a Web server. The following section compares key aspects of both types of classrooms: teacher presence, discussion and collaboration, and access to resources.

The teacher is a physical presence in the face-to-face classroom, as opposed to the online environment where he/she is a virtual presence, and we are amazed at how we are able to teach students in all parts of the world from our homes when we teach online. In conventional classrooms, teachers may work in teams, whilst in electronic online classes teachers may be hundreds, even thousands of kilometres apart, and yet are able to teach and team-teach simultaneously. The teacher may not be a physical presence, but is present as a facilitator who prepares and distributes materials, sets class work tasks, encourages discussion and evaluates tasks.

It is also possible to include guests, specialists, and visitors in virtual classes, as is possible in the face-to-face situation.[4] Specialists and guests may also be included from anywhere in the world, and it is possible for them to participate over a longer period of time as traditional constraints such as the time available disappear. A guest might make input such as posting readings or comments at any time he/she is available from his/her office or home, without the cost of plane tickets and other constraints. Participants may retrieve and respond to messages at a time convenient to them. Nor are common times and venues necessary for students to meet, as course material can be distributed electronically via the course distribution list and accessed at any point in time.

In relation to classroom discussion and collaboration, online discussions held via discussion threads and bulletin boards are possible. Discussion threads occur when one e-mail message may be sent to all linked e-mail addresses simultaneously. On a bulletin board, a message may be placed on a central web site, for instance, and can be accessed and responded to by readers at any time (Warschauer, Turbee and Roberts, 1996). Generally, students may be encouraged to participate in discussions by being asked to submit at least one comment per lesson. This prevents the possibility of dominant or lurking students. As participants become more familiar and comfortable with the technology, they tend to participate more frequently (for example, Albrekston, 1995; Karyan and Crowe, 1997; Johnson and Huff, 2000; Nunan in Kahmi-Steyn, 2000). Albrekston (1995) also found that computer-mediated discussion enabled more inhibited students, in particular, to participate more than in the face-to-face situation. Johnson and Huff's (2000) study of campus-based and distance Social Work students revealed that the students perceived online discussion a useful tool for collaboration, and that it minimised feelings of isolation.

In relation to resources, students traditionally visit the library in order to gain access to books, journals and other material. In electronic classrooms, material may be placed on the class website, and

4 Refer, for example to the study conducted by Hodgkinson-Williams and Mostert (2005).

students also have unlimited access to the Web in order to access information. In the traditional class, assignments are physically handed in and assessed, whereas electronic assignments are submitted via e-mail and may be posted as 'models of good practice' on the website for other students to read as well. This, of course, with the writers' permission, since there are ethical considerations when using learners' work as models for public viewing. Assessment and feedback may also be provided electronically.

Despite the benefits listed above, many questions arise about the challenges posed by online classes. Foremost, critique is directed at the extent to which students and teachers require face-to-face contact. It has been established by some researchers that the lack of personal contact has not hampered student performance in any way, although some participants have noted feelings of isolation (for example Czerniewicz, 2001). Others have praised the benefits because they found the nature of online classes sufficiently collaborative (such as Zafeiriou et al., 2001; Cunningham, 2000; Lally and Barret, 1999; and Johnson and Huff, 2000). However, Lally and Barret (1999) add caution that the construction of an effective online community may depend on the provision of adequate opportunities for socio-emotional discourse and the establishment of co-operative frameworks for learning. It is also felt by teachers that more opportunities for reflection should be encouraged in online communities, and to encourage interaction.

Another challenge is whether computer applications can help improve student performance in basic language skills areas. Here, we need to examine various factors. We need to look into the specific skill areas, grade levels, and content areas in which computer applications are most effective. It is also important to examine the kinds and levels of students who seem to benefit from the use of computers, as is the need to look at the kinds of computer applications that are most effective. Student attitudes also need to be studied, in order to determine whether the use of computer applications can improve students' attitudes towards school and learning, and whether improved attitudes necessarily result in better performance. Equally important is research into teacher attitudes. As mentioned earlier in the section on international studies, a study of teacher-attitudes suggests that teachers who participate actively in a computer-mediated environment have a more positive attitude to its use in the classroom (Koszalka's, 2001). An especially significant challenge is the need for work in the South African and African contexts, particularly in relation to issues around the acquisition of English as a second or additional language. From a sociocultural perspective, any work situated in the English language classroom context warrants some consideration of communication, dialogue and interaction in that context, thus the need for an examination of computer-mediated communication, which is highlighted as being essential in online environments.

Computer-mediated communication: Facilitating dialogue and democracy

The term 'computer mediated communication' (CMC) was coined by Hilz and Turoff (1978 in Murray, 2000) in their study of computer conferencing. The term includes communication via e-mail, bulletin boards, chat rooms, discussion lists and the WWW. It refers to the ways in which telecommunications technologies have merged with computers and computer networks to give us new tools to support teaching and learning (Brush and Uden, 2000), or, in Herring's early view: 'communication that takes place between human beings via the instrumentality of computers' (Herring, 1996: 1). CMC therefore provides a means to develop and implement new forms of collaboration among groups of people, regardless of their location.

As alluded to in the Introduction, the two main types of CMC are synchronous communication (where users communicate with one another in real time via chat programmes or video conferencing) and asynchronous communication (which occurs where there may be a delay between when the message is sent, and when it is responded to, such as e-mail, discussion threads and bulletin boards). Asynchronous communication does not depend on participants being online simultaneously. Learners are allowed more opportunities for productivity and participation because of time and location independence and new access opportunities. Learning therefore no longer requires exclusively face-to-face social interaction, a point supported by Blakely (in Zafeiriou et al., 2001: 2), who says 'Learning is becoming both a personal and participative activity. It is no longer something that requires a group activity, in which participation is limited to the immediate social interaction'.

Empirical evidence suggests that CMC has positive effects on facilitating the acquisition of skills such as writing and discussion (Cunningham, 2000; Warschauer and Healy, 1998), as well as democratising the teaching-learning environment (Warschauer, 1996a; Huff and King, 1988; Tella, 1991). Warschauer and Healy (1998), in their study on student attitudes to online e-mail writing tasks, find that students maintain a more positive attitude to online writing tasks, which in turn could improve their general writing skills.

In relation to classroom interaction and discussion, students sometimes do not interact extensively with their peers or teachers in face-to-face classrooms. Harman (in Warschauer, 1996a) found that electronic discussion helped students increase their amount of communication with the teacher and with other students as well. CMC is also said to have a more equalising effect than face-to-face discussion. This is in relation to participation (such as gender-based participation), as well as social status. Face-to-face discussion may be unbalanced, with just one or two participants dominating the floor, whereas students who traditionally did not participate in face-to-face discussion tend to participate more in electronic discussion (Warschauer, 1996a).[5] Warschauer (2004b) also cites studies where student participation was found to be greater in three areas: student talk versus

5 In Warschauer's (1996a) comparison of the equality of student participation in face-to-face and electronic discussion, each mode was correlated to factors such as nationality, language ability, time spent in the United States and student attitudes. Warschauer (1996a) finds that students participate more equally in electronic discussion and use language that is lexically and syntactically more formal and complex than in face-to-face discussion.

teacher talk, directional focus of student talk, and equality of student participation.[6]

In relation to participation it was found that electronic communication brought in an equalising opportunity among male and female students in the classroom. McGuire, Kiesler and Siegel (1987) show that women make the first proposal as often as men in electronic discussion, compared to only one-fifth as often in face-to-face discussion. Tella's (1991) study of Finnish girls supports the issue of gender-based participation. She demonstrates that although Finnish girls traditionally have less access to and proficiency with computers than boys, when girls were participants in an international English language e-mail project, they participated as much as the boys. Herring's (1996b) study, however, found gender-based differences in male and female participation: he shows that a male discourse style (for example, debate and freedom from rules) dominates the Net. He shows that female CMC is characterised by politeness, support, consideration and appreciation, and that in his study, males participated more frequently than females. When the females did participate they were ignored or criticised. Allen (in Murray, 2000), on the other hand, argues that women have more positive attitudes to CMC than men, especially in terms of e-mail.[7]

CMC is also thought of as democratising the learning environment because it is an accessible medium that reduces social status cues (such as accent, handwriting, voice quality, appearance, race) (Herring, 1993b). In another study, Huff and King (1988) demonstrate that topics proposed by lower-status group members were accepted equally in electronic discussion, but were only rarely accepted in face-to-face discussion.

Thus, to a great extent, CMC can facilitate more equitable participation opportunities among students. Lally and Barret (1999: 151) refer to this as the 'equalisation of community members'. Their study of student teachers established that the absence of non-verbal

6 Warschauer (2004b) cites studies by Chun (1994), Kelm (1992), Kern (1995), and Sullivan and Pratt (1996).

7 Allen (in Murray, 2000) shows that women feel more comfortable with the electronic medium than men.

cues inhibited some of the participants. They also found that communication anxiety relating to technical fears (such as if a message was sent or not), and message inappropriacy, was felt by some of the participants.

From the discussion thus far it is evident that students and teachers with access to ICTs have alternatives to face-to-face classroom participation. However, online learning can be done 'for better or for worse'. It is necessary to have substantial interaction and communication among participants for successful online learning to take place. Interaction enriches the online environment, dispelling the view held by critics that the online environment is sterile and impersonal (Kearsley, 1998). Research on the effectiveness of computers and new technologies in language teaching and learning is an ongoing process. What can be done with computers and teachers' and learners' responses to technology is constantly changing, however, as more research is conducted we get closer to the role technology can or should play. This is vital and it is exactly what my study attempts to do. As Lee (2000) says, if properly implemented, the use of Net technology contributes significantly to experiential learning, motivation, enhanced student achievement, authentic materials for study, greater interaction, individualisation, independence from a single source of information and global understanding.

Having examined some of the key debates and evidence surrounding the differences between face-to-face and online classrooms (teacher presence, discussion and collaboration, and access to resources), as well as issues relevant to CMC (teacher-presence, collaboration, and democracy), I would like to draw specific attention to the emergence of computer-assisted language learning (CALL) at this point. In sections to follow I trace the route taken by CALL in relation to language acquisition theories by deconstructing behaviourist, communicative, and integrative approaches. Thereafter I examine specific Net-based strategies that are relevant for the English classroom.

Exploring computer-assisted language learning (CALL)

Computer-assisted learning (CAL) software was originally used for stand-alone desktop computers. Computer-assisted language learning (CALL) is the application of CAL to language learning and teaching, and may in fact be viewed as an eclectic field that borrows from CAL and Applied Linguistics (Cunningham, 2000). Historically, CALL applications such as language laboratories that comprised a series of booths with a cassette deck, microphone and headphone were used in language acquisition in the 1960s and 1970s (Singhal, 1997). Students followed instructions and were monitored by the teacher at a central control panel. This was based on a behaviourist stimulus-response model. The premise was that the more the students practised drills, the better they would acquire the language. The idea is based on the principles of Skinner (1953) who saw language acquisition as behaviour and habit-formation. The views on language acquisition have since shifted, with acquisition seen as an interactive and communicative process that integrates the various skills. Thus, while the language laboratory method succeeded in linking language and technology, it was pedagogically unsound, leaving students bored, and with little interaction between them and the teacher. This is not to say that the behaviourist approach is dispensable, a point to which I return a little later in this chapter. However, although CALL applications had their beginnings in language laboratories, they are not so confined. The programmes are extensive, as is indicated in Figure 1:

General category	Sub-category
Tools	Text processors Voice processing programmes Communications programmes
Instructional programmes	Drills and practice Tutorials Exploratory programmes Simulations, games, hypermedia
Databases	Information sources Text corpuses Hypermedia
Testing programmes	Computer-based language tests

Fig. 1: CALL Programmes. Adapted from Cunningham (2000)

As stated in the previous section, CALL originated and was initially utilised in the behaviourist tradition with drill-like exercises. However, a marked transition followed, as a result of shifts in how language was taught. These shifts were characterised by a move from memorised drill dialogues to more communicative, creative self-expression and the negotiation of meaning (Warschauer, 2000d). Intrinsic too, is comprehensible input, the incorporation of authentic materials and realia. While initially placing emphasis on tutorials, simulations and tests, the move has been towards human-to-human communication, giving language learners with Net access unlimited access to native speakers and other language learners the world over.

Historically, the forty-year period characterising CALL may be divided into three main stages, all of which parallel shifts in language acquisition theory: behaviourist or structural CALL, communicative CALL, and integrative CALL (Warschauer, 1996b; Warschauer and Healy, 1998). The stages are not as clearly distinct as they appear to be, as there are overlaps and synergies between the stages. One therefore needs to be cautious in describing these stages in an evolutionary manner, which considers 'most recent' best. There are strengths in the behaviourist approach, for example, that may work successfully with particular types of learners or in particular contexts. Certain students may for instance benefit from repeated pronunciation tasks. Therefore it would be short-sighted to dismiss a particular approach completely in favour of another. The following table (Figure 2), as adapted from Warschauer and Healy (1998), reflects the journey taken by CALL over the years more conclusively:

Stage	**1960s–1970s Behaviourist/ Structural Call**	**1980s–1990s Communicative Call**	**Twenty-first Century Integrative Call**
Technology	Mainframe	Personal computers	Multimedia and Internet
English-teaching paradigm	Grammar-translation and audiolingual	Communicative language teaching	Content-based English for Specific Purposes/English for Academic Purposes/ sociocultural/ critical
View of language	Structural (a formal structural system)	Cognitive (a mentally-constructed system)	Socio-cognitive (developed in social interaction)
Principal use of computers	Drill and practice	Communicative exercises	Authentic discourse
Principle objective	Accuracy	Accuracy and fluency	Accuracy, fluency and agency

Fig. 2: History of CALL. Adapted from Warschauer and Healy (1998)

Behaviourist CALL

The first appearance of CALL in the 1960s and 1970s featured repetitive language drills, or the drill and practice method (Lee, 2000). The model, referred to by Warschauer (1996b: 1) as 'drill and kill' was based on the behaviourist model of learning, with the computer being used as a mechanical tutor. The model was used mainly for drills, translation tests, and grammar instruction. As stated earlier in this section, despite critique of the behaviourist approach (for instance, by Stevens, 1989), CALL drills may still be used today, the rationale being, according to Warshauer (1996b: 1) that:

- repeated exposure to the same material is beneficial to learning;
- computers are ideal for carrying out drills. Machines do not get bored presenting the same material, and offer non-judgemental feedback;

- computers can present material on an individualised basis, thus allowing students to work at their own pace.

Several CALL tutoring systems were originally designed around behaviourist principles, the Programmed Logic for Automatic Teaching Options (PLATO) system being one of the earliest and most popular. The PLATO system is an e-learning and computer-based instructional system which offered a range of self-paced programmes in reading, writing, mathematics, science, social studies and life and job skills to learners ranging from pre-school to adult level. The reading and writing programmes, which were initially implemented in 1963, utilised vocabulary drills, grammar explanations and drills and tests. Behaviourist CALL fell out of favour in the late 1970s and 1980s because the behaviourist approach to language learning was rejected on theoretical and pedagogical grounds. This led to the second phase of CALL, based on the communicative approach to language teaching that was prominent in the 1970s and 1980s (for example: Hymes, 1971).

Communicative CALL

Communicative CALL emerged in the 1970s and 1980s as a reaction to the behaviourist approach. Proponents of communicative CALL, such as Stevens (1989) and Underwood (1984) felt that CALL should focus more on *using* forms rather than on the forms themselves, that is it should allow for more authentic communication. Communicative CALL corresponded to theories that recognised that learning was a creative process of discovery and expression. Underwood (1984) made the following premises about communicative CALL: it teaches grammar implicitly, rather than explicitly; it allows students to generate original utterances rather than prefabricated utterances; it evaluates everything that students do, or rewards them with instant congratulatory messages; it avoids telling students that they are wrong, and allows for multiple responses; it uses only the target language; and it creates an environment in which using the target language feels natural and authentic.

Stevens (1989) suggested that CALL courses should build on learners' intrinsic motivation, and that they should also allow for interactivity. Programmes included activities that stimulated discussion, writing, and critical thinking, and communicative CALL programmes appeared to be superior to behaviourist programmes. However, by the late 1980s, many teachers felt that communicative CALL was not working as well as it could have been (Lee, 2000). It was felt that the communicative approach led to language being taught compartmentally, albeit within a communicative framework. This led to a more integrative, networked approach, and the challenge was to design integrative CALL programmes that were more content-driven and project-based.

Integrative CALL and network-based language teaching

Because communicative CALL was critiqued in certain spheres for using the computer in an '*ad hoc* and disconnected fashion' (Kenning and Kenning in Lee, 2000: 6), teachers were urged to move away from a cognitive view to a more socio-cognitive one that advocated real language use in meaningful, authentic contexts. Integrative CALL, which is based on the use of multimedia and the Net, seeks to integrate the language learning skills of reading, writing, speaking and listening, as well as technology more meaningfully into language teaching and learning, giving the learner more agency. Multimedia allows a variety of media such as text, graphics, sound, animation and video to be accessed at a single machine. Multimedia includes hypermedia, that is, all multimedia resources are linked, enabling learners to take control of the learning situation with the 'click of a mouse'. Hypermedia provides advantages for language learning in the following ways: it creates a more authentic language learning environment, where listening, for example is combined with seeing, as in the real world; it is quite simple to integrate skills into a single activity because of the variety of media; students have more control over the learning process because they can work at their own pace, as well as go forward and backward in a non-linear fashion, as the links allow and as they need to (they can spend more time with aspects they need to, and skip certain aspects altogether as they need); and finally, hypermedia focuses on content, language, and learning strategies simultaneously (Warschauer, 1996b).

Innovative teachers may use the Net to help create a learning environment where authentic communication is integrated into all aspects of a course, and with the Net providing opportunities for instruction, research, collaboration, and publication (Mak, 1995a). Students can search through Net files and access materials such as newspaper and magazine articles, radio broadcasts and videos (see examples provided by Brown, 1999; Pathak, 2001; Scotellaro, 2002; Pickard, 2002). They can then publish their own texts or materials on the Web. This can be done collaboratively, within the same class, or by linking up with classes at other institutions, in other countries even. Students can then provide feedback on one another's work, like in the case of Santos' class, described by Warschauer (2002c) as an example of an integrated approach.[8]

Use can also be made of real-time audio and audio-visual chatting, such as through NetPhone and CUSeeME technological tools, which enable participants to see and hear one another while communicating. Audio chatting technology involves sound systems that may be accessed via the Net, where participants may listen to one another. Video chatting enables participants to see one another while chatting. However, these are not being used extensively at the moment in countries such as South Africa, largely due to the lack of access to the relevant technology in educational institutions, cost factors, and limited bandwidth, as discussed in the Introduction.

We can also make a further distinction between CALL and network-based language teaching (NBLT). NBLT involves the use of computers connected to one another, where human communication is the focus, rather than the tutorials, drills and simulations, which are the focus of CALL. NBLT utilises non-synchronous tools such as e-mail and discussion threads, and can also use synchronous tools such

8 As I explain in Chapter 3, in the project described in this book my students were able to utilise online Net sources and participate in communicative activities via discussion threads on web courses. The creation of Web pages was, however, technologically beyond their ability at the time.

as chat rooms and video-conferencing. O'Dowd (2004: 112) summarises NBLT as beneficial for foreign language teaching for the following reasons: it supports interaction and reflection; it encourages equality of participation among learners; it provides an authentic environment for learners; it facilitates collaborative construction of knowledge; it allows learners to work with hypermedia; and it facilitates intercultural contact. The context of NBLT has not, according to Kern and Warschauer (2000) been studied sufficiently, or in depth, but they emphasise the need for a holistic, socio-collaborative approach that goes beyond a study of linguistic features. They say:

> Network-based language teaching does not represent a particular technique, method, or approach. It is a constellation of ways which students communicate via computer networks and interpret and construct online texts and multimedia documents, all as part of a process of steadily-increasing engagement in new discourse communities (Kern and Warschauer, 2000: 11).

Although computers can serve a multitude of purposes, as indicated above, they constitute the medium, or the methods and approaches that are implemented. Thus CALL is only effective in how we, the human element, put it to use (see also Garret, 1996).[9]

Some challenges in South Africa and beyond

Despite the benefits of ICTs and online learning as discussed in the previous section, and given the minimal incentives in South Africa, technology has not made an extensive impact on education thus far.[10] Teachers are not yet suitably technically proficient to make their own programmes, and commercial developers do not have the necessary pedagogical background to ensure that the programmes are of suitable quality. South African teachers are also not yet offered sufficient

9 Cited in Warschauer (1996b: 7).

10 There is some work on the impact of multimedia such as 3-D games, as well as the development of digital archives.

training courses in order to work within a technological environment, as was found in research conducted by the South African Institute of Distance Education (SAIDE, 2003; also *Draft White Paper on e-Education*, 2004). Computers are also not yet intelligent enough to be fully interactive, as required in an integrative approach.

Another reason for the minimal impact of technology in the educational context is that learners are not adequately computer literate. Thus I selected an approach that is partly communicative and partly network-based to implement in the project described and analysed in this book. I was further limited in that the higher education institution selected for study did not have adequate facilities to utilise for a fully integrative approach, and it was beyond budgetary constraints at the university to install additional hardware and software at the time of my research. Such decisions are important to consider in the context of a developing country when designing a project of this nature.

The specific sources of Internet-based applications relevant for use in the English classroom and which are relevant to this book are described and critiqued in sections to follow.

Sources of Internet-based applications

As I have maintained thus far, the use of Net enhanced applications in the language classroom is not new, but is an emerging development in South Africa and other developing countries. It is necessary to examine what has been done elsewhere, as is suggested in the SAIDE Report (2000b) *Lessons in the applications of educational technologies in South Africa*, in order not to perpetuate mistakes. For example, the Report cites instances where technology-based projects were unsuccessful because of their high operating costs, the problems with adaptation to local conditions, and the lack of skilled personnel. The Report maintains that South Africa appears to be repeating the same mistakes as other developing countries, rather than 'leapfrogging' them, despite the local and international experiences. Chisholm et al. (2004) and Warschauer (2002a, 2002b, 2003a, 2003b, 2004b, 2005, in press)[11] also cite such common weaknesses in the implementation of technology in developing countries. Ultimately, success depends on the teacher's ability to integrate technology in the classroom and the curriculum:

> The intrepid and creative teacher will venture into this virtual realm, find authentic resources, and use them to make the second language classroom a marvellous place to learn (Leloup and Ponteiro, 2000: 4).

There are several Net-based applications that can be used in the English classroom, provided of course, that the infrastructure and resources are available. These applications are described by Leloup and Ponteiro (2000), and Marcos (1994). To provide an overview of the field, and because this work is located within the context of a developing country, where ICT-use is still an emerging practice, I include descriptions of the current practices in the following section, although I have only chosen to implement the use of the Net, e-mail, and discussion threads in my online course, which are less intensive than full web-use for the developing country context. The following applications, although not exhaustive, are constantly updating and upgrading. The list also serves as an indication of where we are at in South Africa:

11 Warschauer (2002a, 2002b, 2003a, 2003b, 2005, in press) describes these weaknesses in three case studies: India's 'Hole in the Wall' project, where computer kiosks were introduced in streets for children to use in an attempt at non-invasive education. They were not taught to use the technology and subsequently did not use the technology to learn, rather to play games and paint. In Ireland's Information Age Town project, towns were encouraged to submit technology plans to show how they would incorporate technology into the town. The town that won extensive ICT systems, could not fully operate the systems because they were not trained sufficiently in its use. The town that was the runner-up won ICTs to a lesser value but was more successful because the people focused more on training. In Egypt's Model Lab project, a US-funded computer laboratory was established at an Egyptian university. However, the laboratory remained closed for bureaucratic reasons, and because staff and students were not given suitable training and access to the equipment.

- e-mail
- electronic lists
- electronic journals and weblogs
- streaming audio and video, and podcasts
- remote access to libraries and databases
- chat, audio and video conferencing
- Web course management

E-mail

The most commonly used online tools are e-mail, bulletin boards, and chat rooms. Of these tools e-mail is the most commonly used Net application. It allows individuals from anywhere in the world to communicate with others without the constraints of time zones. Messages can be sent at the sender's convenience, regardless of whether the receiver is present at that time. The message can be opened and responded to at the recipient's convenience. E-mail is used by educators around the world, and language teachers in particular can integrate e-mail based activities such as e-pal (electronic penpal) programmes into their curricula to encourage student interaction. Learners across the world may be matched depending on the learning context, or needs (such as course of study, level of English, age of learners, and so on), through several contact websites, or by requests through listservers.

I included in my pilot case study an e-pal project that was conducted with students, the details of which are presented later. Several other studies of e-mail use have been conducted in the field, such as those by Ho (2000), Sakar (2001), Mello (1998), Liao Chao (1999), Jor and Mak (1994), Lee (2004) and Greenfield (2003). The following summary of relevant research provides a cross-section of studies conducted in the field using e-mail and e-pal projects. For convenience, the research has been tabulated according to the relevant study and its findings:

Researcher	Method	Findings and/or recommendations
Ho (2000)	International collaborative project between two schools in Singapore and Birmingham.	Participants' confidence, awareness and understanding of both cultures were enhanced. Their language skills and creativity were developed.
Sakar (2001)	E-mail exchange between Turkish students at the University of Bahcesehir and other international foreign language students. The study was based on Hymes' (1974) communicative approach, and the intercultural communication approach (Belisle, 1996; Berenfield, 1996).	The project provided an opportunity for reading and writing practice, and had a positive impact on cultural awareness.
Mello (1998)	International collaborative exchange between students in Sao Paolo, Korea, and Japan.	The study recommends that teachers must have the same objectives and maintain contact for the duration of the project. Students should be paired with students of a similar age and level of English to prevent drop-outs and lack of interest. Student training is essential.
Liao Chao (1999)	Exchanges between students in Taiwan, and partner countries including Australia, Germany, Ireland, Romania, United States. The study used Hymes' (1974) communicative language teaching model.	Recommendations include technical training for students. Students also need to be taught how to ask questions, in particular, those of a cross-cultural nature.
Jor and Mak (1994)	Two international projects involving 250 students from eleven universities. The students participated in an integrated writing course.	Their recommendations include having a good mailing list, adequate access to resources, adequate time to learn and reflect on writing, advance planning, good matches in terms of levels and objectives. They also emphasise teacher collaboration, integration of e-mail into the curriculum, and willingness to embrace new technology. Students wrote for a real audience.

Lee (2004)	The study examined learner perspectives on networked collaborative interaction. Participants included native and non-native speakers of Spanish at the Universities of New Hampshire and George Mason. Strategies included e-mail, discussion threads, and bulletin boards using the Blackboard web management system.	Participants were able to produce a wide range of discourse structures and develop grammatical competence and L2 lexicons. The only reported adverse effect was because of the different time zones timing was not appropriate for synchronous exchanges.
Greenfield (2003)	The study examined secondary ESL students' attitudes and perceptions of a collaborative e-mail exchange project between a class in Hong Kong and one in Iowa. The purpose of the exchange was for learners to participate in an integrated writing course.	The researcher found that students' reading, writing, grammar and listening skills improved. She further reports that the Taiwanese students perceived that their confidence grew as a result of the project.

Fig. 3: Summary of research findings of e-mail exchange projects

From Figure 3 it is evident that practitioners and participants across the globe are demonstrating an interest in e-mail exchange projects. Of particular interest, the findings indicate that skills and competencies in writing, speaking, reading, listening and grammar improve. However, some of the studies rely on self-report data, which is not generalisable. On a positive note, cross-cultural awareness also appears to improve. An obvious difficulty is establishing common times for synchronous exchanges, such as using chat rooms, if participants are located in different time zones. Researchers recommend, however, that participants have an interest in the use of technology, and that teachers maintain contact during the course of the project. Other key recommendations include training for teachers and learners, as well as integration with the curriculum, rather than stand-alone projects. Distance learning is also reportedly enhanced by e-mail applications, where e-mail has been found to facilitate communication and interaction (Odendaal, 2001).

E-mail can therefore be used creatively in the English classroom. However, e-mail, like other forms of technology, will not solve language problems. Success depends on the innovative teacher to develop ways of utilising it in the classroom to satisfy specific goals, and based on learners' needs (see Warschauer, 1995). Students may be disoriented if they are not very proficient at using computers and e-mail, which is particularly true in the context of developing countries.

To summarise the above findings and recommendations, e-mail exchanges in the teaching-learning situation are reported to motivate students and foster positive attitudes to language learning and the cultural beliefs of others. Reading and writing skills, well as grammatical and L2 lexical structures, are said to improve.

Concerns discussed by Moran and Hawisher (1998) and Warschauer (2004a) about the casual nature of online writing, as well as its graphic (as opposed to text) dominance that could be detrimental to language acquisition, are dispelled by Danet (2001) and Moran and Hawisher (1998) who compare e-mails to the different genres of writing. For example, students would be taught that e-mail conversations are far more casual and social than the formal language requirements of collaborative projects that are going to be published. To this end, Mak (1995a, 1995b) recommends that the language of e-mail be incorporated into English courses, together with how to write clearly, effectively and to tolerate cultural and geographical differences. The findings of the studies on e-mail use, as well as their implications for English teaching and learning are worthy of consideration for teachers wanting to implement similar strategies in their teaching. Of note are the findings regarding English language teaching and learning, given the context of English as an additional language in developing countries.

Electronic discussion groups and listservs

Another application of an Internet-based technological approach is electronic discussion groups or listservs, which use e-mail to provide a forum where people can participate in professional dialogue and share resources. In his Introduction to *E-mail for English Teaching*, Warschauer (1995: 1) describes how a teacher in New York, teaching English pronunciation to Spanish speakers needs help from colleagues around the world and posts a question on a listserv. Within half an hour her question is answered. Several lists exist for language teachers, where questions and suggestions may be posted, such as EDNET and EDUTEL (lists which discuss the relationship between computer networking and education), TESL-L (international discussion for ESL teachers), TESLCA-L (international discussion on computer-assisted language learning), Language Learning Technology International Discussion Forum and the International E-mail Classroom Connection.

Because participation can enhance professional development for teachers, electronic lists provide participants with the 'floor' to network, address common issues and perhaps solve problems. Murphy's (2000) doctoral study bears reference here. She elicited teachers' beliefs about the use of online technology in the teaching of French as a second language on a listserv she created for the purpose of the study. She found that teachers responded positively to the use of listservs, because it gave them the opportunity to interact and communicate. Lee's (2004) study summarised in Figure 3 also bears reference. She found participation on listservs helped ESL students produce a wide range of discourse structures and develop grammatical competence and L2 lexicons.

Electronic academic journals

Electronic journals can reach a wide readership, and while some are freely available, others require subscription. This is important in countries where access to journals is limited. Articles include links to other sources because of the hypermedia or hypertext nature, making them very accessible. Examples of electronic journals in the field of English language include *Language Learning and Technology (LLT)*, *Teaching English as a Second Language Electronic Journal (TESOL-EJ)*, *Online Educator*, *Calico Journal* and *Academic Exchange Quarterly*, all of which are American-based. Subscriptions and submissions are done electronically. Articles may be submitted, edited and printed electronically, which facilitates the publishing process. African journals include African Journals online (www.ajol.info).

Some students might find approaching a teacher an intimidating experience if they are shy or lack confidence in speaking English. Journals may help facilitate communication between teacher and students, as well as encourage writing skills. Tillyer's (1993) study, for instance, shows how students maintained greater contact with their teacher via e-mail journals than in regular face-to-face consultation sessions.

The use of print-based dialogue journals to encourage reflection and writing has benefits in ESL learning. However, as Warschauer (1995) comments, weekly submissions and waiting for teacher-feedback is tedious. He says this is facilitated by the use of electronic journals. Wang's (1993) study of student writing in electronic and print format shows that students wrote more, and asked more questions electronically than they did in print medium. Electronic submission permits teachers to respond electronically as well, although it is probably true that teachers who do not return student work timeously, will probably not do so electronically either! Should the teacher wish, public journals may be created (with student permission), where entries may be submitted to a bulletin board for other students to read and comment on, creating student-student interaction as well.

Weblogs, or blogs are web-based publications which are updated regularly by 'bloggers', as the writers are known.[12] They function as online diaries or journals and cover a range of topics and issues such as, but not limited to, politics, education, topical and social issues, popular media and culture, career and workplace news, and updates on personal lives. Bloggers might include photographs and hyperlinks to related sites, and encourage comments and discussion on their entries.

In the educational context, blogs might be used in a variety of ways. Wikipedia (http://en.wikipedia.org/wiki/Blog) details how blogs can be used as an electronic scrapbook for school excursions, where learners can upload photographs, texts, as well as audio and video recordings of places visited. Other uses include online courses, news-

12 http://en.wikipedia.org/wiki/Blog Last accessed 4 May 2006.

letters and teacher training materials. Data available on blogs provide a rich source of research material. Huffaker (2004), for instance, analyses teenage blogs in America to ascertain how teenagers construct their identities in the online medium.

Audio and video technology and podcasts

Streaming audio and video technology allows learners to listen to news, sports, weather and music broadcasts throughout the world. Two common streaming formats, *RealPlayer* and *Media Player* (technology which enable audio broadcasts) can be freely downloaded. Such practices add vastly to any English teacher's repertoire of authentic materials. Pickard (2002), for instance demonstrates how audio and video technology (such as news sites) contribute positively to English second and foreign language classrooms. Students may listen to a news programme as a listening exercise, and summarise the news as a speaking or writing activity. A study conducted by Meskill and Mossop (2000) on teachers' use of ICTs in the classroom finds that the use of electronic, audio- and video-texts increased student motivation, and that the role of the instructor shifts from a central one to a peripheral one. Other multimodal devices impacting on education include MP3 players and I-pods, which could be utilised by teachers in English teaching and learning. New vocabulary, for instance, could be sent as message texts, and quick quizzes could be administered to students via such devices.

Podcasts (a contraction of iPod and broadcast) are digital media files that are distributed over the Net, that can be downloaded automatically and played back on media players and computers.

Libraries and bibliographies

Library catalogues and bibliographic resources are available on the Net, thus providing remote access to databases. Examples such as the *Emerald* and *ERIC*[13] databases make it possible for teachers and learners to locate mini-bibliographies and articles online. This option is very useful to researchers, and enables them to search literally hundreds of databases around the world. Researchers are able to retrieve texts and graphics, and save the results on their own computers.

Chat, audio, and video conferencing

Real-time or synchronous communication may take place via chat, conferencing, and messaging programmes. Applications such as *Internet Relay Chat* (*IRC*), which refers to chat software that may be installed for online chat over the Net enable synchronous conversation among participants anywhere in the world. Users 'talk' by typing messages, which can be seen by all other users participating in the conversation. Foreign language students can participate in voice conversation, and be seen using conferencing programmes such as *CUSeeMe* and *MSMeeting* that enable participants to see one another while communicating. In a study by Pratt and Sullivan (1994, in Warschauer, 1995), the effects of computer-networking on ESL was studied at the University of Puerto Rico. Two ESL classes were studied, one that met once or twice a week in an online environment, and the other that met in a traditional face-to-face classroom. The researchers found that students participated more in the online environment than in the face-to-face environment, and that the students' writing improved to a greater extent in the online class, when pre-and post-writing tasks were compared. Pratt and Sullivan (1994, in Warschauer, 1995) further found that the online class was more

13 The Education Resources Information Centre (*ERIC*), is a free online database of journal and other education literature, and is sponsored by the Institute of Education Sciences of the United States Department of Education.

student-centred, while the face-to-face class was teacher-dominated. Similar results were found by Hartman et al. (1991) and Mabrito (1991, 1992).[14] Their research shows that less able ESL writing students communicated more in an online environment than in a face-to-face environment, made more input in relation to peer editing, and incorporated more revisions into their own texts (in Warschauer, 1995).

Web course management systems

Web course management software is designed to create and manage online courses. Web courses can be conducted entirely online, or can also run parallel to traditional face-to-face courses as an extension or support effort, with teachers making course notes, syllabi, glossaries and extended reading available to students. Students may also engage in discussion threads on web courses. Examples of web course management software include *WebCT*, *Blackboard* and *Nicenet*. Because of bandwidth limitations, and the cost involved (*WebCT* for instance requires a licence), instructors may opt for course managers such as *Nicenet* or *Blackboard*.

As referred to earlier in the section on South African research, one study into Web course management systems in the South African context was done by Cronje and Murdoch (2001), who examined the use of *WebCT* at Rand Afrikaans University in South Africa. They elicited data on the use of the system, training, infrastructure and institutional support. They found that lecturers who had a general interest in technology wanted to keep up with the use of technology in their teaching. Lecturers indicated that it also offered benefits such as increasing the opportunity for interaction, developing students' computer skills and decreasing the administrative burden. Problems included that it took up too much time, it provided little academic interaction with students, staff did not benefit in terms of incentives such as promotion if they used the system, there was not enough support available, participants found the technology intimidating, and

14 Their studies are cited by Warschauer (1995).

that there was too little knowledge about *WebCT* to utilise it optimally at the time.

In another South African study, although not designed around language issues, but on a broader university-wide e-Learning implementation project, Van der Merwe (2004) evaluated the e-Learning initiatives and *WebCT* use at Stellenbosch University. She used her findings to make recommendations for managing change in higher education, as well as for the integration of ICT at institutional and classroom levels, and finally to improve the e-Learning project at the university. Another study conducted by Muianga (2005), who researched the impact of a Web component in two Masters courses at a university in Mozambique, revealed that students responded positively to blended learning which utilised online web courses and face-to-face strategies.

From the above applications and activities, it is inevitable that there are differences between conventional and web-based applications to language teaching and learning, however, both essentially have the same objective: to promote the acquisition of English language. The following section provides some clarity on these differences.

Some differences between conventional and web-based language teaching

Mak (1995a) says that there are four kinds of activities on the Web that are relevant for language learning: instructional, publishing, research and collaboration. Several distinctions may be made to ascertain how language learning on the Web can be different from conventional classroom learning within the framework of instruction, publishing, research and collaboration. The following table, adapted from Mak (1995a) is an indication of some of the differences:

Conventional language learning	Web-based language learning
Linear presentation	Hypertext, multimedia
Not very motivating	High motivation
Receptive learning	Self-paced, self-accessed learning
High teacher control	High learner control
One-to-many (teacher to students)	Individual and many-to-many
Limited resources	Unlimited, updated information
Interaction with fellow classmates	Contact with classmates, native speakers and professionals

Fig. 4: Differences between conventional and web-based language learning. Adapted from Mak (1995a)

In relation to publishing, the differences between conventional language learning and Web-based language learning include differences in how material is presented. As stated earlier in this chapter, traditional, print-based materials are generally presented in linear format, while on the WWW, information is presented in hypertext, which enables the learner to take multiple routes. That is, learners may access glossaries for words they do not understand, or even listen to the pronunciation of a word they find difficult by highlighting particular aspects of the text that are hyperlinked. Learners may read up on the background of the author, or even look up other works by the author. In some instances, learners might ask the author or editor of a text questions, and receive feedback as well, completing the interactive nature of the process.

The multimedia possibilities of the Web include graphic, auditory, and visual texts, to a greater extent than non-web teaching and learning. Users are therefore exposed to a wider range of multimodal Web-based materials in contrast to traditional print-based materials. This promotes a more learner-centred or autonomous approach that appears to facilitate greater interaction among teachers and learners, as well as with outside professionals if necessary (Mak, 1995a, 1995b; Derewianka, 1993; Kajee, 2002, 2003). Learning can therefore be more self-paced than receptive.

Learners also have a collaborative audience to communicate with, including native speakers of English, as well as other ESL learners and professionals. They are able to interact in real situations and collaborative class projects may be done across continents. The learner is not limited to the teacher and fellow classmates as an audience. Students are far more motivated to write when they know that their work is being shared with others, and may even be published on the Web (Mak, 1995a, 1995b; Warschauer, 1996a).

Students are encouraged to draft, edit and rewrite before submitting a piece of work. According to Mak (1995a: 3), this encourages them 'to transcend the physical and psychological boundary of the language classroom and enter into the real world, the international community'. However, the differences should also not be over-simplified. While the Net has the potential to provide high learner control, and increased opportunities for student interaction, it is not straight-forward, and much depends on pedagogy and how the technology is used.

New technologies and the Net are therefore changing the way we traditionally perceive education. It is for these reasons that I wanted to find out more about teaching and learning in online environments. My project however, focuses on the instructional, research and collaborative aspects of Mak's (1995a) model.[15] This is discussed in more detail in Chapter 3. Having examined the changes brought about by the use of Net technology, I believe it is inevitable that there are implications for the role played by the teacher. The next section examines the shift in the teacher's role.

The changing role of the teacher

Education policy documents indicate that teachers' responsibilities are changing. With the impending increase in the utilisation of ICTs in the classroom, these changes are compounded. There are four possible areas in which the role of the teacher changes: pedagogical, social,

15 I did not take my students through to the task of publishing for a worldwide audience because their training did not extend to Web page design at the time. Because we used an internal Web management system, which required a class key and password, their work was published for the classroom audience.

managerial, and technical (Berge, 1995). Pedagogical conditions encompass teachers' duties as facilitators in the online classroom; social conditions include creating an environment suitable for suitable facilitation; managerial conditions include organisational and administrative tasks; and technical conditions encompass knowledge of the ICT system, hardware and software. It might not be possible for the teacher to fulfil all these roles simultaneously. The roles also presuppose that teachers are technologically competent to manage the CALL classroom, and if not, technical support is necessary, which off course has implications for budgets in already financially-strained institutions.

The SAIDE Report (2000) on ICT-use in South Africa also indicates that with technological changes, it is obvious that the role of the teacher changes too. The traditional role of the teacher as central and dominant in the teaching-learning process has undergone a paradigm shift, not only as a result of the use of new media in the classroom, but because of general shifts in how learning is viewed. In the technology-enhanced classroom we begin to rely more on information technology as the source of data and information, and less on the teacher as the source of information (Cunningham, 2000). The teacher's role, though it changes, is no less important. The role played by the teacher becomes one of facilitator of learning: guide, motivator, correspondent, challenger, materials' designer.

The collaborative role of the teacher is also foregrounded with the use of technology. The use of computer applications facilitates networking among teachers, who may form support and interest groups, especially if they are new to the field. Such groups are invaluable in providing assistance in identifying new material, methodology and when technical problems may be experienced (Cunningham, 2000). There are numerous such CALL support groups and listservs that currently exist for teachers who would like more support, and as several researchers such as Singhal (1997), Warschauer (1997), and Brown (1999), as well as policy documents remind us, teachers would benefit greatly from training.

Because the teacher has become a facilitator of learning, rather than 'sage on the stage', he/she will find, select, and offer information in a variety of ways on the basis of what his/her students must learn in order to meet their diverse needs (Warschauer and Healy, 1998). As facilitators, teachers should be aware of the material available on the Net, as well as the Net-based strategies that may be harnessed in the classroom. Teachers should respond to students' current needs. Although training is an obvious prerequisite for teachers to be able to use ICTs effectively in their teaching, the results of the SAIDE (2003) Report *Computers in Schools* bears testimony to the lack of formal teacher training opportunities in South Africa. The report indicates that only eleven certificated courses on training teachers to use ICTs in their teaching currently exist in South Africa, of forty-one tertiary institutions surveyed, including universities, technikons, and colleges. The reality for South Africa and other developing countries is therefore a far cry from the recommendations made by researchers in developing countries. Introducing ICTs into the classroom has implications for the budget, pre- and in-service teacher training, as well as for the learners. So, while researchers recommend that technology be integrated across the curriculum of teacher-education programmes, the reality is still quite distant in developing countries.

Conclusion

While the use of CALL and technology-enhanced learning environments appears to be promising, the constraints must also be considered because they can lead to limited success in attaining objectives, even failure. In order to overcome some of the constraints, the role of the teacher must be emphasised. Constraints include teachers' and, or students' lack of technical and theoretical competence, teachers' and, or students' lack of interest, cultural impediments, financial barriers such as the cost of hardware, software, maintenance, and lack of infrastructure (O'Dowd, 2001, 2004; Jones, 2001; Lee, 2000). The need for training is therefore vital. Such an approach calls for a framework that integrates electronic literacy into the language learning classroom (O'Dowd, 2001).

Despite the limitations, the learning potential of technology cannot be overlooked. Technology has opened up a whole new world of teaching and learning opportunities, but we are reminded that computer networks must supplement, not replace teachers (Mak, 1995a, 1995b). Warschauer (2000b) adds about the Internet in particular:

> The Internet does not constitute or prescribe a particular teaching method; rather, it is an important medium bringing together tens of millions of people throughout the world. The existence of the Internet provides the potential for purposeful, powerful use of online communication in language writing classes. It is up to us to give life to that purpose and thus achieve the full potential of computer networks in second language teaching (2000b: 9).

Nor can we expect results simply by purchasing elaborate hardware and software. Computer technology should be used to supplement and enhance good teaching practice. As Schneiderman (1997,vii) says, 'We must do more than teach our students to 'surf the net,' we must teach them to make waves'. However, we are also reminded that technology should not take over the language classroom, it should be embraced in order to allow educators to do those things they are unable to do themselves.

Chapter 2
Theorising learning, communities of practice, literacies, and identity

The previous chapter examined key issues that I consider significant in this book: the nature of online learning; the paradigm shift from face-to-face teaching and learning to teaching and learning in a virtual environment; the notion 'computer-mediated communication' and its role in the teaching and learning of English; the concept 'computer-assisted language learning'; and specific online applications and activities practices (such as e-mail, e-journals, the WWW, audio and video streaming, and web course managers) that are appropriate for the teaching and learning of English.

Here I present the theoretical framework of my study on online communities of practice. First I examine views on the shift from the Industrial Age to the Information Age (Castells, 1996). I draw on constructivist principles of meaning-making, and establish links between Vygotsky's (1978) Sociocultural Theory of Learning, Lave and Wenger's (1991, 1996, 2002) Situated Learning, and Communities of Practice (COP), as well as Rogoff's (2003) views on Communities of Practice. I further suggest, on the basis of the concept 'literacy as social practice', that participants' home, community, and school electronic literacy practices, with emphasis on ICTs, impact on their classroom electronic literacy practices. To this end I draw on the concept 'literacy as social practice' and New Literacy Studies, in particular, the views and theories of Gee (1996, 1997, 2000), Street (1984, 1993, 1998, 2003), Barton, Hamilton and Ivanic (2000) and Lankshear and Knobel (1997, 2004). I also argue that how learners construct their identities while making meaning is fundamental to participation in a COP. Thus I include discussion of Castells' (1996), Norton (Pierce's) (1995, 1997, 2000), and Hall's (1992) work on identity, which positions identity within a non-essentialist, post-structural framework. I extend their work on identity, to include the construction of identity in online environments.

Shifting from an Industrial Age to an Information Age

Digitisation is characteristic of the move from an Industrial Age to an Information Age.[1] Thus the shift from the Industrial Age to the Information Age is largely marked, among other things, by technology becoming increasingly accessible to a larger audience. With the proliferation of the WWW, some people in developed contexts have unlimited access to information and unlimited opportunities for communication, giving rise to what is called the 'information technology revolution' (Castells, 1996: 5), which is 'reshaping, at accelerated pace, the material basis of society' (Castells, 1996: 1). However, while this may be an accurate observation in developed countries, it is not always accurate of countries such as South Africa, where access to technology is minimal, sometimes even non-existent for certain socio-economic groups, especially those from disadvantaged communities.

Because the Information Society is one that is able to draw on information effectively, a key feature of such a society is its information and communication networks. It is inevitable then, that the dependence on the new modes of information flow gives power to those in a position to control the flow of information (Castells, 1996). This view resonates with the position taken by Feenberg (1991) and Warschauer (2002a, 2002b, 2003a, 2003b, 2004b, 2005, in print), as introduced earlier in this book: that the digital divide should not be considered a bipolar division between 'haves' and 'have-nots'. Rather, it is about political, economic, institutional, cultural, and linguistic issues of class and power. In my project on online communities of practice among participants with limited previous access to the use of ICTs, issues of power are fundamental. I examine the extent to which such participants negotiate meaning, and argue that the configuration of communities cannot overlook the identities participants construct in online spaces, and how they position themselves in relation to technology. While it is

1 The Information Age is also referred to by theorists and researchers as the information society, knowledge economy, and new economy. In this book I use the term Information Age.

inevitable that the Information Age has implications for education and learning, these implications are not without challenges.

Some challenges for education and social inclusion

It has been argued that the Industrial Age was characterised by control, conformity and compliance (Reigeluth in Cronje, 1997). In the traditional classroom, the teacher plays a central dominant role, and communication is limited. In the Information Age, on the other hand, the focus is on the process to teaching and learning that promotes inclusive education, autonomy and co-operation, shared decision-making, initiative and networking among teachers and learners. The learner is greatly valued in this process, and the teacher-centred approach is *passé*.

In South Africa, inclusive teaching and learning is recommended in the *Green Paper on Higher Education* (1996) to narrow societal divides. Inclusion has social consequences, and of great concern to policy-makers and educationalists is the possibility that the use of ICT could further marginalise communities without access to technology. Chapman (1996) for example, argues that society should exploit technology to provide education for democratic, socially inclusive, economically advanced communities.

Warschauer (2003b) points out that access to technology goes beyond quantifying those with and without access, and that a more significant factor is the use of technology for social transformation. In his book *Technology and Social Inclusion: Rethinking the Digital Divide* (2003b), he presents illustrative case studies of the implementation of ICTs in under-resourced contexts: India's 'Hole in the Wall' Project, Egypt's Model Lab, and Ireland's Information Age Town. As noted in Chapter 1, all three cases demonstrate that introducing technology to under-resourced contexts does not automatically ensure a socially transformed society if participants are not sufficiently prepared for its use. Thus, he critiques the instrumentalist approach, and emphasises the need for a four-pronged approach to incorporate social, human, physical and digital resources.

Social inclusion refers to 'the extent that individuals, families, and communities are able to fully participate in society and control their own destinies, taking into account a variety of factors related to economic resources, employment, health, education, housing, recreation, culture, and civic engagement' (Warschauer, 2003b, online, page 5 of 7). He goes on to say that there are many ways in which the poor can be included, even though they may lack resources. Even those who are more privileged, may face exclusion on the basis of age, disability, sexual preference or gender.[2] Inclusion is therefore not merely about resources, but also about control over life circumstances. In an interview with Raven, Warschauer says 'Technology for social inclusion de-emphasises the notion of bridging divides and instead looks at the broader goal – achieving social inclusion for all – and then considers the role that technology can play within that' (2005, online, paragraph 6).

In my project I implement an ICT intervention in my English class, not only with the purpose of introducing resources into a minimally resourced environment, thus narrowing the digital divide, but to examine how participants make meaning in such an environment. I investigate their ICT practices, participation and construction of identity as a means, not of what they do, but of who they are (Castells, 1996). One may question then, whether the use of technology contributes to social inclusion. Underpinning how participants position themselves and make meaning, I argue that it is necessary to examine the concept 'learning'. In the sections that follow I discuss notions and principles of learning from a constructivist perspective, before going on to examine sociocultural approaches to learning and communities of practice.

2 Kajee (2005b) demonstrates social exclusion in relation to disability in her case study of a blind student using technology in an inclusive setting, that is, with sighted peers in an English class.

The notion 'learning'

Numerous theories have been posited to explain how people learn, or how they move from one state of knowing to the next. Some of these theories have been accepted more readily than others, therefore a brief overview of the theories might help to provide insight into how learning occurs, and why certain practices are promoted over others. Martin (2000) summarised some of the main theorists, as well as their foci, as follows:

Theories	Theorists	Learning process	Locus of learning	Examples of practice
Behaviourist	Thorndike, Pavlov, Watson, Guthrie, Hull, Tolman	Change in behaviour	Stimuli in the external environment	Behavioural objectives, competency-based education, skills development, training
Cognitivist	Koffka, Kohler, Lewin, Piaget, Ausubel, Bruner, Gagne, Vygotsky	Internal mental processes	Internal cognitive structuring	Cognitive development, metacognition, learning how to learn
Constructivist	Van Glaserfield, Ernest, Candy	Constructing understanding of the world	Search for meaning, understanding the whole and parts.	Generation of new mental models to fit in with the old. Constructing own meaning.
Humanist	Maslow, Rogers	Personal act to fulfil potential	Affective and cognitive needs	Self-directed learning
Social learning	Bandura, Freire, Rotter	Interaction and observation in the social context	Interaction of person, behaviour, environment	Mentoring, co-operative/ collaborative learning.

Adult learning	Knowles, Jarvis, Kidd, McClusky, Mezirow	Self-directed learning through life experiences	Change in life circumstances	Andragogy, self-directed learning, simulation, work-based learning
Student development	Chikering, Gilligan, Magolda, Perry	Development of the whole person	Collegiate environment	Identity, development, moral development

Fig. 5: Overview of learning theories. Adapted from Martin (2000: 2)

Figure 5 is not meant to suggest that the theories are mutually exclusive. The theories apply to face-to-face learning, however, I draw on them in this work on online learning because the key concepts of learning that are underpinned remain consistent. I have located my study within the broader framework of constructivist principles of meaning-making, and draw on key sociocultural principles provided by Vygotsky (1978).

Constructing an understanding of the world

Constructivism, as a philosophy of learning, is based on the premise that we construct our own understanding of the world we live in by reflecting on our experiences. We generate our own rules and mental models in order to make sense of our experiences. Learning is therefore a process whereby we adjust our mental models to accommodate new experiences. Tobin's (1990: 30) view of constructivism as 'a theory that assumes knowledge cannot exist outside the bodies of cognisising beings […] Knowledge is a construction of reality' is therefore fitting. The view highlights the notion that new experiences are interpreted and made sense of in terms of previous experiences. Candy (1991) adds that because individuals give meaning to events and ideas, knowledge cannot be taught, but is learnt or constructed and built up by the learner.

Constructivism essentially takes two broad forms: cognitive constructivism and social constructivism. Cognitive constructivism[3] focuses on a learner's internal cognitive processes and cognitive structure during learning, while social constructivism expounds the role of human mediation and the social context in shaping learning (Appleton, 1996). Both views are important in how we learn, however, for the purpose of my study, I draw more strongly on social constructivism because of my focus on participation, literacy as social practice, and identity.

In essence, the guiding principles of constructivism, as provided by theorists such as von Glasersfeld (1990), Derry (1992) and Colburn (2000) are:

- Learning is a search for meaning, therefore learning must start with issues around which students are trying to construct meaning;
- Meaning involves understanding wholes as well as parts, and it is necessary that parts must be understood within the context of the whole. The learning process should therefore focus on concepts, rather than isolated facts;
- The mental models that students bring with them in order to understand the world must be understood in order to teach well;
- The purpose of learning is for an individual to construct his or her own meaning, not just to memorise the right answers. It is therefore important that assessment is part of the learning process, not an isolated entity, ensuring that students are provided with feedback on the quality of their learning in an ongoing manner.

While it is possible to create meaningful constructivist learning environments in face-to-face situations, I investigate these possibilities in blended spaces, and ask how participants with limited knowledge of online participation, construct meaning in these unfamiliar spaces. Their online participation has implications for education, and teaching

3 Cognitive constructivism, based on Piaget's (1977) work, encompasses two main areas, the first on being the 'ages and stages' component that predicts what children can or cannot understand at particular ages. Second is Piaget's (1977) theory of development that describes how children develop cognitive abilities.

and learning in relation to curriculum, teaching strategies and practices, the learning environment, the role of the teacher and learner, and materials-design.

The traditional view of learning has a tendency to locate objectivist/behaviourist views and constructivist/cognitivist views at different ends of a continuum. Cronje (2000) argues that this view is problematic because it limits any learning experience as either objectivist or constructivist. His argument is that the view caters for learning that may be low, for example on stimulus-response methodology, and high on scaffolded constructivism, but it does not cater for learning experiences that may be high on both. This is also evident in South African educational policies, which view the 'old' and 'new' systems as appears in Figure 6:

Old view	**Current view**
Passive learners	Active learners
Examination-driven	On-going assessment
Rote learning	Critical thinking, reasoning, reflection and action
Content-based syllabus broken down into subjects	Integration of knowledge. Learning is relevant and connected to real-life situations
Syllabus is viewed as rigid and non-negotiable	Learning programmes are seen as guides that allow teachers to be innovative and creative in designing programmes
Emphasis is on what the teacher hopes to achieve	Emphasis is on outcomes – what learners become and understand
Behavioural approach to learning and assessment	Cognitive approach to learning and assessment
Assessment of isolated knowledge and discrete skills	Knowledge, abilities, thinking processes, metacognition and affect assessed
Individual learning and products	Collaborative learning and products

Fig. 6: South African government's changing view of education. Adapted from Cronje (2000)

With the introduction of constructivist environments, our assumptions about learning also change. Grabinger (1996: 667 in Reeves 1998) presents the major changes in our shift in assumptions about learning, which articulate with Cronje's (2000) views on old and new perspectives on education: old assumptions include the fact that people are able to transfer learning with ease by learning decontextualised concepts; learners are recipients of knowledge; learning is essentially behaviouristic; learners are passive recipients; skills are best acquired independent of context; and assessment is decontextualised. New assumptions challenge these notions: people need both context and content, as it is difficult to transfer learning; learners are active constructors of knowledge; learning is cognitive and in a constant state of growth; learners bring their own experiences to the learning context; knowledge and skills are best acquired within realistic contexts; and assessment is best realistic and holistic.

Because of the changes in the assumptions about learning, new challenges arise for designers of constructivist learning environments, which Wilson defines as follows:

> a place where learners may work together and support each other as they use a variety of tools and information resources in their guided pursuit of learning goals and problem-solving activities (1996: 5 in Reeves 1998, online).

I agree with Reeves (1998) who proposes that developers of constructivist learning environments adhere to the following goals in order to meet the challenges of learning:

- provide students with experience in the knowledge construction process;
- provide experience in and appreciation for multiple perspectives;
- embed learning in realistic and relevant contexts;
- encourage ownership and voice in the learning process;
- encourage the use of multiple modes of representation; and
- encourage self-awareness of the knowledge construction process.

These I attempt to simulate in my online environment. Constructivism also has an impact on the curriculum and instruction by promoting curricula that are customised to students' prior knowledge. I discuss this further in Chapter 4 where I present the Foundation in English courses which provide the content basis of my study. Also, in relation to pedagogy, teachers using the constructivist paradigm would shape their teaching strategies to student responses and encourage students to analyse, interpret and predict information. Within this paradigm teachers also rely more on open-ended questions and promote extensive dialogue among students.

From the above it is evident that the learning environment, and teaching strategies in constructivist approaches promote interaction to make meaning. We should therefore draw attention to 'how' to teach, rather than 'what' to teach in the constructivist paradigm, and emphasise the need to redesign the typical classroom, as teaching strategies must be congruent with learning processes (Yager and Lutz, 1994). They say that to improve student learning it is necessary to focus on a change in teaching. Their perspective is that constructivist teachers encourage and accept student autonomy, initiation and leadership, and encourage students to interact with one another and with teachers. These key principles are also conflated with the guiding principles of self-direction, as well as Knowles' (1975, 1980) theory supporting adult learning. Pereira (1996) shares their view that learners must be responsible for their own learning and adds that there is need for a supportive community within which students may interact and negotiate meaning without fear of making mistakes.

In summary, the paradigm shift from an Industrial Age to an Information Age has presented the South African educational system with new concerns around how teachers can best implement technology in under-resourced environments, while still focusing on learning. Thus, I focus on a perspective of learning from a constructivist stance, which places learners as constructing their own understanding of the world. The view resonates with Government's changing view of education, which places learners, rather than teachers at the centre of the learning process. This notion I argue as central to my position on learning.

Key principles of learning

Seven principles of learning underpin constructivist theory: context, interest, scaffolding, metacognition, responsibility, community, and modelling (Bickmore-Brand, 1996). The principles of context, interest, and scaffolding begin with the learners' knowledge base. They emphasise starting where the learner is at, and using their background knowledge to establish a context, which they perceive as relevant. The principles relate to central issues in constructivist theory, where knowledge, which is stored as schemata or frameworks, and new knowledge is assimilated or accommodated into these frameworks (see also Pereira, 1996). It also emphasises the need for knowledge to be contextual and relevant to the learner.

The principle of metacognition relates to the students' ability to think about how they learn (Pereira, 1996). If learners are able to contextualise learning, they are able to control it, thus constructivists acknowledge that students must learn how to learn. The next key principle provided by Bickmore-Brand (1996) is when learners develop the ability to accept responsibility for their learning (Pereira, 1996; Downes, 2000).

In relation to community, Pereira (1996: 29) says, 'The development of a supportive community of learners provides an environment in which experiences can be examined and ideas constructively tested.' Learners should not feel that they are isolated entities, they should feel that they are part of a supportive community they can share and interact with. They should have the freedom to express and debate ideas in an environment that is free from ridicule. The principle resonates with Lave and Wenger's (1991, 1996, 2002) and Rogoff's (2003) communities of practice. The idea of experimenting with new knowledge and negotiating meaning is central to constructivist thinking. The final principle, modelling, is designed around the view that learners should be able to work co-operatively where they are able to observe and learn from others, which is pivotal in a community of practice.

Vygotsky's (1978) sociocultural theory of learning

Vygotsky's theoretical contributions to the development of education are widely known among educational theorists. In the 1930s Vygotsky argued that social experiences shape our ways of thinking and interpreting the world. He regarded learning and education not only as central to cognitive development, but as 'the quintessential socio-cultural activity' (Moll, 1990: 1). The capacity to teach and learn is therefore fundamental to human beings. Central to Vygotsky's theory is the belief that biological and cultural development, do not occur in isolation (Vygotsky, 1978). Where Piaget (1977) believed that cognitive growth occurred in stages, with a fixed endpoint, Vygotsky believed that development is not a product, but a process. Thus, his approach may be characterised according to three themes:

- a reliance on genetic (developmental) analysis;
- the claim that higher mental functions in the individual have their origins in social life; and
- the claim that an essential key to understanding human social and psychological processes is the tools and signs used to mediate them (Wertsch, 1990: 112).

Vygotsky's view was that the route to understanding the mind lay in specifying its origins. In this regard he was influenced by Piaget (1977), among other psychologists. His second point is that mental functioning in the individual is found in social activity. He said:

> Every function in the child's cultural development appears twice: first on the social level, and later, on the individual level; first between people (inter-psychological) and then inside the child (intrapsychological). This applies equally to voluntary attention, to logical memory, and to the formation of concepts. All the higher functions originate as actual relationships between individuals (Vygotsky, 1978: 57).

According to Vygotsky (1978), individual cognition occurred in a social situation, thus shifting emphasis away from the individual to the group, the group therefore being vital to the learning process for all participants. One may learn through interaction with other individuals and more knowledgeable peers in social situations to negotiate meaning (refer also to Jaramillo, 1996). Subjects therefore develop their own interpretative meaning of acts while communicating with others.

The third point is that higher mental functioning is mediated by tools and signs. Vygotsky (1978) argues that human activity can only be understood if we take into account the tools or signs that mediate this activity. For instance, Wertsch says:

> These forms of mediation, which are the products of the sociocultural milieu in which they exist, are not viewed as simply facilitating activity that would otherwise take place. Instead, they are viewed as fundamentally shaping and defining it (1990: 113).

Vygotsky's focus on mediation was the human communication system, namely, speech. His focus was how language, and speech, in particular, were interrelated with aspects of social and individual activity. As Tudge (1990: 156) says 'language, (is) a tool of immense power, (and) ensures that linguistically created meaning are shared meanings, social meanings'.

All three points are central to my work in the sense that I focus on students who are novices with technology, and I examine how they develop during their use of technological tools. Second, I acknowledge that learning does not occur in isolation, but through interaction with others, and third, I acknowledge that students mediate knowledge through their use of language, and in this study, technology, both of which serve as mediating tools and signs.

Another key concept established by Vygotsky is the zone of proximal development (ZPD). The underlying assumption behind the concept is that psychological development and instruction are socially embedded, and in order to understand them one must analyse the surrounding society and its social relations (Hedegaard, 1990). Vygotsky (1978) explained the ZPD thus:

> The child is able to copy a series of actions which surpass his or her own capacities, but only within limits. By means of copying, the child is able to perform much better when together with and guided by adults than when left alone, and can do so with understanding and independently. The difference between the level of solved tasks that can be performed with adult guidance and

help and the level of independently solved tasks is the zone of proximal development (in Hedegaard, 1990: 349).

Thus, the ZPD bridges the gap between what is known and what can be known (Riddle, 1999). In addition, the ZPD also provides the process through which children, with assistance, come to be socialised into the dominant culture (Tudge, 1990). It is through collaboration with another person, either an adult or a more competent peer in the ZPD, that leads to culturally appropriate development. The notion articulates well with Lave and Wenger's (1991) view of apprenticeship as assisted performance, and Rogoff's (2003) views on guided participation, as is discussed later in this chapter.

As shown in previous sections,[4] schools[5] historically have not constructed environments where students play an active role in their own, as well as the education of their peers (Riddle, 1990; Schutz, 2002). Vygotsky's (1978) theory requires teacher-learner and learner-learner collaboration to make meaning. Riddle (1999) says that this leads to reciprocal learning and makes the classroom a community of learning. Schutz (2002: 4) adds:

> when it comes to language learning, the authenticity of the environment and the affinity between its participants are essential elements to make the learner feel part of this environment. These elements are rarely predominant in conventional classrooms.

This too, is underscored by Lave and Wenger's (1991) view of assistance and legitimate peripheral participation in communities of practice.

Scaffolding and reciprocal teaching are effective strategies in the ZPD. Scaffolding allows for the teacher to provide students with the opportunities to extend their current skills and knowledge, and requires

4 For example, the work of Reeves (1998) and Cronje (2000).

5 Note that I move between research conducted in schools and in the higher education context because my students are in their first year of study and just out of school (for the most part). Furthermore, studies located in the higher education context are minimal, and I believe that school-based research has an impact on my study to some extent. In addition, the issues and challenges remain the same, even though the context might differ.

that tasks be simplified so that they are manageable and motivate students to pursue instructional goals. Studies cited by Riddle (1999)[6] demonstrate that reciprocal teaching shows advantages over other instructional strategies. Lave and Wenger's (1991) Situated Learning Theory concurs with Vygotsky's Sociocultural Theory in terms of its conceptual framework, and has implications for online environments.

Situated learning and communities of practice

Learning may be equated with co-participation (Lave and Wenger, 1991). Wenger (1998) asserts that situated learning theories regard learning to be interactive relationships between people and their environments. Their theory advocates learning in a specific context, and focuses on how individuals become members of communities of practice (COPs). They see COPs as sets of relations among people, activities and the world, over time, and in relation to other overlapping COPs (Lave and Wenger, 1991, 1996). Rogoff (2003) also asserts '*Humans develop through their changing participation in the socio-cultural activities of their communities, which also change*' (Rogoff, 2003: 11) (italics in original). She suggests that children, for instance, learn the skills and practices of their community by engaging with others who may contribute to structuring the process to be learned. Adults may provide guidance and help adjust participation according to proficiency. COPs therefore emphasise the interconnectedness of people, learning, practice, participation and the social world. The figure that follows, adapted from Barab (2000), illustrates the relations among practice, meaning, identity and community:

6 Studies cited by Riddle (1999) such as Brown and Palincsar (1989), Driscoll (1994), and Hausfather (1996).

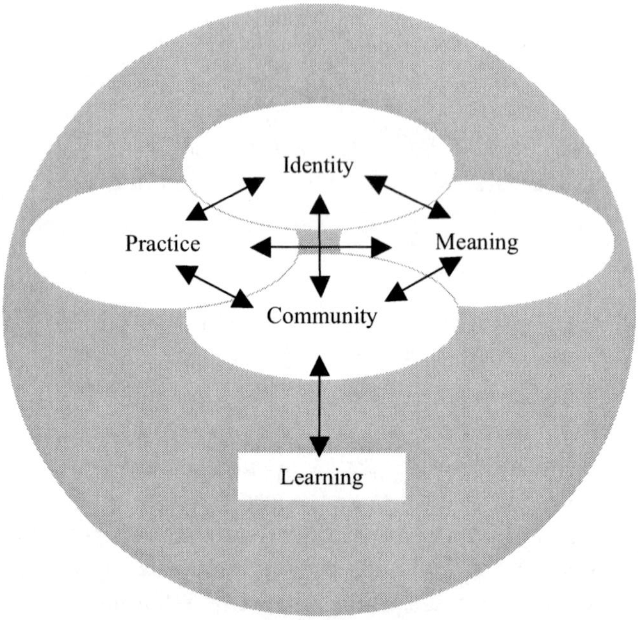

Fig. 7: Relations between practice, meaning, identity and community. Adapted from Barab (2000)

In her original diagram, Barab (2000) represents the different entities (meaning, identity, practice, and community) separately. What I found useful was the identification of the different entities. However, I also found the diagram limiting in that she does not illustrate the interaction or relationship between the entities. Thus I have adapted her diagram to include arrows to illustrate the symbiotic relationships, which derive from assistance and guided participation within a community.

Rogoff (2003) argues that development occurs as a process where a person gradually increases his/her participation and belonging to society's various communities of practice. These communities may include the social, school, family and career groups with which the student chooses to identify. Communities share their social practices, which include the language, tools, documents, images, symbols, criteria, procedures and regulations. Knowledge is integrated in the doing, social relations and expertise of the communities.

People construct their identities in relation to the communities in which they participate, and move along a continuum of learning, from legitimate peripheral participation, to full participation. Legitimate Peripheral Participation (LPP) refers to the 'relations between new-comers and old-timers, and about activities, identities and artefacts, and communities of knowledge and practice' (Lave and Wenger, 1991: 29). Wenger (1998) uses the terms 'marginal' and 'peripheral' participation, where the latter leads to full participation.[7] Lave and Wenger's (1991) use of the terms 'newcomers' and 'old-timers' refer to novices and experts, or more able participants, respectively. Lave and Wenger (1991, 1996) describe the relationship between novices and experts as an apprenticeship. In their view, learners are the 'apprentices', and teachers are the 'masters' (1991: 29).[8] I prefer the view, as discussed earlier that teachers are facilitators of the learning process, because I think that 'masters' implies superiority, with the learners or 'apprentices' as followers, rather than co-constructors of knowledge. Lave and Wenger (1991) also perceive situated learning to be more than 'learning by doing', but as an integral and inseparable aspect of social practice. They continue that situatedness:

> implied emphasis on comprehensive understanding involving the whole person rather than 'receiving' a body of factual knowledge about the world; on activity in and with the world; and on the view that agent, activity, and the world mutually constitute each other (Lave and Wenger, 1991: 33).

Thus, they propose that LPP is 'a descriptor of engagement in social practice that entails learning as an integral constituent' (Lave and Wenger, 1991: 35).

Peripherality suggests that there are varied ways of being located in fields of participation. Lave and Wenger (1991) view the move from

7 Refer, for example to the Carr et al. (2004) study of participation using a COP framework in an Economics course at the University of Cape Town.

8 The term 'apprenticeship' arose from Lave and Wenger's (1991) observations of Vai and Gola tailors in Liberia, Yucatek midwives in Mexico, US navy quartermasters and butchers, and members of Alcoholics Anonymous.

peripheral participation to more intensive participation as an empowering position, as is the prevention from participation a dis-empowering one. They also emphasise that LPP is not in itself an educational form or pedagogical strategy. LPP takes place whatever the context. Learning therefore implies involvement in new activities, the ability to perform new tasks, and the ability to master new understandings. These, according to Lave and Wenger (1991), do not occur in isolation, they are part of a broader system of relations, which arise from social communities.

In order to participate in, and become a member of a community, newcomers need access to the community, which resonates well with Warschauer's (2003a, 2003b) views on social inclusion. Access includes access to activities, old-timers, other members, information, resources, language, and opportunities for participation. Engaging with the technologies and tools of the practice is therefore vital. Thus, in an ICT environment, for example, access to ICTs and knowledge of their use are essential.

Changes in the community and in identity are intrinsic to the process of participation. Language is therefore central to the development of the community, with peripheral participants learning to 'talk' in the same manner as full participants.[9] Situated Learning theory shares key concepts with Vygotsky's (1978) Sociocultural theory. Lave and Wenger's (1991) concept, like Vygotsky's, is based on learning as a social phenomenon. In essence, Situated Learning theory states that the goal of education is the negotiation of meaning, and they emphasise that education therefore cannot be examined in isolation. The interconnectedness of persons learning and participating and the social world is therefore central.

The learning theories discussed thus far have not taken cognisance of the introduction of ICTs in society, which has the ability to provide

9 Aldrich (2001) says that it is this knowledge of the language and the stories of the community that enable participants to become members of the community. Hildreth, Kimble and Wright (2000) add that the stories and narrations that are used in a community results in the transition from novice to expert. As newcomers' stories become accepted into the community, they become legitimate members of the community.

infinite opportunities for social interaction. In his book, *The Virtual Community*, Rheingold (1993) explains that it is inevitable that people will build virtual communities, with the availability of CMC. He says:

> Virtual communities are social aggregations that emerge from the Net when enough people carry on those public discussions long enough, with sufficient human feeling, to form webs of personal relationships in cyberspace (Rheingold, 1993: 6).

While I agree with Rheingold's (1993) view about the building of virtual communities, I do not view this as an inevitable conclusion. In developing countries, considering the scarcity of technological applications, I believe that learners will have to be helped to create and participate in these communities.

In the technology-supported learning environment, theoretical support for the collaborative and social aspects of computer usage is essential if pedagogical approaches are to be developed. I found that a communicative framework based on Vygotskian (1978) Sociocultural theory and Lave and Wenger's (1991) Situated Learning theory most relevant for understanding how learners work towards achieving higher order learning outcomes using ICTs because computers are now increasingly recognised as part of the social context of classrooms. This would be true for developed countries, rather than most developing countries. Therefore, while collaboration and peer instruction was once only possible in shared physical space, learning relationships can now be formed in cyberspace, with ICTs as a cultural tool that students use to mediate and internalise their learning (Riddle, 1999) .

The special features of online communication provide an array of new ways to link learners, which makes online learning a potentially powerful tool for collaborative learning (Warschauer, 1997b: online, 15 of 22). Warschauer counters Rheingold's (1991) argument presented earlier, and cautions that not all educators feel equally strongly about online communication, and that online activities can be used in the traditional transmission style, which may lead to ICTs not having the transformative effect as anticipated. The connection between communities of practice and technology in online learning environments is further explained by Duncan and Leander (2001). In order to create a community, they too emphasise the need for participant interaction. Communities may develop in class discussions between facilitators and learners, and among the learners themselves. These are enhanced by the adoption of Net-based strategies such as discussion threads, bulletin boards, listservs, chat facilities, and engaging students in e-mail projects.

While the latter online practices have been adopted by some teachers willingly, not all practitioners are enthusiastic about the possibilities of creating online communities of practice. Some, such as McMahon (in Alexiades, Gipson and Morey-Nase, 2001) found the authenticity of using the WWW questionable because of the breadth of the information available, and because its use can result in feelings of isolation. Jonassen (in Alexiades et al., 2001) further suggests that the use of technology reduces the opportunity for active interaction with other learners, especially when the communication is personally or culturally unfamiliar. However, several research studies, as discussed in the previous chapter, praise the benefits of online interaction.

Although online communities of practice are obviously collaborative because of the electronic networks involved, and users are able to maintain contact with individuals at other locations, those individuals may in turn belong to other COPs. This could expand worldwide, with anybody who has an interest being a member. This is the antithesis of Lave and Wenger's (1991) original view of COPs. Brown and Duguid (2000) therefore expanded the notion COP to 'network of practice' to describe more diffuse networks. In relation to language teaching, the term network-based language teaching (NBLT),[10] as discussed earlier, is appropriate. In my study, only the e-pal section of the course involved global collaboration. This is explained in more detail in Chapter 3.

To illustrate the workings of an online COP, in a study conducted by Alexiades et al. (2001), a group of students from an Australian school, in collaboration with students from the James Cook University were located on a remote island to work on an ecological project. They had to maintain contact with the school using laptops. The students were in an authentic ecological island environment and were mentored

10 Please refer, for example, to O'Dowd's (2004) doctoral study of NBLT and the development of intercultural communicative competence.

by the university students, perpetuating the notion of cognitive apprenticeship (Lave and Wenger, 1991). The mentors engaged in modelling, coaching and scaffolding, and provided students with reminders, feedback and support. The apprenticeship began with students observing from the boundary, and gradually moving to the centre of the community as functional agents.

In the local South African context, a study on student reflection and meta-reflection conducted by Granville and Dison (2005) illustrates how students at a South African university engaged in an English Academic Literacy course designed around face-to-face community of practice principles.[11]

Beyond communities of practice

While COPs is an influential theory, it is not without criticism, and some claim it is in need of review and elaboration. It can be claimed for instance that COPs do not effectively deal with issues of power and identity. Therefore I draw especially on aspects of power and identity in online discourse and participation in my work, using COPs as the building blocks.

Thus far I have presented theories around COPs. It is not inevitable that COP principles translate well into online practice. The implications for practice need further refinement. Vygotsky's (1978) Sociocultural Theory of Learning, as well as Lave and Wenger's (1991) and Rogoff's (2003) Situated Learning and Communities of Practice theories support the basic tenets of online learning in the following respects:

- The move away from the individual to the role of the individual within a learning community;
- The need for interaction among participants;

11 Granville and Dison's (2005) study was also conducted with students studying the Foundation in English Course that I examined in my study, albeit in a different year.

- The theories state that learners acquire knowledge when they are more autonomous, rather than when the teacher plays a central, dominant role, a situation supported by the role of the online facilitator;
- Learners process knowledge when it is presented at a level higher than they are used to, and that such tension results in learners moving from the periphery of a learning community to central participation.

Learning is not limited to knowing. My study lies at the interface between learning as meaning-making, language, and the use of new technologies. I argue that there is a symbiotic relationship between language and literacy, hence an examination of key concepts surrounding literacy adds value to my work. In the section to follow, I examine literature surrounding the concept 'New Literacy Studies', where literacy is conceptualised as a social practice.

New Literacy Studies: Providing a lens for literacy as social practice

Literacy has long been a central concern of educationalists, as a means of socialisation, and as an end in itself (Goodfellow, 2004). Literacy has become a 'lens' through which to look at educational practice more critically, he adds. Thus, in this study I examine the notion of literacy more closely, because of its relationship with language. Barton and Hamilton (2000:8) provide the following six propositions as a framework for the nature of literacy:

- Literacy is a social practice;
- Different literacies are associated with different domains of life;
- Literacy practices are patterned by social institutions and power relationships, and some literacies are more dominant, visible and influential than others;
- Literacy practices are purposeful and embedded in broader social goals and practices;
- Literacy is historically situated;
- Literacy practices change and new ones are frequently acquired through informal and formal learning and sense making.

Gee (1996) suggests that in New Literacy Studies (NLS) literacy is not a skill, but a contextualised practice, thus NLS treat language and literacy as social practices rather than technical skills to be learnt in formal education. The concept requires that language and literacy be studied as they occur naturally in social life, taking into account context and their different meanings to different cultural groups. Gee (1996) argues:

> [T]he traditional view of literacy as the ability to read and write rips out of its sociocultural contexts and treats it as an asocial cognitive skill with little or nothing to do with human relationships. It cloaks literacy's connections to power, to social identity, and to ideologies, often in service of privileging certain types of literacies and certain types of people (1996: 46).

He adds that reading and writing only make sense when studied in the context of social and cultural (and historical, political and economic) practices of which they are part (Gee, 2000).[12]

Street (1984) too opposes the autonomous model of reading and writing as literacy in favour of an ideological model, which attempts to understand literacy in terms of social practice. Thus, there are many literacies that occur within varying social contexts. Barton, Hamilton and Ivanic (2000: 1) agree 'Literacy is situated. All uses of written language can be seen as located in particular times and places. Equally, all literate activity is indicative of broader social practices'. In adopting a framework of literacy as social practice, literacies are positioned in relation to the social institutions and power relations that sustain them, education being one such institution (Street, 1995; Gee, 1996). Thus the teaching of one type of literacy could privilege certain groups, while disempowering others who have not had access to that dominant literacy. On the other hand, not exposing learners to that dominant literacy serves to exclude them from society at large. Barton and

12 This is based on the idea that reading and writing are situated within specific Discourses, with a capital 'D' (Gee, 1996). Gee (1996) uses the term 'Discourses', rather than 'discourses', which refers to stretches of language. A Discourse, he says is a way of being together in the world (for example, gangs, classrooms, being gay, and so on), and learners may belong to several Discourses simultaneously.

Hamilton (2000) agree that there are different literacies associated with different domains in life, and as Gee (1996) adds, home is the primary domain, and school, secondary, thus what learners bring from the home is valuable, though often marginalised in the school environment.

Barton and Hamilton (2000) distinguish further between the concepts 'literacy practices' and 'literacy events'. Literacy practices are the ways of utilising language that people draw on in their lives. Practices are what people do with literacy, and are shaped by social rules that regulate the use and distribution of texts, prescribing who may have access to them. Thus literacy practices overlap with Lave and Wenger's (1991) and Rogoff's (2003) notions of communities of practice. Practice provides a link between reading, writing, and the social structures in which they are embedded, and which they help shape. Literacy events are activities where literacy has a role. They are observable episodes that arise from practices and are shaped and situated within a social context. In my study of an online classroom, I analyse messages posted to discussion threads as literacy events[13] situated within the broader literacy practice of the utilisation of ICTs in the higher education English classroom.

New Literacies are associated with the changes that are intrinsic to life. Different levels of change and practices have emerged with the introduction of digital and electronic media. Lankshear and Knobel (1997) refer to the use of digital and electronic media as technological literacies. Reading and writing, for instance require new practices, such as using hyperlinks, the use of semiotics in e-mails and chat rooms, being able to read different elements of Web pages, such as icons, menus, and understanding when to launch different media, such as to download music and video files or copy images. NLS embrace these changes, and highlight the importance of what learners bring to the classroom from outside of it.[14] The introduction of digital and electronic media such as computers, the Net, and cell phones has therefore

13 Please refer also to de Pourbaix's (2000) study of how university students communicate in virtual spaces, in which she uses social practice as her theoretical framework.

14 Please refer, for example, to Knobel and Lankshear's (1997) mapping of in-and out-of-school technology practices of a group of Australian students.

changed what it means to learn, know and do things (Knobel and Lankshear, 2002). Much of the cyber lives of young people is text-based, such as e-mail, sms, chat, and discussion boards, although in the developing context of South Africa, this is more true of sms-text than e-mail, chat and discussions boards if one were to consider learners from under-resourced backgrounds. Presently too, we may note vigorous use of YouTube and Facebook where the internet is available. Goodfellow (2004) therefore recommends the exploration of the nature of textual interactions. If these are not explored, he cautions that it could lead to feelings of marginalisation and frustration among learners. His work on the linguistic analysis of discussion thread postings of distance education students as small-scale literacy events bears reference (Goodfellow, 2004). In my study, I examine the electronic literacy practices that participants have been exposed to, at home and in their high schools. I examine these practices in relation to ICTs and the electronic literacy practices they are exposed to at university.

Literacies, like other uses of language, involve social identities. Gee (1996) says there is a reciprocal relationship between language and identity. He adds that literacy- and identity-association can occur in the classroom through active apprenticeships in academic social practices, and emphasises the importance of apprenticeship in acquiring new social identities and literacies, as do Lave and Wenger (1991) and Rogoff (2003).

Thus far, I have shown how my study will be underpinned by learning and sociocultural theory. I have shown, by reviewing key concepts surrounding New Literacy Studies and New Literacies, that the teaching of one type of literacy cannot be justified, as there are multiple literacies which are embedded in cultural practices, and which vary with time and place.

Following Gee's (1996) 'take' on the reciprocity between language and identity, I argue that it is not just participants' electronic literacy practices that need to be examined, but how they construct themselves in relation to the above-mentioned changes that are fundamental. Thus, I shift perspective to examine notions of the construction of identities in communities of practice.

Hall (1992) argues that old identities, which stabilised the social world, are in decline, giving rise to new identities and fragmenting the modern individual as a unified subject. As Castells (1996) explains:

> In a world of global flows of wealth, power, and images, the search for identity, collective or individual, ascribed or constructed, becomes the fundamental source of social meaning. This is not a new trend, since identity, and particularly religious and ethnic identity have been at the roots of meaning since the dawn of human society. Yet identity is becoming main, and sometimes the only, source of meaning in a historical period characterised by widespread destructuring of organizations, delegitimation of institutions, fading away of major social movements, and ephemeral cultural expressions. People increasingly organize their meaning not around what they do but on the basis of what they are (Castells, 1996: 3).

This crisis of identity (Hall, 1992) is seen as part of a wider process of change, which is dislocating the central structures and processes of modern societies, and undermining the frameworks that gave individuals stable anchorage in the world.[15] Thus, as indicated by Castells (1996) above, people increasingly make meaning, not on the basis of what they do, but on they basis of what they are, or believe they

15 To illustrate the shift in the construction of identity, Hall (1992: 275–7) identifies three concepts of identity: enlightenment subject, sociological subject, and post-modern subject. The enlightenment subject is based on the concept of the human as a unified, centered individual, which emerged at birth and continued throughout the individual's existence. The sociological subject saw the subject as significant only in relation to others who mediated to the subject values, meanings and symbols. Here identity is formed in the interaction between self and society, and bridges the gap between the inside and outside. The subject was thus not composed of a single, but several identities. The post-modern subject is conceptualised as having no fixed, permanent identity. Identity becomes a 'moveable feast' (Hall, 1992: 277). Thus, Hall says, the subject is decentred, dislocated. This is characteristic of late modernity, and with modern societies in constant change, it illustrates a theme of discontinuities (Hall, 1992: 277). In my study I examine how participants position themselves in their discussion of course readings, in relation to the identities they construct, from a non-essentialist, post-modern perspective.

are. In *The Power of Identity*, the second of his trilogy *The Information Age*, Castells says: 'Identity is people's source of meaning and experience' (Castells, 2004: 6).

From a sociological perspective, all identities are constructed, and that the social construction of identity takes place in a context marked by power relationships (Castells, 2004). The question is how are these identities constructed, and how does this position participants in an online environment? I explore these questions in the chapters in which my findings are presented.

In relation to writing in a second language, Matsuda, Canagarajah, Harklau, Hyland and Warschauer (2003) show that learning to write in a second language is not just the accumulation of technical linguistic abilities, but is related to identity, that is, how one sees oneself and is seen by others, as a student, as a writer, and as an ethnolinguistic minority. Thus, writing is interwoven with multiple, unstable, ambivalent identities as young adults, as immigrants, and often as people of colour.[16]

In relation to participants' constructions of identity in their postings on discussion threads, I refer to the work of Bonny Norton (Pierce) (1995, 1997, 2000) and Ivanic (1998). In her work on language and identity of immigrant women, Norton (Pierce) (1995, 1997, 2000) uses 'identity' to refer to how people understand their relationship to the world, how that relationship is constructed across time and space, and how people understand their possibilities for the future. She refers to West's (1992) view of identity as it relates to the desire for recognition and affiliation (in Norton, 1997). This desire is inseparable from material resources in society, where those with access to such resources are accorded access to power and privilege. Thus identity shifts as social and economic relations change. Human agency and subjectivity

16 Lam's (2000) study of Almon, a teenage Chinese immigrant who writes to a transnational group of teenagers on the Net, is an example. The study shows how his correspondence relates to his developing identity in the use of English. In their study of adult immigrants' writing, Doyle and Song (2005) say further that many people appear to be afraid of writing because it is in writing, much more than in speaking, that people have to express their identity. Their study illustrates how the adult students of English as a Foreign Language construct their identities through their writing.

(Weedon, 1987) are also foregrounded in her argument. Weedon's (1987) theory of subjectivity, for instance, also defines the multiple nature of the subject, subjectivity as a site of struggle, and subjectivity as changing over time.

Ivanic's (1998) work with mature-age students and how they construct their identity through their writing is also relevant. In her study, Ivanic (1998) examines students' discoursal constructions of identity, and says that they construct a sense of self in their written texts. Their identity may be constructed differently each time, because people have multiple identities. Ivanic (1998:11) says that people '(identify) simultaneously with a variety of social groups'. She adds:

> Every time a writer constructs a discoursal self, which draws on less privileged possibilities [...] they are like a drop in the ocean, infinitesimally redefining the possibilities [...] which will in turn be available for future writers (Ivanic, 1998: 28).

In summary, drawing on findings from New Literacy Studies and identity studies, there is an emerging need to explore the use of new electronic and digital literacies, and how learners construct themselves, their identities and make meaning through their use.

Constructing identity through technology

With new technologies networking the world, computer-mediated communication produces a vast array of virtual communities (Castells, 1996: 22). Castells (1996) emphasises that we should locate technological change in the social context in which it is taking place, and by which it is being shaped. He adds 'We should keep in mind that the search for identity is as powerful as techno-economic change in charting new history' (Castells, 1996: 4). Thus a study of identity within a technological framework is relevant to my work on online communities of practice.

In the borderless world of the Internet and computer mediated communication, where anonymity and the creation of persona are not uncommon, the construction of virtual identities is inevitable. In her book *Life on the screen: Identity in the Age of the Internet*, Turkle (1995: 9) argues '[The Internet] links millions of people in new spaces that are changing the way we think, the nature of our sexuality, the form of our communities, our very identities'. She continues 'The Internet has become a significant social laboratory for experimenting with the constructions and reconstructions of self that characterise postmodern life' (Turkle, 1995: 180). Users adopt identities that are multiple: real and virtual selves. Lam's (2000) ethnographic study of Almon's written correspondence with a group of peers on the Net, mentioned earlier, bears reference.

Identities may be constructed through personality, social roles, relationships and shared values. These may be manifest through the use of language, names and social cues such as emoticons in virtual environments. In his study of identity and language use in teenage blogs, Huffaker (2004), for example describes how American teenagers constructed their identities through their disclosure of personal information, their choice of online names and avatars, and the use of emotive features.

Netspeak, or the language used on the Internet, as discussed in the previous chapter, is not always compliant with traditional language use. Examples include the use of acronyms, such as LOL (laugh out loud) and emoticons, such as smileys (☺) to convey mood in the absence of facial expression and gesture. In the representation of persona, participants may choose to use their own names or nicknames to construct their chosen identity.[17]

To recapitulate: my focus on online identities adopts the post-modern view of the subject as decentred, and identity as multiple and shifting. I examine how participants construct their identities through the use of language, name and emotional features, and analyse how they position themselves in relation to their responses to course themes, readings and social issues.

17 Bechar-Israeli (1995, in Huffaker, 2004) found in his study of names used in chat rooms, that they could be categorised as follows: real names, self-related names, technology-related names, names of objects, plays on words and sounds, names related to literature, films, fairy tales and famous people, and provocative or sexual names.

Conclusion

This chapter of the book provides a theoretical and conceptual framework by examining relevant learning theories, and linking these to projects exploring the link between learning, literacies, and identity in online environments. I began by presenting the basic elements of a constructivist approach, then establishing a link between constructivism and the learning theories of Vygotsky (1978), Rogoff (2003) and Lave and Wenger (1991). I established connections between language and literacy studies by referring to New Literacy Studies, where literacy is conceptualised as a social practice, and the advent of technology is viewed as a new literacy. I presented Gee's (1996) view that literacies entail social identities in apprenticed-communities, and went on to deconstruct identity based on the views of Castells (1996), Hall (1992) and Norton (1995, 1997, 2000). In summary, these theories provide a conceptual framework, which together provides a basis for my journey into online communities of practice, in particular, around issues of electronic literacy practice and identity-construction in online environments. In Chapter 3 I present the research design and methods to be used in the project located at the University of the Witwatersrand in South Africa.

Part II

Design, methodology and implications

Northumbria University
Library & Learning Services
Coach Lane Campus
Items borrowed

Title: Constructing identities in online communities of practice : a case study of
ID: 2006764543
Due: 04/03/2009 23:59

Total items: 1
04/02/2009 14:44

Please keep your receipt in case of queries

Chapter 3
Designing the project

Having established connections between overlapping concepts in sociocultural theory, communities of practice, literacy, and identity, as well as why a study of literacy and identity in online communities is valuable in relation to this exploration of technological environments, I present the research design of my project, which I named the Online English Project (OLEP).

I present the qualitative case study as the most appropriate approach to my research, as well as the planning and implementation of the first and second semesters of the study which are shown as Phases 1 and 2. A multi-faceted approach to collecting data in the study is also provided, as is the participant sample, with a view to providing the overall design of the project.

Recapitulating the key research questions

The motivation for this project arose from my interest in the field of ICTs in English teaching. My interest arose from my observations that undergraduate students appeared to be more empowered when given the opportunity to use online strategies, alongside their face-to-face classroom engagement. This was a valuable insight, compared to the conventional teacher-centred classes, where students were seemingly less stimulated by the teaching-learning process. Despite setbacks such as the current lack of infrastructure and resources at many South African universities, as well as student and teacher under-preparedness for online learning in South Africa, I was motivated to further explore this field that was relatively new to me.

To remind the reader, my work is framed by the question 'To what extent do English non-mother tongue speakers in a university English classroom engage in communities of practice in online spaces?'

Recognising that communities of practice involve negotiation of meaning, participation and the establishment of relationships, all of which are facilitated by the construction of participant-identities, I ask the following sub-questions:

- What are the electronic (ICT)-literacy practices of higher education English non-mother tongue speakers, and how do these practices shape their perceptions of ICT-use in an English language classroom?
- What relationships do the participants develop in online environments?
- How do the participants construct identities in online environments?

I conducted a qualitative case study of the implementation of selected ICT interventions in a higher education English classroom in South Africa, with participants who had limited previous exposure to ICTs.

Presenting the qualitative case study

Qualitative research is often regarded as a 'soft' science, concerned with exploratory, personal research and consequently open to bias. However, I found Denzin and Lincoln's (1998), Cohen et al. (2000), Yin (1994) and Nunan's (1992) views of the qualitative case study particularly suitable for the following reasons:

- That it is multi-method in focus
- That qualitative researchers study things in their natural settings
- It provides real life focus
- That it examines real people in real situations
- That it presents and represents reality and provides a sense of being there
- That qualitative researchers attempt to make sense of, or interpret, phenomena in terms of the meanings people bring to them
- That it uses thick description.

It was important for me to be able to observe students at length and have conversations with them about their work, and this would not have been quantifiable. I found that the approach helped me explore issues relating not merely to participant use of ICTs within the classroom, but to how the participants made meaning and constructed their identities in the online medium. The qualitative approach has also been successfully adopted by other researchers in the field of ICTs in the language classroom.[1]

Although I adopted the case study, I acknowledge the weaknesses cited by Cohen et al. (2000). They criticise case study research for its weakness for following the interpretative paradigm of seeing research through the eyes of participants, as well as for its lack of generalisability, leaving case studies closed to cross-checking, which may lead to selectivity, observer bias and subjectivity. I was conscious that as teacher-researcher, this could be problematic for me. Therefore I relied on a multi-method approach, and kept a diary where I recorded notes of informal discussions and observations. I explain the methods in more detail later in this chapter.

However, despite the possible weaknesses acknowledged by theorists, my focus on the case study as a research approach were its benefits, such as those elucidated earlier. The strengths then are its flexibility, intensive focus on the participants, and its reliance on thick description.

Project plan: The Online English Project (OLEP)

In Figure 8 that follows I present a diagrammatic representation of OLEP, which provides the phases of the project.

1 Refer, for example, to qualitative studies conducted by O'Dowd (2004), Warschauer (1996a), and Kern and Warschauer (2000), as well as qualitative case studies discussed in Chapters 1 and 2.

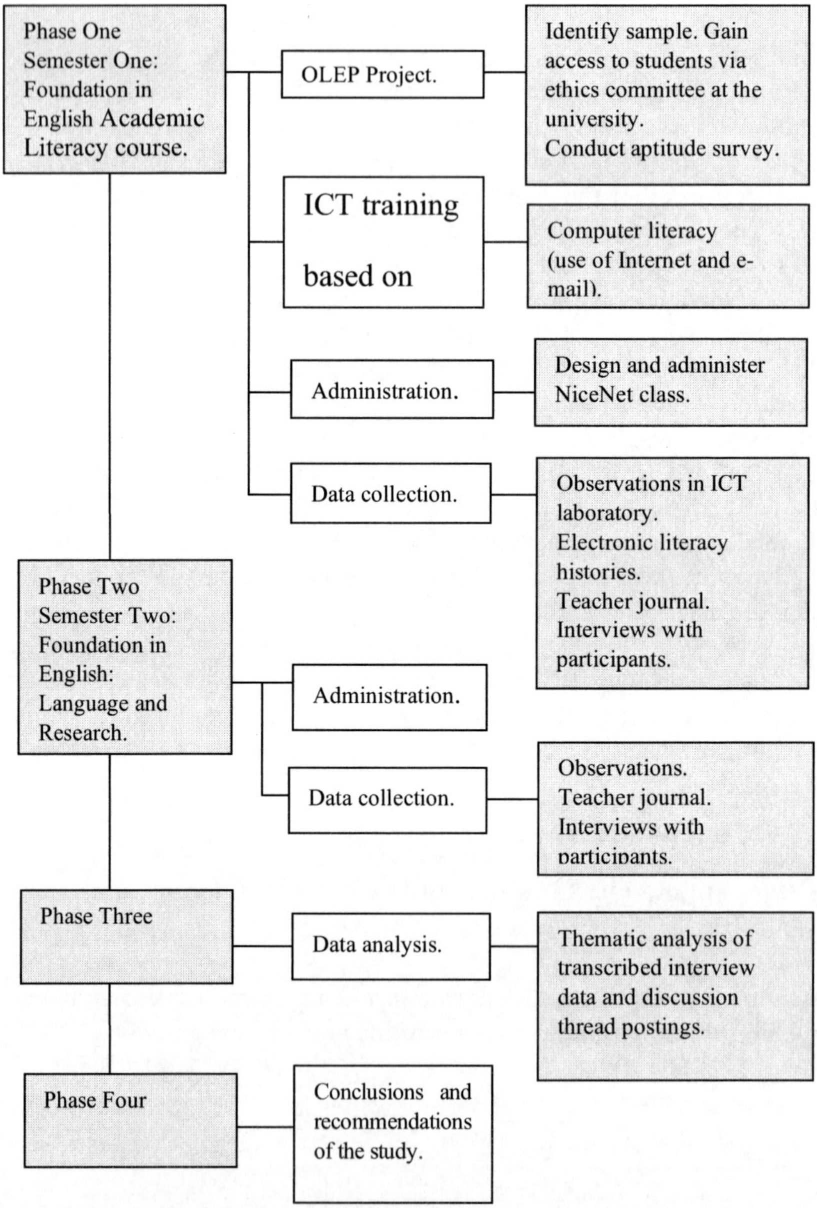

Fig. 8: Online English Language Project (OLEP): Research design

Phases One and Two: Case study at the University of the Witwatersrand

The University of Witwatersrand is situated on the outskirts of Johannesburg's busy central business district in Braamfontein, South Africa. The institution originated as the South African School of Mines in Kimberly, in 1896, and became the Transvaal University College when it transferred to Johannesburg in 1904. In 1910 it was renamed the South African School of Mines and Technology. It was granted full university status as the University of the Witwatersrand in 1922. Student numbers grew rapidly from 6 275 in 1963 to 10 600 in 1975, and 16 400 by 1985 (www.wits.ac.za). Since 2000, the University has been undergoing major plans to expand and modernise in terms of physical, academic, and technological infrastructure.

Although the University originally served a white student population, increasingly, black students have been admitted since the onset of democracy in the country in 1994. A substantial number of international students from more than sixty countries, speaking more than seventy different languages, have also been admitted over the years. The University website provides the following demographics:

Student headcount (2003)	24 381
International students (2003)	1300
Black student headcount (1996–2003)	8185 – 15 820

Fig. 9: Student demographics at the University of the Witwatersrand. From www.wits.ac.za (November 2004)

In its Mission Statement, the University declares that the fundamental role of any university is to promote freedom of enquiry and the search for knowledge and truth. The University therefore sees itself at the industrial and commercial centre for education and research of the highest quality. The Mission Statement continues:

> Wit's mission is to build on this foundation in a way that takes account of its responsibilities within South Africa today; and to maintain and enhance its position as a leading university in South Africa, in Africa, and in the world by

> sustaining globally competitive standards of excellence in learning, teaching and research (www.wits.ac.za, November 2004).

The University is therefore committed to academic freedom and excellence, and playing a leading role in addressing historical disadvantages in the education of students previously disadvantaged by the apartheid era. Included in the purpose statement is to ensure that graduates achieve levels of skills and knowledge that are comparable world-wide, thus, among the University's immediate priorities is to ensure that campuses are well-resourced.

Generally, students register for degrees spanning three years. If their matriculation points do not meet the requirements for university entrance, they may enter via a special selection process. If they are successful they are generally accepted over an extended curriculum spanning four years. They are advised on curriculum issues by a curriculum planning unit. Two of the language modules they might be required to study in the Discipline of Applied English Language Studies (AELS) is Foundation in English: Academic Literacy, and Foundation in English: Language and Research. The discipline AELS, and the two Foundation courses are presented in detail in Chapter 4, where I describe and analyse the data.

The participant sample

Students who register for the Foundation in English course may do so for one or two semesters. As outlined in Chapter 4, students who do the Foundation in English: Academic Literacy module may continue onto Foundation in English: Language and Research in the second semester, or they have the option of doing English or African Literature. Each week consists of one lecture period, and three tutorial periods. The students meet as a group in the lecture period, where lectures are conducted by staff members. In the remaining periods they attend tutorial groups of about thirty-five students each.

My Academic Literacy tutorial group consisted of thirty-five students in the first semester. At the end of the first semester, seventeen students remained, while eighteen students left to pursue the other courses on offer. In order to make optimal use of staff, the tutorial groups were reorganised so that seventeen new students from another tutorial group joined my group, bringing the total number of students in semester two to thirty-four.

Of the thirty-four students, twenty volunteered to be part of my research project, however, not all twenty students participated in the online course, OLEP. I have provided character sketches of all twenty participants in order to provide the reader with a more holistic picture.[2] All twenty volunteers were interviewed. In the analysis I use extracts from the interview transcripts and discussion threads to support my discussion. More specific participant demographics in terms of age, gender, nationality and language are described in sections to follow.

The participants ranged in age as follows: six were under twenty, thirteen were in the age group twenty-one to twenty-five, and one was in the age group twenty-six to thirty. There were thirteen males and seven females in the study. All were in their first year of study at the university, however, their choice of degrees varied, as the following figure shows:

Degrees of study	**Student number**
Bachelor of Arts (BA)	7
BA Social Work	1
BA Dramatic Arts	1
BA Fine Arts	1
BA Economics	1
Bachelor of Commerce (B Com)	1
LLB (Law)	8
Total	**20**

Fig. 10: Sample participants' degrees of study

2 Please refer to the Appendix for the character sketches of all participants. Participants' real names are not used to maintain their privacy.

In terms of the regions from which participants came, sixteen were from various regions in South Africa, while four came from SADC or other countries. The figure that follows elaborates:

South African students		**SADC and international students**	
KwaZulu Natal	3	Teheran, Iran	1
Limpopo	3	Shanghai, China	1
Giyani	1	Morewa, Zimbabwe	1
North West	1	Maputo, Mozambique	1
Northern Province	2		
Gauteng	3		
South Africa (specific regions not provided)	3		
Total	**16**	**Total**	**4**

Fig. 11: Participants' regions of origin

The intention of this study is not to draw comparisons between local (South African) and international students. The reason for including international students is that they were all in the same class, studying the same course, and were non-mother tongue speakers of English. Their prior use of technology did not influence the results of this study in any way, because none of the international students had used technology in their learning previously. Oscar, Farzana, and Xing had used e-mail previously, while Natalie had had some lessons in computer literacy in school.

All of the South African participants were from disadvantaged backgrounds, having spent most of their formative schooling in under-resourced schools in the rural areas or townships, where they had been learning English from primary school. The students from the SADC regions, as well as China and Iran, had been learning English since high school.

Of the twenty participants, not all used the *Nicenet* system. For more clarity on issues of participation, in the following section I present the students who participated in the system, and those who did not. Thirteen participants (65%) were active in the programme, most having been in my class from the first semester. Seven students did not participate in the programme, the majority being new to my class, having joined in the second semester. However, I have included them in the study in order to present a more composite picture of participants' views on online learning. Once again, the purpose is not intended to be comparative.

First and second semester (old) students		**Second semester (new) students**	
Used	**Did not use**	**Used**	**Did not use**
Herman	Natalie	Zinhle	Mabela
Farzana	Sibonelo	Adam	Leonard
Precious	Nothando		Musa
Lucky	Lindiwe		
Xing			
Oscar			
Elsie			
Ernest			
Alex			
Blessing			
Mbali			
11	**4**	**2**	**3**

Fig. 12: Student use of *Nicenet*

I elaborate in Chapter 4 the reasons why certain students participated in the web course, while others did not.

Data collection methods and techniques

Having obtained informed consent from participants and the ethics committee at the University,[3] I opted for a triangulated multi-method approach to data collection, which included the use of questionnaires, observations, individual interviews, written data such as electronic

3 The University Ethics Committee requires that research conducted at the university be cleared ethically to ensure that participants' rights are not infringed.

literacy histories and postings from discussion threads, and facilitator journals.

Participant and manager questionnaires

I designed a survey questionnaire to elicit data from the student participants before the intervention began, about their access to, and proficiency with computers, e-mail and the Internet, as well as their views on the use of ICTs in the English classroom. The questionnaire consisted of two main sections. The first section was designed to elicit biographical data such as participants' age, home language, gender, and the degrees towards which they were studying. In the second section I asked questions and used Likkert scales to ascertain students' English proficiency, as well as their access to and proficiency with ICTs. I included questions around how they learnt to use computers and the Internet. Figure 13 from the participant questionnaire illustrates its structure:

2.1 How would you rate your proficiency in the following English skills? Please indicate the most suitable response with a cross (X).

	More than adequate	Adequate	Less than adequate	Not adequate
Reading				
Writing				
Speaking				
Listening				

2.4 How would you rate your proficiency in using the following:

	More than adequate	Adequate	Less than adequate	Not adequate
Computer				
E-mail				
Internet				

Fig. 13: Extracts from survey questionnaire: English and ICT proficiency

A Likkert scale ranging in choice from strongly agree, agree, disagree, strongly disagree, to don't know was used to ascertain how students thought using ICTs, including the Internet might help them in the English classroom. Here data around the following issues were elicited: reading, writing, listening and speaking skills; vocabulary; pronunciation; intercultural communication; and communication with the teacher and other learners.

Open-ended questions on the questionnaire gave students an opportunity to explain how they learnt to use computers and the Internet. The final question was also open-ended and asked for reasons why they would or would not like to use ICTS including the Internet in the English classroom.

I tried to avoid common pitfalls such as overly long questionnaires, confusing instructions, complicated design and ambiguous questions. Thus my questionnaire which served to capture data from the thirty-four students in the first semester at the University of the Witwatersrand, and seventeen new students in the second semester, was designed to accommodate the linguistic needs of English non-mother tongue speakers in a simple and accessible format, as shown in Figure 14:

Do you have regular access to a computer?

	Yes	No
Where you live		
At your institution		

Do you have regular access to the Internet?

	Yes	No
Where you live		
At your institution		

Fig. 14: Extract from survey questionnaire: Computer and Internet access

In addition to student questionnaires, two School Managers were asked to complete questionnaires in order to establish a more comprehensive view of ICT use in the Faculty of Humanities and in the School of Literature and Language Studies, namely the Head of

School, and the Head of Information Technology for the Humanities. Open-ended questions addressed the following issues:

- ICT-policy and technology planning at the University;
- the incorporation of technology in the Humanities classroom;
- the extent to which online learning was being implemented at the University;
- responses of staff members and students to the use of ICTs in teaching and learning;
- their perceptions of the possible benefits and challenges of online learning;
- ICT facilities in the School for staff and students,
- staff and student training; and
- the role of online learning within the School, and in particular, in the teaching and learning of English.

Observations

The purpose of the observation, one of the typical methods adopted in the case study, is to probe and analyse with a view to establishing generalisations. Observation methods are beneficial on several accounts: non-verbal behaviour may be observed and commented on, a feature that may be overlooked in other methods such as questionnaires. The description of ongoing behaviour as it unfolds is also enabled through observations.

Vital to observations is the role played by the observer, namely, the observer as participant and non-participant. As course facilitator, I played the role of participant observer when students went to the computer laboratory. The predicament here could be the issue of bias and subjectivity. As a member of the class group, I had to be conscious of the fact while I could assist students if they needed help logging on, I was not there to teach them during observation sessions, but to observe their ICT practices. Thus I tried not to interfere in their practices. Non-participant observers on the other hand, remain distant from the goings on of the unit, and do not become members of the group.

Because the observation write-up may be prone to vague descriptions and inconsistent categorisations, which does not contribute to reliability and validity, the use of an observation schedule helped me prevent imprecision in terms of data collected. The schedule helped me categorise participant behaviour, thus contributing to reliability and validity in the process. The systematic coding methods I opted to use, and which I decided on prior to my observation sessions enabled me to record particulars of what I was looking for, and the types of events I was interested in.

I made provision for observations of the computer laboratory being used, and allowed for field notes including the following:

- laboratory layout, notices, the number of computers, the number of working computers;
- the number of students in the laboratory, in queues to use computers, and the number working per computer;
- students' ability to get connected to the Net, and to the *Nicenet* class if that was the purpose of their visit;
- independent, pair or group work;
- requests for assistance, and from whom; responses to requests for assistance.

Observations are not to be considered fault-free, and I was aware of some of the problems with which they are associated. Among these are that I had to be sufficiently vigilant to observe all that was occurring. This is not always possible as classroom dynamics operate on several layers. To me, one of the major problems is that one can only observe the observable – what appears on the surface. In order to examine in detail, it is necessary to make inferences, which may or may not be valid. Therefore, I triangulated the data gathering process with additional methods such as interviews. An option would be video-recording, but even this is not without bias if one needs to focus on all students equitably. An additional problem was that the participants went to the laboratory in their own time, when other students were busy working on the computers, and I could not guarantee ethical clearance if I recorded students who were not part of the study. Because the laboratory was a general Faculty laboratory, I had to make arrangements with students about when they would be working with the computers so that I could observe them in small groups or individually.

The observation as a research method is open to subjectivity on the part of the researcher, and, as already stated, in order to circumvent subjectivity, I adopted a triangulated approach that included other instruments such as questionnaires, interviews, written data and facilitator journals. In all, I observed six computer laboratory sessions during semester one, and six in semester two, ranging from one to two hours per session. I arranged for participants to inform me when they were going to the laboratory, so that I was able to observe about 75% of the participants working on computers at least once.

Interviews

Interviews are productive in terms of gathering data for case studies as they focus directly on the case study topic. Individual semi-structured interviews were held with twenty students towards the end of the project. I feel comfortable using semi-structured interviews, which rely on a basic interview guide, which may be elaborated on during the course of the interview. I also did not feel bound by the order of the questions. Therefore, I found the flexibility offered by the semi-structured interview an attractive option.

Each interview was audio-recorded and transcribed in order to ensure accuracy. Interviewees were given copies of transcripts to comment on for accuracy, and in order to ensure member-checking as a form of validity. Audio recording might allow for greater accuracy, although the presence of an audio recorder could also distract or hamper certain interviewees. It is inevitable too that transcription loses data from the original encounter.

Furthermore, non-verbal body language, which may add richly to meaning and are therefore important in an interview, will also be omitted in transcription. Thus I noted relevant non-verbal gestures during interviews where necessary. The advantage of audio-recording, however, is that I was not hampered by making extensive notes during the interview.

In relation to content, the interview schedule consisted of two main sections, namely, biographical details, and ICT and Net-based practices. Students were asked as a means of triangulating the questionnaire discussed earlier, about their access, proficiency prior to and after the implementation of the project, as well as their Net-practices such as frequency in logging on and sites accessed. Figure 15 illustrates selected interview questions:

Section 2: ICT-practice, proficiency and access

2.1 Did you have access to computers and the Internet at high school?

2.2 Do you have regular access to a computer

2.2.1 Where you live?

2.2.2 At your institution?

2.3 Do you have regular access to the Internet

2.3.1 Where you live?

2.3.2 At your institution?

2.6 How often do you log on to the Internet

2.6.1 For class use?

2.6.2 For personal use?

2.7 For what purposes do you log on, and what types of sites do you generally visit?

Section 3: Internet-based classroom and English practices

3.1 Have you enjoyed being part of the online class? Why?

3.2 Are you using computers and the Internet in any of your other courses?

3.3 Do you think there are advantages to using computers and the Internet in class? If so, what are they?

3.4 Do you think there are disadvantages to using computers and the Internet in class? If so, what are they?

3.5 Has the use of the Net helped you communicate better:

3.5.1 With your lecturer? If so, in what way?

____

____

3.5.2 With fellow students in class? If so, in what way?

____

____

3.5.3 Have you been using the e-pals system? If so, how many students have you been communicating with? ______________

3.5.4 What do you generally communicate about? ______________

____

Fig. 15: Extract from the student interview schedule

Written data from participants and the researcher

I wished to elicit rich data from students around their thoughts and feelings on their early encounters with electronic literacy, in particular ICT literacy practices and thus I decided to borrow from the literacy history method of eliciting data, by asking participants to write literacy histories around their electronic literacy practices, which I called electronic literacy histories. The electronic literacy history is an autobiographical account of participants' early encounters with ICTs, and provided valuable input on their feelings and perceptions of electronic literacy practices. Especially significant was the detail they provided on their feelings of disempowerment, not being proficient in the use of ICTs, as well as how they positioned themselves in relation to ICTs.

The second type of written data was messages posted to discussion threads in the online class. In order to analyse participant-identities as constructed in online environments, I found it necessary to refer to my own, as well as participants' extracts from the discussion threads. I posted a question around course readings each week, and participants were asked to respond to the issues and discussions that emanated. I conduct a discourse analysis of some of the postings or written data in relation to language use and the construction of identity.

Facilitator journal and journalistic notes

I kept a reflective journal over the year in which the research was conducted, where I recorded my thoughts on the project, as well as notes on relevant informal conversations with participants who 'popped in' to visit with queries, or if we happened to meet around campus. I found the informal conversations very helpful, but needed a more formalised way of recording them, which the journal provided. I also used the journal in which to reflect on the project as it unfolded, and it helped me modify some of my strategies as the course progressed. Essentially, the journal helped me grow personally, as well as professionally.

I was aware that the use of journals has been critiqued for their subjectivity and bias, however, I believe that the journal gave me a lens through which to reflect on my own practice, and because it was a rich source of data, especially when used in conjunction with other methods such as observations and interviews. Having described the methods of data collection, Figure 16 summarises these for the reader.

Method	**Participants**	**Instrument**	**Analysis**	
Survey	34 students 2 School Managers	Survey questionnaire Questionnaire and conversations	Statistical and thematic: Biographical and background details. Thematic: Access and policy issues within SLLS.	Overarching theoretical framework: Communities of practice
Observations	Six groups in Semester One Six groups in Semester Two	Observation schedule	Thematic: Identity (Hall, Norton, Castells).	
Interviews	20 students	Interview schedule	Thematic Framework: Identity (Hall, Norton, Castells).	
Written data	20 students	Electronic literacy histories Extracts from discussion threads	Thematic Framework: Electronic (ICT)-literacy as social practice (Gee, Street, Knobel and Lankshear). Framework: Identity (Hall, Norton, Castells).	
Facilitator journal and journalistic notes	Facilitator	Journal Observation schedules	Thematic: Identity (Hall, Norton, Castells).	

Fig. 16: Matrix of data collection and analytical methods

Figure 16 shows that the themes selected for analysis transcend across all the data collection methods, making it possible to cross-check findings from one particular method with another. The intention is also that responses relating to questions around identity-construction, participation, and relationships will underpin and form the basis for answering my primary research question on the extent to which communities of practice are enabled in online environments.

Conclusion

In this chapter I presented the project, by discussing the first two phases, namely the planning and implementation of OLEP.[4] The multi-method approach to collecting data in the study is also described with a view to securing, as far as possible, the reliability and validity of data, methodology, instrument design and participant sample.

Chapters 4 and 5 present a thematic analysis of data collected from the range of instruments described in Chapter 3. In Chapter 4, I present participants' ICT-practices, in- and out-of the university, in relation to themes such as access and proficiency, as well as a framework for literacy as a social practice. Chapter 5 raises issues of negotiation, participation and identity in online environments.

4 Phases Four and Five are presented in the data analysis and concluding Chapters respectively.

Part III

Electronic literacy and identity

Chapter 4
Electronic (ICT) literacy as a social practice: Issues of ICT access, proficiency and practice

In the previous chapter I presented the research design of my project as a four-phase intervention, where I described the first two phases, the planning and implementation of Online English Project (OLEP).

In order to explore the research questions, the next phase, Phase three, which describes and analyses the data comprises two chapters, to handle two specific areas that enable me to explore the extent to which participants engage in online communities. The first area I examine is their electronic literacy practices, with specific focus on ICT-literacy. Then, I look at their online interactions and construction of identities. The question concerning the electronic (ICT) literacy practices of higher education English non-mother tongue speakers, and how these practices shape their perceptions of ICT use in an English language classroom, is addressed. I draw primarily on the work of researchers and theorists such as Barton, Hamilton and Ivanic (2000), Street (1984, 1993, 1998, 2003), and Gee (1996, 1997, 2000), who suggest that the conventional view of 'literacy' is narrow, and that literacy is not a skill, but a social practice that is embedded in broader social goals. They say further that different literacies are associated with different domains of life, and that literacy practices are patterned by power relationships and social institutions. Literacy is also historically situated, and the practices change, in particular, in this case, with the introduction of new electronic technologies into the teaching-learning environment.

Let me first describe the context of the School of Literature and Language Studies (SLLS), the discipline, Applied English Language Studies (AELS), and the Foundation in English courses. I describe the technological provisions within the school and discipline, to provide a context for the use of ICTs across the School. Thereafter the *Nicenet* online component is described. At this point I explore participants' in- and out-of-school ICT-literacy practices in terms of ICT access in their former high schools, homes, and at the university. Then I examine participants' ICT-literacy practices in relation to their proficiency, and how they learnt to use the media. The next section examines learners' Internet and online (*Nicenet*)-literacy practices in relation to frequency of access, the types of sites they visit and their views on the benefits and challenges of the use of ICTs. I conclude the chapter with personal reflections on participants' ICT-literacy practices.

In Chapter 5, I analyse the data thematically in relation to Lave and Wenger's (1991, 1996, 2002) concept 'communities of practice', in order to establish the extent to which participants engage in communities of practice. I establish the extent to which they participate, negotiate meaning and develop and sustain relationships in online communities. This is in response to my second query, 'What relationships do the participants develop in online environments?' Participants' interaction is examined in relation to Lave and Wenger's (1991, 1996, 2002) concept 'legitimate peripheral participation', where participants initially engage as novices, or 'new comers' and are assisted by more proficient participants, or 'old timers' in order to participate fully within the community of practice. Then I examine how participants construct their identities textually, in relation to broader social issues, and moving beyond communities of practice, in response to my third query, 'How do participants construct their identities in online environments?' This examination I draw on the work of Hall (1992), Norton (Pierce) (1995, 1997, 2000) and Ivanic (1998). Uncorrected data texts from discussion forums are used as the basis for analysis.

The analysis of students' electronic literacy practices, relationships, participation, negotiation of meaning, and their construction of identities provide a framework for understanding my primary research query on the extent to which communities of practice are enabled in online environments, given that the characteristics are key elements of communities of practice.

About thematic analysis

Although thematic analysis is most often used in ethnographic studies,[1] I found aspects of such an approach appropriate for the analysis of data gathered for this book. Thematic analysis focuses on identifiable themes and patterns of living and behaviour (Aronson, 1994). Patterns of experiences within transcribed conversations are listed, and these may take the form of direct quotes or paraphrasing. The data may be related to already classified patterns. This structure I adopt within the patterns identified in communities of practice and self-directed learning. Within these patterns I combine and code related themes and sub-themes to provide a more holistic view of the issues concerned which would have been fragmented on their own. Seen from this perspective, a narrative emerges on participants' ICT-literacy practices, their access and proficiency with ICTs, and their participation in online communities. In the following section, I present the background of the School of Literature and Language Studies (SLLS), the discipline, Applied English Language Studies (AELS), and the Foundation in English courses, on which my study is based.

About the School (SLLS), the Discipline (AELS), and Foundation in English at the University of the Witwatersrand

The School of Literature and Language Studies (SLLS) is located within the Faculty of Humanities at the University of the Witwatersrand (Wits). The School is organised in Disciplines which offer a range of courses and programmes, including African Languages,

1 Refer, for instance to Norton's (1995, 1997, 2000) studies of language and identity among immigrant women in Canada, and Brice-Heath's (1983) work with children's language use in two communities in the United States.

African Literature, Applied English Language Studies, Classics, English Studies, French, German, Portuguese, Spanish, IT for the Humanities, Italian, Linguistics, Media Studies, Publishing Studies, and South African Sign Language.

My enquiry covered two Foundation in English classes over one year within the discipline Applied English Language Studies (AELS). I considered Applied English a suitable choice for a language-based course because of its concern with the study of English language as a social practice in multilingual contexts. The discipline functions at the interface between language, literacy and the social context, and academics within this area are interested in the origins of language practices in English, their social effects and implications for intercultural communication. The discipline offers students undergraduate and postgraduate degrees in the field of English Language Studies.

Both Foundation courses address academic literacy and served as the basis for my study. Foundation in English: Academic Literacy focuses on language in a sociocultural context. The skills and practice focus is writing in specific genres such as autobiographical or narrative writing, comparisons and contrasts, and arguments, as well as oral skills. The content basis is established through particular themes such as the transition from school to university, HIV/AIDS, polygamy and gender issues. Students are provided with a range of interesting and provocative readings as core material. Over the course of the semester skills are scaffolded, or presented at levels of increasing complexity. The course structure includes formal lectures of forty-five minutes once a week, and smaller group tutorials of forty-five minutes each four times a week. Students are given the option to attend an academic development tutorial every week where academic literacy skills may be developed more extensively. Students may also make appointments with lecturers and tutors for private consultations. Students are assessed formatively and summatively in oral and written contexts, and are given the opportunity to rewrite essays based on self, peer and tutor feedback. Comprehensive assessment criteria are used. Written and oral feedback is provided formally and informally.

The second semester module, Foundation in English: Language and Research has a strong research focus, unlike the Academic Literacy course offered in the first semester. As explained already, students have options with regard to courses they could choose to study in the second semester: Language and Research, Literature, African Literature, or Legal Discourse (the latter in the case of Law students). For this reason, there is generally a re-organisation of students into tutorial groups, that is, students do not necessarily remain within the same class groups in the second semester.

Students work in groups to conduct research on language issues over the course of the fourteen-week period, and compile a research report, which they present in written and oral form. They attend formal lectures on different aspects of research, and simultaneously start their research projects in tutorials. Research articles on various language issues such as language policy, naming practices, language varieties, language attitudes, and translation and interpreting are also discussed in tutorials. Students select their own research groups and produce a research topic, questions, methodology, and instruments. They collect data within the prescribed period, analyse the data, and present their findings orally to the tutorial group, and then in a written report.

Next I look at an overview of the current technological landscape of SLLS. I do this in order to provide contextual detail on issues such as technology planning and policy, as well as staff access to, and use of ICTs in teaching and learning. These issues are important because, for staff members to utilise ICTs effectively in their teaching practice, it needs to be supported at university-wide level. Furthermore, to overcome teacher under-preparedness and apprehension staff members require suitable access to ICTs, and to be professionally trained in its use as a teaching tool. Additional views on the incorporation of ICTs into Humanities syllabi are elicited from two School Managers, namely the Head of School, and the Head of IT for the Humanities.

The technological landscape in SLLS

Technology planning

The intention to integrate technology into teaching and learning at an institution is usually located within its technology plan or policy. Such a plan or policy may drive the use of technology across the university. I established that a technology plan does not exist at the institution. According to the HIT, the Faculty and University computing committees of which she is a member were never able to articulate a concrete policy that was agreeable to all parties. However, both the HOS and HIT articulated the need to incorporate technology in Humanities classrooms for the following reasons:

> The Humanities are no longer just paper based disciplines or areas of study. Quite a lot can be done using computers and on the Internet to assist with writing, research and creative work (HOS).

> [...] because more and more research resources are being digitally distributed and information literacy is becoming more vital to successful research (HIT).

Although the integration of technology into teaching and learning does not appear to have been planned at the university, staff and students do have access to technology. The following section expands on staff access and their use of technology in their curricula and teaching practice.

Staff and student access to ICTs in SLLS

As stated earlier in this chapter, staff access to, and proficiency with ICTs, are important in overcoming teacher under-preparedness for the incorporation of ICTs in their teaching. In SLLS at present, most staff members have computers and printers. All staff members have Internet access. Students in SLLS have access to one teaching laboratory in the School, with forty workstations, a stand-alone server, and one heavy-duty printer. This laboratory has a foldaway partition, so that when the laboratory is needed as a teaching laboratory, it might be divided into two venues with twenty workstations each, where one section is used in which to teach, and the other may be used by students for their own purposes. This partition, however, does not eliminate noise or interference from each section. All students have Internet access in the laboratory. Students also have access to other computer laboratories on campus, such as in the main library, which are similarly equipped.

Using technology in teaching and learning

At the time of this study, technology had been incorporated into very few courses in SLLS, specifically, it has only been introduced in Media Studies, Modern Languages and AELS. One such course, Internet Literacies is a second year Applied English module which I co-ordinated and taught at the time of this project. In this course students learn about the ways in which computer technology is changing language, literacy, and communication. Students apply their understanding of technology and cyber culture to projects that may involve authoring web pages and designing web sites.

At the time I undertook this project, the use of technology in teaching and learning was not the norm in the SLLS. One of the reasons suggested for the limited extent to which online learning is being undertaken within SLLS, is the lack of central budget (HIT). There are also challenges in terms of staff training. Academic staff members are not formally trained to use technology in their teaching and learning, unless they choose to attend selected training courses. Students also do not receive formal training, although, in courses where technology is utilised students could benefit from it. The HIT added:

> The general view in the Human Sciences is that such learning should be reserved for postgraduate students who work on their own. Staff members are also reluctant to interact with the technology which is what is needed for a successful implementation of technology-enhanced learning at an undergraduate level.

It is the view of both Managers that students could benefit from the implementation of online learning. Students would benefit by being empowered to use technology for various purposes, as well as have access to wider research resources. Staff too would benefit from modernised, innovative course delivery. However, one of the challenges associated with implementing technology in the classroom remains the need to constantly upgrade equipment to keep up with changes, about which the HIT felt 'what is worse than not implementing technology-enhanced learning, is the use of outdated technology'.

This book is therefore clearly located against a backdrop where the use of ICTs in teaching and learning is not the norm. The next section describes the online component, which I designed and ran parallel to the face-to-face Foundation class, using the *Nicenet* system. Thereafter an overview of the participant sample is presented, as well as their access, proficiency, and views on ICTs.

Online English Project: The *Nicenet* online component

OLEP involved the design of an online intervention, using the *Nicenet* web course management system, to run parallel to the face-to-face tutorials. As explained in the section on web course management systems in Chapter 1, *Nicenet* is a free web course management tool that provides users with the following basic facilities:

conferencing page where participants may engage in discussion;
link sharing, where other relevant sites may be loaded;
documents page where documents may be uploaded;
class schedule, where timetables and course outlines may be uploaded;
list of class members;
personal messages, where participants may access messages sent to them.

Other web course management systems such as *Blackboard* could have been used, but, the download time in South Africa was much slower than *Nicenet*. *WebCT*, another popular system, to which the University is licensed, was a little complex, in my view, to use with my undergraduate students who had little previous experience with ICTs. This is an important consideration in developing countries. Although I had done training courses in all three systems, I found *Nicenet* most suitable for my purposes, the only facility lacking being chat rooms. However, as my research did not involve the use of chat rooms, this did not matter at the time.

The Foundation in English participants were given a detailed Handout with instructions on how to join the class. I also assisted students who experienced difficulty signing on. Topics were linked to class discussions around readings and assignments. *Nicenet* offers conferencing links, where teachers and students may engage in asynchronous discussions. Link sharing allows for the teacher, as well as students to post suitable useful links such as other articles or web sites. I also included the e-pal link. I received a posting on the TESL listserv from a teacher in China, who was interested in his students communicating with English-speaking students, and sharing cultural experiences. This will be discussed in more detail in the section on global e-pal communities in Chapter 5, which examines communities of practice in detail.

The documents link allowed me to post documents such as model essays for students to read. I also included hints on writing the examination, such as examination preparation, study techniques, and time management. The section 'Class Members' enables all participants to see who had joined the class, as well as to get other members' contact details. I found the link useful to ascertain which students were registered for the class at any particular point in the project.

ICT-literacy practice: Living the digital divide

Drawing on Warschauer's (2002a, 2002b, 2003) and Feenberg's (1991) views, as presented earlier in this book, the digital divide should not be considered a bipolar division between 'haves' and 'have-nots'. Rather, it is about political, economic, institutional, cultural, and linguistic issues of class and power. I was conscious of the social presence of my participants, that is, who they are, and where they come from, also bearing in mind that providing them with ways of utilising technology was not just a means of providing them with access, but a means of social inclusion and mobility. Hence, my focus in this section on ICT-practice is not only to highlight the presence or absence of ICTs, but serves to draw attention to issues of electronic literacy practice, social development, and inclusion and exclusion, in Warschauer's words: 'an overemphasis on the mere presence of computers or Internet connections, without corresponding emphasis on social mobilization and transformation, can squander resources while leaving inequity intact' (2003b: 303).

In fact several participants in my study commented on the marginalisation and lack of power they felt on entering university from disadvantaged backgrounds, because of their lack of access to technology. In their view white students had previous access to ICTs at home or in school. They regarded this as being compliant with the historical polarisation of race and politics in South Africa. Thus, the view is consistent with Gee's (2000) reference to social practices being studied within social, cultural, historical, political and economic contexts. Street (2003) also says that research requires language and literacy to be studied as they occur naturally in social life, taking into account context and their different meanings for different cultural groups. Considering South Africa's past, it is not surprising that many black students from under-resourced rural and township schools and environments come to university under-prepared for the dominant academic and technological discourses of such an environment. In the following sections I therefore focus on participants' electronic literacy practices, with specific focus on their ICT-literacy practices. Taking into account that literacy is socially situated, and that learners bring with them dominant home discourses and out-of-school practices to the classroom, I focus on ICT access in their high schools, at home, and at university. Then I explore ICT-practice in terms of participants' proficiency, and Internet and online (*Nicenet*) practices, such as their frequency in logging on, and the sites they access. Finally I examine their views on ICT use, in terms of the possible benefits and challenges. In the thematic analysis extracts of interview transcripts and electronic literacy histories are examined, and reference is made to field notes and diary entries.

In-school ICT-literacy practices: About access at school 'A computer is a luxury, you only get to see it'[2]

Of the twenty participants, the majority did not have access at school or at home. Of the South African participants, fifteen (75%) said they did not have access to computers and the Internet at school, with only one stating that he had had previous access. The student who had ICT access at school said:

> LUCKY: [We had] just a lab but it was not easy, I was stealing time to go there, but here at the varsity to be told how to use the Internet, it's not really a big work. I don't think we have to be told to do that. OK, it's an easy thing I would say. Some students don't do this. Ja, others type their assignments [for them].[3] It's just the fear. People are just afraid. There's nothing to be afraid of.[4]

Lucky was fortunate that his school had a computer laboratory, but he acknowledged the difficulty in getting access to use the computers. His use of 'stealing time' to use the computers shows that this was not always an easy task, that time to use computers was not provided for, or that it was not always permitted. This relates to Warschauer's (2003a, 2003b) findings on the model laboratories set up in Egypt, where equipment was not installed or used because of bureaucracy and gate-keeping. Lucky's reference to fear is a common emotion felt by participants with minimal previous ICT-experience, and is indicative of the technophobia felt by several participants at the outset of the project.

Students who did not have ICT-access at school expressed some of the problems they experienced when they entered university and had to

2 Sibonelo.

3 It is a common occurrence at the University for students who are not computer literate to pay others to type out assignments.

4 Note that extracts have not been corrected grammatically or otherwise to maintain authenticity.

compete on equal terms with students who had previous access to technology:

> SIBONELO: We had no computers. No computers in school, only the teachers had access. In the office – only one computer for all. The area I come from, Limpopo is one of the poorest. A computer is a luxury, you only get to see it.
> ELSIE: No, we didn't [have computers]. We had a problem when we came here in first year to university we had to type and do all sorts of things. It is so hard when you come from a disadvantaged school.
> ADAM: Ja, the principal had it, but if he could use it? (*Shrugs, raising shoulders.*) The teachers could use his [computer], but not the students. Now there is computers for the students in the school. We didn't have it, now they do
> LEILA: How does this make you feel?
> ADAM: Well...like it's not fair, but it's better for them.
> LEILA: Did you have access to computers and Internet at school?
> LINDIWE: No, nothing.
> LEILA: So when you got here, what happened?
> LINDIWE: (*Laughs*) Whew, it was very difficult. You have to learn even how to use a mouse!
> ERNEST: No, never at school. We used to see all this computers and things on TV and we thought one day we would use it. Now they are getting it in school. They are fortunate. They must appreciate it, it is a resource for the future.
> ALEX: No. The principal, the teachers are saying all the time, be computer literate. With no computers?

It is evident from these responses that most of the students were from under-resourced schools, where in some cases only principals, and sometimes teachers had access to ICTs. Adam's doubts about whether the principal was computer literate is also typical of what Warschauer (2002a, 2002b, 2003a, 2003b) talks about in Egypt and Ireland, where technology was purchased (in Ireland's case, won) at great expense, but not used, partially because of bureaucracy, and because people were not sufficiently trained in its use. A common thread that emerged is that the participants were encouraged by teachers to use ICTs in preparation for university, even though they did not have access at school, for instance, Alex's comment 'The principal, the teachers are saying all the time, be computer literate', was applicable to other participants who felt the same way. Another thread is the dissatisfaction felt when participants arrived at university, but were excluded from one of the dominant academic practices of the institution, that is, ICT proficiency. Lindiwe, for instance commented on feeling uncomfortable that she could not use computers when she got to university. This issue was obviously recognised by the participants' high school teachers who encouraged the use of ICT. There is also an indication that ICT is currently being introduced to schools (refer for instance to Adam's and Ernest's comments),[5] the implication being that new students entering university might be better-prepared for its use, provided, of course, that they use the equipment, and that their teachers are trained in its use.

Of the SADC/International students, three had access at school, while one did not. Xing, for instance, speaks about his high school in Shanghai:

> XING: In my high school in Shanghai we had some computer lessons. Now my classmates in Shanghai have their own computers, so we have a lot of opportunities. It helped me when I got here. With the Internet I think I'm good at it.
> LEILA: And do you use the e-mail to keep in touch with people back home?
> XING: Yes, we talk to each other and ...actually we have a lot of opportunity to use the Internet because there are many Internet cafes in Shanghai. Everyone uses it. Even you can use public phones and your phone card to log on.

Xing's comment on being able to log on to the Internet using phone cards was new to me. It is obvious that had Xing remained in Shanghai, he would have been exposed to technology of a far more sophisticated nature. He was obviously also motivated to use e-mail to maintain contact with family and friends in Shanghai. This was common among the other foreign students, as well as those from outside South Africa, such as Natalie, Oscar and Farzana.

Oscar, who is from Zimbabwe, did not have previous access to ICT at school. However, as an older student, who is also an artist, he had been exposed to technology through his work:

> OSCAR: Not so much access, but I had a knowledge of computers since I started travelling to and from Europe. But I wasn't a computer genius that time. I started using computers in 2002 [...] when I got my first e-mail address when it was

5 ICTs are being introduced to schools in poorly-resourced areas as a result of donations by companies and parastatals, as well as initiatives such as GautengOnline and SchoolNet Africa, discussed earlier in this book.

pressurizing me to get contact with the outside world because of a growing number of contacts I was having.

LEILA: When you say you were travelling to and from Europe, where were you travelling, and for what reason?

OSCAR: In 1999 I was invited by Germany for an exhibition because two years before that, in 1997, I exhibited for the Clintons[6] and I was the youngest artist there and I was the best seller. What I was doing there was unique. I was the first artist to do Bushman paintings from rocks on textiles because people travel from all over Europe to see those paintings, so I thought of putting it on textiles so they would have that memorabilia in their own homes, so they organized me an exhibition in Europe.

LEILA: Did you keep in touch with these people, you say that is why you have an e-mail address?

OSCAR: Actually I keep in touch, it was someone in Europe who said I must do this. Compared to other mediums like phoning it [e-mail] is cheap and fast.

Oscar was motivated to use ICTs because of a need to sustain contact for his work. Of all the participants, Oscar appeared to be more motivated than his classmates, and was always keen to learn more. Oscar made an interesting transition during the course of the year. He often brought along an *mbira*[7] to class at the beginning of the year, but halfway through the first semester this was replaced with a digital camera, which he used to take pictures of everyone in class. He would then e-mail them to anyone who was interested. In the second semester he started to bring along a laptop to class, on which his group would work on their research project, showing his transition to using technology. Students also often listened to music on his laptop. His view that he was not a 'computer genius' at the time he started his travels implies that he considers himself very proficient during the course of the project. As an exhibiting artist he was probably in a better position to purchase equipment, and he also had a sponsor in Germany.

6 His reference to the Clintons is former President Bill Clinton and his wife Hilary. As a point of interest, Oscar brought me photographs of himself, with Hilary Clinton, posing with one of Oscar's fabric paintings. He also brought along a portfolio of his work in the hope of selling his art.

7 An African hand-held piano played with the thumbs.

Out-of-school ICT-literacy practices: About access at home 'You must understand where we are coming from. Even lights is a fairly new thing, even TVs and videos'[8]

Lelliott, Enslin and Pendlebury (2000), in their paper on online education in Africa, emphasise the more urgent needs such as education, health care and access to basic amenities in Africa, which take precedence over the introduction of technology. Many of the participants used this argument as well when commenting on ICT access in the home. Of the local students, only one participant had access to ICTs at home, while fifteen did not. One of the latter fifteen participants, Adam, said that he sometimes went to Internet cafes if there was something urgent he had to do, but also commented on the expense involved. Others said that the only access they had was at university. Mbali commented on the need for more basic amenities, which receive priority in the home.

> MBALI: You must understand where we are coming from. Even lights is a fairly new thing in some cases, even TVs and videos. Also first we must do the kitchen – the fridge, stove. Computers? No way, maybe with the new generation.
> ERNEST: Not even at home, Leila, it was impossible to think of a computer. I could go to town I think to use Internet café, but I wouldn't know how to use it.

All of the South African participants were receiving Financial Aid packages[9] from the University in order to study, therefore comments such as those by Mbali are hardly surprising, that purchasing computers was not a priority compared with furnishing a home with necessities.

All four of the international students had access to ICT in the home. Natalie, who had access at her home in Maputo, was considering getting a computer in South Africa, while Xing and Farzana also had computers at home in South Africa. It should be noted that Farzana's father was a PhD student at the University at the time of my study, which might have made the use of a computer necessary at home. The

8 Mbali.

9 Financial Aid is awarded to certain students who come from disadvantaged homes.

family is also originally from Iran, and maintained, like Xing, regular e-mail contact with friends and relatives back home.

Finally, Oscar had a laptop which he had purchased from funds he obtained selling his art work:

> LEILA: OK, do you have access to a computer where you live and on campus?
> OSCAR: I have, I can say because I have my laptop.
> LEILA: Do you have e-mail access on your laptop?
> OSCAR: I have, but where I am living now they don't have access, they have to connect it.
> LEILA: What made you decide to get a laptop?
> OSCAR: I couldn't carry a PC around – you can't walk around with it. When I travel I just pack it in my bag. Everything is there – my music, my videos, my stuff like my school work.

Participant access to ICTs, both at home and at school, was obviously limited, and participants felt marginalised by the divide this created between them and students with greater access (refer to students comments discussed earlier about access across the race groups). In the next section, I look at participants' views on access to ICTs at the University.

University ICT-literacy practices: About access on campus 'You are still typing...and you have to go'[10]

University of Witwatersrand offers all students ICT access in computer laboratories, however, participants do not consider the resources sufficient or suitable. The majority (60%, or twelve participants) found ICT resources on campus limited and unsuitable. Eight participants felt that computer access at the University was suitable.

Of the participants who found ICT access at the University of the Witwatersrand is suitable, Lucky, a drama student said that he also had access to a computer laboratory in the Drama Department. However, the laboratory did not have Internet access, so he had to use the Internet in one of the other laboratories, which is something he needed to do

10 Elsie.

daily in order to check his e-mails. Mabela commented that the access was 'very good' although two of the computer laboratories were quite crowded. He found the new laboratory in the library more accessible, with about fifty workstations.

Of the participants who found access unsuitable, the majority complained that the laboratories were overcrowded, and that they sometimes had to leave just when they were busy typing, either because the laboratories were booked, or because they had other classes to attend. Elsie, for instance said:

> ELSIE: And they tell you right now, not even thirty minutes before 'We are going to have a tut.' It's so much to share... you are still typing... and you have to go... Ja, you just have to leave everything even if your assignment is due [...].

Elsie could, however, be misguided about being forced to leave the laboratory while she was busy, because I have observed a teaching timetable posted at the entrance. The timetable indicated when the laboratory was being used as a teaching venue. The problem, the technician said, was that students did not read the timetable and notices, and then got upset if they had to move to accommodate classes.

I had similar experiences when I taught another course in the laboratory, and other students were busy working. Despite booking the laboratory in advance and the timetable stating that the laboratory would be occupied for a teaching session, students would have to be asked to leave, something they were not very happy to do. As stated in Chapter 3, a further problem was that the Humanities laboratory had a foldaway partition running down the middle of the room so that two laboratories of twenty workstations each could be created and that a class could be taught in one section, while students who were not part of that class could use computers in the other section. This situation was not ideal as the class being taught could be heard in the other section.

Sometimes students employed innovative tactics in order to get computer access on campus. Xing's comments may be taken into account:

> XING: I like to use the computers here, but the situation is not good. There are twenty thousand students in Wits, and the computers are not enough.
>
> LEILA: Do you have a lab in the Commerce department?

XING: No, I use FNB and Senate House,[11] and I have friends in Medical School, I use their computers.
LEILA: Do you have access there?
XING: Well, not really, I swipe their cards.

In order to gain access to a computer laboratory, students are required to swipe their student cards. They are not allowed to use the cards belonging to other students. However, this appeared to be the only way Xing found of getting access to computers.

Participants therefore found the number of computers insufficient, and said that sometimes the computers did not work. I observed during several of my observation sessions as well that certain computers were not working, once as many as six of the forty (Field notes, April, May, June, 2004). In addition to issues of access, I thought it important to establish the extent to which participants were proficient in the use of ICTs, because of the impact this could have on their participation. In relation to proficiency, students were given a proficiency questionnaire at the beginning of the year, and I later asked them about their proficiency during interviews.

ICT-literacy practice: Student proficiency 'I make mistakes, lose the file, start again.'[12]

In this section I asked participants to rate their proficiency with ICTs. At the beginning of the year participants indicated that they were generally lacking in proficiency in computers, e-mail and the Internet, as is shown in Figure 17:

11 First National Bank building and Senate House are two of the buildings in which computer laboratories are located.
12 Ernest.

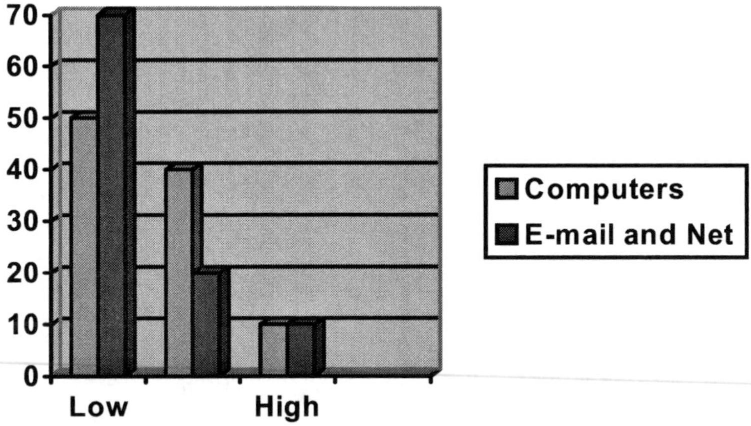

Fig. 17: Student ICT proficiency at the beginning of OLEP

According to Figure 17, over two-thirds of the participants (70%) of the participants felt that their e-mail and Internet proficiency was not adequate, while half (50%) felt they were not very proficient in the use of computers. Predictably, however, by the end of the course, most participants felt that their proficiency in computer-use, e-mail and the Internet had improved to a great extent. Although most of the participants had not used computers at school and did not have access at home, Figure 18 demonstrates how participants rated their proficiency at the end of the online course, and indicates that they were actually attaining proficiency quite rapidly as a result of the online intervention:

Degree of proficiency	**Student numbers**	**Student names**
Good	11	Xing, Oscar, Zinhle, Adam, Precious, Natalie, Lucky, Mabela, Leonard, Alex, Blessing
Average, still learning	7	Herman, Farzana, Elsie, Nothando, Lindiwe, Ernest, Mbali
Not good at all	2	Sibonelo, Musa

Fig. 18: Student ICT proficiency at the end of OLEP

As indicated above, most of the participants felt that they were quite proficient at using ICTs, and that they had learnt a substantial amount about computers by the end of the course. Adam, for instance, felt that he was suitably proficient to be able to teach someone else what he knew. Of the participants who felt they were still learning, Farzana felt that perhaps speed was a problem, something that other students such as Lindiwe and Ernest also commented on:

LINDIWE: In the beginning I was slow, like one by one (*gestures with fingers*) [...] I was typing. But it showed me how to type, still I type like that (*laughs*).
ERNEST: Now I say it is getting OK. First it was so slow, now I am learning to do it. But I make mistakes, lose the file, start again.

Elsie describes how she went about learning to use *Nicenet* with assistance from another student:

ELSIE: Um, it's... it's... after the *Nicenet* class I was helped by P... [another student] because I tried to see you but you were out. He came, he helped me with my password and I was able to register myself. The instructions were quite simple to follow, very clear. My password had expired and I had to get another one. The first person I e-mailed was Oscar 'cos when I opened my messages I found this topic of polygamy and it was so interesting, and I asked him what he thought... it was quite fun, like talking out of class.
LEILA: So would you say your proficiency is quite good now?
ELSIE: I am improving more every day.

Elsie shows how, with guidance and assistance, she was able to move from being a peripheral participant to an active member of the online class, reminiscent of Lave and Wenger's (1991, 1996, 2002) and Rogoff's (2003) theories on how participants move from the periphery, to the centre of the COP.

As referred to earlier, Sibonelo (14 September 2004) suggested that his background played a role in his lack of proficiency. Of all the participants, Sibonelo, a Law student, often commented on the disadvantaged socio-economic circumstances leading to his arrival at university. He displayed a strong sense of justice and often quoted from the *Constitution* (Act 108, 1996) to support human rights issues.

SIBONELO: Ja, I'm not so good, because the background I come from is very disadvantaged. We had no computers. No computers in school, only the teachers

> had access. In the office – only one computer for all. The area I come from, Limpopo is one of the poorest. A computer is a luxury, you only get to see it.

Thus, despite enjoying access to equal resources and support at the University of the Witwatersrand, the digital divide was conspicuous in class, where I was conscious that I too was in a position of advantage and privilege. I recognised that I was very much a 'have' because I had ICT access at home and at work, testimony of my more privileged circumstances. Concerns such as these indicate the greater power struggles, where students who have access to the dominant discourses and practices are privileged by the higher education system, while those who do not feel justifiably disempowered. In the section that follows I explore another facet of participants' ICT practice, namely, how they learnt to use the medium.

ICT-literacy practice: Taking multiple routes in learning to use ICTs

As referred to in the previous section, I also found participants' views on how they learnt to use ICT relevant. I stated in the Introduction and earlier in this chapter that the University does not provide computer literacy courses for students. Students may pay to attend such courses, and certain departments get senior students to teach newcomers the basics. The following table, with data elicited from the interviews, demonstrates the multiple routes taken by participants to become computer literate.

How learnt	Number	Student names
Friends	4	Herman, Precious, Elsie, Blessing
Family	1	Farzana
School (mostly international students)	4	Farzana, Natalie (only the basics), Xing, Lucky (a little)
Short course in computer literacy	4	Mabela (failed), Sibonelo (still not good), Leonard (failed), Zinhle (course was adequate)
Self-taught	4	Oscar, Nothando, Adam, Ernest
Notes	1	Elsie
Previous university	1	Musa
Another department	1	Lindiwe (senior student tutors in the Geography Department)
Observing/asking others	2	Alex, Mbali
Practice	2	Herman, Lucky
Laboratory technician	1	Herman
Lecturer	1	Elsie

Fig. 19: Learning to use ICTs

The most popular methods included being taught by friends, attending a short course, and being self-taught. Three of the international students had some previous access to computers at school, where they became computer literate, however, they had not used the Net at school, or as a teaching-learning tool. Of the four participants who paid to attend different short courses in computer literacy, two, Mabela and Leonard, failed. Participants also described how they became computer literate in their electronic literacy histories. Leonard commented that not being able to use ICTs left him feeling 'less worthy' than other first year students:

> I feel less worthy if I do not have ICT use. If you make it here it is not the end of the road. I went to a course, but even the course was a waste. I went with M.... but even with a friend its not the best thing if two don't know. You can feel stupid (Electronic literacy history).

His use of 'less worthy' and 'stupid' indicate that he felt disempowered and marginalised that he was not proficient in the use of ICT. Only one participant, Zinhle, felt that the course she attended was good, while Sibo felt that the course he attended was not helpful at all, as he was still lacking in some of the basic skills. Generally, these participants still observed others and asked for assistance, for instance Sibo said 'as I watch other people and they help me, I am learning'. Still others, such as Alex and Mbali, relied on help from other students:

> ALEX: When I got here at Wits it was a big shock. All the students could type, even I used to see this at home with some varsity students. They say they are computer literate. I did not know what to do. I did this short course but it wasn't enough, so other students in class they show me a lot. Also I ask.
> MBALI: I watch other students in class. They know what to do. Then I do it. Then I also ask if I need help. Computers make me to feel like something. Everywhere, all over the world, it's computers, for jobs, studies, everything. Now I feel like something.

Students were therefore primarily reliant on guidance and assistance, further evidence that they functioned in COPs. Mbali went so far as to say that computers give her a sense of being 'something', which is reminiscent of Feenberg's (1991) views about ICTs being related to issues of class and power, and Gee's (1996) perspective on power and literacy, in this case, electronic literacy. Mbali equated computer literacy with a sense of power, status and achievement. She also recognised the need for computers in relation to jobs and studies, reminiscent of Fang and Warschauer's (2004) findings on the combination of English and technological skills providing valuable job market skills. In her electronic literacy history Mbali wrote about her very early fascination with the electronic, in this case, her family's first television set. She recalled:

> My family got the first TV. It was so joyous. We used a car battery to charge the TV. Then we will sit around, laugh, watch. Even the neighbours, they came to visit when it was time for tv. It was regular. Sometimes the battery will fail, and we can do nothing...we would wait for my father to charge (it), then we can watch again. But sometimes even the neighbours get jealous for this – we had the tv (Electronic literacy history).

Watching television became a communal experience, with neighbours coming over to watch as well, although Mbali's comment on their jealousy indicates that the family had become a 'have' and gained prestige upon getting a television set, which could have distanced them somewhat from the rest of the community. She mentions also that the set had to be charged using a car battery, which was common practice in areas lacking electricity.

Similar experiences were noted when students used or got cell phones for the first time. They found that their cell phones created better opportunities for communication and socialisation. As is analysed later in Chapter 5, participants transferred their cell phone messaging skills to their discussion thread postings, for instance by using abbreviations and symbols to reduce the time needed to write messages, or as a substitute for non-verbal cues (Murray, 2000).

Mbali further described an early computer experience in her electronic literacy history: her aunt had a computer at home, but she kept it covered with some fabric to keep the dust off, and none of the children were allowed to use it. Mbali wrote about how an older cousin said that a computer must be used, or it would be outdated, but still the little cousins were instilled with fear and awe that something would happen if they touched it. The computer remained an expensive ornament. Mbali wrote: 'There is always this fear if you touch it something will happen' (Electronic literacy history).

Conversations with other participants over the year revealed similar views of computer and electronic literacy as a route to eventual success. However, as mentioned earlier in this thesis, Warschauer (2002a, 2002b, 2003a, 2003b, 2004b) also cautions against the determinist view that suggests that the mere presence of technology will bring about social change. Rather change and inclusion lies in how technology is utilised.

Elsie accredited the facilitator for her computer literacy. Elsie often went into full narrative when interviewed, and told me of her experiences in attaining computer literacy:

> ELSIE: It was through Leila. I was so scared (*laughs*)...the first time I went to the lab I had a password and username...but... but it just didn't work, it made me to be demotivated. But if it wasn't for you, I would not have started because you made it happen for us. I was so scared, I had to talk to myself. I would carry your notes and say everyday 'Today I will do it'. And my password would deny. I will

leave everything. She, Nothando, also helped me. I never thought one day I would use a computer even.

Elsie also gave credit to other students in class for what she has achieved. During the course of the online intervention she also showed concern for other students.[13] In many cases, participants indicated the sense of achievement they felt when they were able to use the technology, and thus gain membership to one of the dominant discourses of the university community (Gee, 1996).

Other participants stated that they were self-taught. Nothando (16 September 2004), for example, described how she was able to solve a problem with her mouse by pretending she was using a laptop. Adam displayed a sense of determination and independence in his attempt to become computer literate. He wrote in his electronic literacy history: 'I said to myself there is no way I will let it pass. I have to know it. It was the opportunity' (Electronic literacy history).

Adam proved to be quite independent as well, and spoke about his mother living and working overseas as a nurse, which no doubt necessitated his use of e-mail as a means of maintaining contact with her (Conversation).

Ernest described the confusion of being a new student at the beginning of the year, where the need to become computer literate, he felt, is almost an additional burden:

> ERNEST: Whew, when I got here it was bad, so bad, sort out registration, residence, bursary...then the classes start and all the lecturers say we must use a computer. We are in first year, we say how can we, it is so hard (*laughs*). Then we start to learn. I tell myself I must do it, I can do it. So I watch, do a few lessons, and I practice, everyday I practice. Some of these students they have computers at home so they know how. They are fortunate. It is important this computer.

13 Elsie consulted and e-mailed me often, in one case regarding a student who had been absent from class for some time. When I investigated, I found that the student was experiencing financial problems, and was also quite ill. I must admit that Elsie provided the stimulus for action so that the student could be assisted. It also so happened that the same student had helped her join the *Nicenet* class when she had difficulties.

Also evident is the barrier between those with access to ICTs and those without, highlighting the sense of inclusion-exclusion. Of the participants who claim to be self-taught, all display a sense of independence, determination, and perseverance to succeed. Such characteristics are intrinsic to self-direction or learner autonomy, and will be expanded on in Chapter 6.

It is evident from the data described thus far that access to ICT practices are limited, and that proficiency, although improving, was limited at the beginning of the project. Most participants were self-taught, and those who displayed an independent perseverance tended to decide what they wanted to do and how to achieve their goals. Common to all participants is the feeling of alienation and exclusion, of not being part of the dominant academic discourse without computer literacy. In the following section I continue examining participants' ICT-literacy practice, this time from the perspective of their Internet and *Nicenet* practices.

ICT-literacy practice: Internet and online (*Nicenet*) practices

As discussed in Chapter 2, as well as in the introduction to this chapter, literacy is viewed as a social practice (Street, 1984, 1993, 1998, 2003, and others). Learners' social and out-of school practices cannot be ignored in relation to the value these add to the classroom. This section examines how often participants used the Net, and the types of sites they accessed voluntarily. It also explores how they use the *Nicenet* class, and their views on the system.

Internet practices

Participants in the study varied with regard to how often they logged onto the Net. Figure 20 illustrates this diversity:

Frequency in logging on	**Number of participants**	**Participants**
Nil	1	Natalie
Every fortnight	1	Lindiwe
1 to 2 times a week	5	Sibonelo, Xing, Elsie, Adam, Musa,
3 times a week	9	Herman, Farzana, Precious, Nothando, Zinhle, Alex, Blessing, Mbali
4 times a week	1	Ernest
Daily	4	Mabela, Leonard, Oscar, Lucky

Fig. 20: Participants' frequency in logging on

Not all the participants logged onto the Internet regularly. Although most logged on three times per week, others, such as Natalie did not generally log on at all. However, at the end of the year, after the examinations, Natalie e-mailed me with queries about her results, indicating that she too had begun to overcome her initial apprehension of logging on.

To establish general patterns of Internet use as a social practice, I also examined the types of sites participants accessed. These sites students accessed voluntarily because the Foundation course does not stipulate that students access particular sites. The data was elicited from interviews and observations. Participants displayed a wide range of interests, some linked to their courses of study, while others were for fun and entertainment. Several participants indicated a preference for free 'sms' sites such as those offered by Vodacom. Here they would send free sms'es to friends and family via the Internet. During an observation quite early on in the project, I read a notice in the computer laboratory stating that students would be banned from using the laboratories should they access free sms sites. When I asked the technician the reason for this he said that students wasted time sms'ing friends, and that students who needed to use the computers for assignments and research were prevented from doing so if all the computers were being used. However, this did not appear to deter some of the participants in this study, as they continued to access the sms sites. Figure 21 presents an overview the types of sites accessed.

Participants	**Types of sites visited**
Herman	Research sites, sites which help with assignments, Chinese e-pals
Farzana	Research sites, Persian newspapers and magazines, Iranian university sites
Precious	Contact friends, sms sites
Lucky	Research sites, plays, playwrights, scripts
Mabela	Music, entertainment
Leonard	Entertainment, sport
Oscar	Music, entertainment, art, sms sites
Elsie	Constitutional court website
Nothando	sms, movies, SABC, university websites
Zinhle	News, jokes
Adam	Research for project on language policy, Chinese e-pals, radio
Musa	Research sites
Lindiwe	Free sms sites
Ernest	Research sites, entertainment, free sms sites,
Alex	Research sites, music, sport
Blessing	Magazines, beauty sites for his girlfriend, news
Mbali	Free sms sites, music, research

Fig. 21: Types of Internet sites accessed by participants

Farzana used the e-mail facility to keep in touch with family and friends at home in Iran. Later in the year she indicated that she would like to return to Iran and had been in touch with Iranian universities to enquire if she could transfer her studies. Her sister, who had also been a student at the University of the Witwatersrand, had returned to Iran in the second semester. Farzana enjoyed being able to use Persian, her home language, and said that the Internet, especially the e-mail helped her feel closer to home.

With regard to music sites, because the computers in the student laboratories did not have audio facilities, students were not able to listen to music, but read up on the sites of radio stations. The laboratory technician also kept the only pair of headphones in the laboratory. Several participants expressed a desire to listen to music, which they would have done if sound cards were installed on all the computers, however, this was reportedly beyond the laboratory budget, according to the laboratory technician.

For many, the Internet and e-mail in particular enabled them to communicate with friends, especially those who were at other universities. The issue of contact and communication will be resumed in more detail in Chapter 5, in the section on 'communities of practice'. In the section that follows I explore participants' use of *Nicenet.*

Online Nicenet *practices*

To reiterate, the purpose behind using the *Nicenet* system was for students to access notes, and to communicate with me and other students online. As shown in Chapter 3, thirteen students participated in the *Nicenet* online class: Herman, Farzana, Precious, Lucky, Xing, Oscar, Elsie, Ernest, Alex, Blessing, Mbali, Zinhle and Adam. Natalie, Sibo, Nothando, Lindiwe, Mabela, Leonard and Musa did not.

Most of the users found the *Nicenet* system relatively simple to operate and found the notes that I had given them to follow quite helpful. Farzana (26 August 2004), for instance felt: 'Yes, [I enjoyed it] very much. It helped me to get a lot of information that I couldn't get in class. I was reading my notes on the Internet class'.

Not all comments were positive. Xing and Oscar said they were a little disappointed with the system because they felt I should have updated it more regularly, and that students should have participated more frequently. Oscar also felt there was some repetition. Remember, Oscar logged on daily to check his e-mail, and spent a substantial amount of time on the computer.

Part of the problem in not uploading new summaries and questions daily was because the majority of students did not access the *Nicenet* class daily. Adam, who found the system easy to access, found the summaries useful, but also felt that the system could benefit from more input. Zinhle also found the articles and summaries useful, but did not participate in discussion. Adam also made use of the e-pal connection, through which he communicated with five Chinese e-pals. This is discussed further in the section on global communities of practice in Chapter 5.

Alex found the system interesting and participated in discussion. In a conversation we had during the year, he said he mentioned the online class to people at home, and that they encouraged him to use as much ICTs as possible, because they attributed status to computer literacy. I found this to be a common occurrence, where participants said that family members would encourage them to get as much exposure to ICTs as possible at university, because they felt it would benefit them in later years.

Mbali mentioned the sense of achievement she had in experimenting with something new, to the extent that she felt she could become the teacher:

> MBALI: Ja, it was so interesting. In the beginning we just helped each other, then we became the teachers. When the other students did not know what to do, we were helping. It was like a reward. We knew something they did not. Ja, we had fun. Even in the second semester it was helpful to others.

While most participants were comfortable talking about their achievements on the online environment, others did not participate as enthusiastically, and the causes and reasons are explained in the next section.

Demotivation and dissuasion from using Nicenet

Students who did not join the online class said they had various reasons for not doing so, including access, busy schedules, demotivation and laziness. Natalie, a Portuguese mother-tongue speaker, did not access the *Nicenet* system. Often she would use her limited English proficiency as a reason for not participating, and it became what I saw as an excuse for not accessing the system:

LEILA: The Nicenet class I set up? Did you access it at all?
NATALIE: No, I didn't, (*laughs*)… too much and my English is not so good. Now I am thinking to have Internet at home. My friend says it's not so expensive, but I have to because it's useful for researching and e-mails, my family.

Mabela and Leonard, who joined the group in the second semester, both felt that they were too busy when they joined my tutorial group to join the class. Both thought that it was just after the June examination and that their results had been disappointing, so they should concentrate on the traditional lectures. However, they considered that the system itself would not be difficult to access, although it might be time-consuming.

Sibo said he was demotivated because he had previous experiences where he did not have access or time, which dissuaded him from participating in the online class. Musa, on the other hand, confessed that he was too lazy to join. Musa had spent the previous year at another university, where he had not passed. He was accepted as a student at the University of the Witwatersrand in the year that my research was conducted.

MUSA: Uh…(*hesitates*) I guess it was just lazy. I had the notes, I kept saying I will do it but it never came up. Not that I experienced problems. It never came up. There was always something else to do at the computer... assignments, research.

Lindiwe attributed her lack of participation to limited time:

LINDIWE: Ja, the thing was it was difficult for time, but if I did have time I would. Because with readings we have to do the whole reading and understand it ourselves, unlike on the *Nicenet* class they give you the summary and everything and that would have helped me.

A key factor around participation on the *Nicenet* system was that it was not a requirement of the course, and many students put it off as being unimportant. However, although the majority of the participants had only started using the Internet in the year that this study had been conducted (2004), they already developed an idea of what they considered the advantages and disadvantages of using the Net. The following section presents their perceptions of the benefits and challenges.

Perceptions of benefits and challenges of using the Net: 'You can't get lost'[14]

In his review of the views of techno-optimists and techno-pessimists, Warschauer (1999a: 11–12) cites Roszak (1994), Postman (1993, 1995) and Birkets (1994) who consider the Net shallow, vacuous, and lacking in critical theory. Joyce actually refers to the Net as 'the zombie's news stand [...] where lots of glossy things wave in the light' (in Warschauer, 1999a: 12). On the other hand, Lanham (1993) and Bolter (1991) regard the Net as facilitating a dynamic approach to learning and critical thinking.

Thus, there are ambivalent views of the contributions of the Net. Participants included among the benefits that the Net provides greater access to information and resources, unlimited access and contact, and that it improves reading and writing skills. The optimists included Herman, Sibo, Natalie, Zinhle, Musa, Lindiwe and Alex. Sibo, for instance said:

> SIBO: Ja, a great advantage because this is an easier way of getting information than the library, if you go there the book is out, pages are torn. The library is good, but on the computer, the information is always there.

However, Mbali added a note of caution when she said that because of the amount of information, users had to learn to be selective. She said:

> MBALI: You must not get fooled that you get everything... you want. You have to choose what is right for what you want. The Net won't give it to you. It will give you everything, you must look for what it is... relevant.

A second advantage reported is that it provides unlimited access outside the classroom. Precious felt that it was helpful if one missed a class, that the Internet, and in particular, *Nicenet*, provided a back-up. However, the reverse is also true; that students might be tempted to miss classes and compensate for work missed by getting their notes online.

14 Nothando.

Lucky commented that class extended beyond regular class time, and that with the use of the Net 'the learning follows you'. Nothando also used an interesting metaphor about using the Net:

> NOTHANDO: Ja, I remember the first time my mum sent me to Jo'burg I said no… I'm gonna get lost. She said take a pen and a paper… she wrote everything down… you get off from here, turn left, turn right… that's a computer, Net… you can't get lost.

Ernest also spoke about the way in which contact improves, although he recognised that sometimes the type of communication might be too casual:

> ERNEST: Oh, ja, there are advantages – definitely. We can contact people, the English improves, but sometimes it is too casual. Also for work – everyone says for jobs you must know the computer, so it is important. Also the Internet brings you into contact with people you never knew before, it's so easy, click, click *(Gestures clicking motion with hand)*.

Adam agreed that it facilitated contact, and that it helped to read the views of other people. Ernest and Mbali mentioned the need for external, global contact. Mbali was also concerned about the need for progress in South Africa. She said:

> MBALI: I think we have to have it, it is a necessity today for everything we do. We are moving out of Third World in South Africa. So the Internet can provide us with progress. We can't say no to progress.

The final advantage reported by Ernest was that reading and writing skills improve, which he felt aids one's prospects in the job market. Here, I expect it was the writing practice that helped participants in terms of writing skills. Some might consider the use of e-mail and discussion thread language as weakening writing skills, because of the non-standard use of the language, for example, the use of abbreviations and symbols. However, when asked by Ancker (2002: 5–6) about the possible debasement of language, Warschauer said he felt that this was not possible, and that the use of language in electronic media should be considered as a different register, of which students should be made aware. In relation to reading, students had to read more, and contribute critically to online and face-to-face discussion of readings, which could help improve reading and comprehension skills. However, this study did not set out to evaluate possible improvement in reading and writing skills, and the views on improvement in these skills remain participant perceptions.

The perceived disadvantages or challenges of the Net were generally attributed to students' fear of technology (or technophobia), lack of skills, limited access, outdated, slow technology, poor time management, and that the Net encourages laziness.

In relation to technophobia, both Herman and Ernest commented that many students are afraid of technology because they had not been exposed to technology before. The strongest disadvantage was attributed to students' lack of skills. Herman, Farzana, Bob, Lindi and Mbali felt that far too many undergraduate students do not have technological skills, which places them at a disadvantage when other students are using technology. They felt computer literate students were being privileged. Mbali commented: 'It's sad when students don't know what they are looking for. They come to the lab and they are lost. No skills'.

A third disadvantage stemmed from lack of access. Here Sibo, Oscar, Alex and Blessing agreed that insufficient access was an issue. Alex articulated the following frustration:

> ALEX: Also it is frustrating if you want to work but the computer labs are full, so there must be more labs. And everyone must have a course when they come here in the first year, or how can they learn?

Oscar felt that although lack of access was an issue, when they were given access, it was actually considered prestigious.

> OSCAR: One big disadvantage here at Wits will be the access of computers. Computer access. It is very hard, I have even been telling some of my family and friends that we are having an Internet class. They were so surprised. They never heard of such a thing before. That is prestigious for us. But I think it is more useful, for someone to be in the mode of learning you have to be eager to find new things, interesting things so that will be good learning (16 September 2004).

Blessing became quite emotional when he commented that white students have better access to ICTs. He associated the situation with the political circumstances in South Africa and what he considered the lack of democracy, implying that it is the black students who are at the greatest disadvantage because they lack access. This raises a theme of power and exclusion, which pervades in both the literature and in participants' experiences. Blessing expressed concern that lack of access ultimately impinged on one's future career prospects. He said:

> BLESSING: Students aren't taught – this makes me angry. This is the disadvantage. If we are not taught, we pick up the skills if we can. White students can do it... if they have computers in school and at home. It becomes a political issue. This is not a democracy. How can we compete for jobs then?

A strong disadvantage that came through from Precious, Natalie, Elsie, Nothando and Zinhle, is the lack of time management when students go on the Net. These participants said that, on one hand, there is insufficient time to use the Net, and on the other, once students are logged onto the Net, they do not manage their time well, to the extent that they miss class, or access sites for entertainment purposes, rather than doing what they need to in terms of research and assignments. Nothando felt there were disadvantages in terms of time, but also felt that the time spent makes students more proficient.

To compound the problem, Xing commented that even if you know what you are looking for, often there is too much to choose from. Leonard also found the extensiveness of information available on the Net to be problematic.

Another concern, expressed by Alex, was that the Net might encourage laziness if students do not apply themselves to the tasks at hand. He felt that there was so much on the Net, but that students must not rely only on the Net for research as there were other methods and libraries still had an important role to play.

Conclusion on participants' perceptions

The use of ICTs in teaching and learning is not common practice in SLLS. Drawing on the work of Barton, Hamilton and Ivanic (2000), Street (1984, 1993, 1998, 2003), and Gee (1996, 1997, 2000), I found in relation to electronic (ICT) literacy practice that the majority of the participants had minimal access to ICTs at home and previously at school, and their proficiency, when they entered the University, was minimal. The theorists argue that different literacies are associated with different domains of life, and that literacy practices are patterned by power relationships and social institutions. This was evident in participants' feelings of marginalisation that they did not belong to one of the dominant academic discourses of the university, in this case, the discourse of ICT-literacy. Most experienced this as disabling, to the extent that it created a divide between them and students who have had better access, usually students of other race groups. The digital divide, which students viewed as a legacy of South Africa's apartheid past, was thus a pervasive presence, not just in the communities from which the participants came, but in the university environment as well. However, participants who were autonomous and motivated appeared to overcome these gaps and attain the skills necessary to succeed.

In terms of Internet use, participants logged on to a variety of sites depending on their interest. In terms of the use of the online class, 65% of the participants in the study participated in the class, while 35%, for various reasons, did not. Participants who used the class found it to be easy, enjoyable, and rewarding to use.

On the whole, participants found that the Net and *Nicenet* offered diverse benefits, including unlimited information, ease of use, facilitation of contact, and some found a general improvement in English skills such as reading and writing. The disadvantages included technophobia, lack of skills, limited access, outdated technology, poor time management and 'laziness'. The divide appears to perpetuate experiences of inclusion-exclusion among participants. One of the most significant fears expressed by participants is that the lack of access to technology could impact on their future commercial, material, and economic prospects, thus widening the divide. This I consider a pertinent fear, which, in my experience, has already made an impact on participants' academic lives. Thus, the possible impact on their future prospects remains unknown.

Having reviewed the participants' home, school and university ICT-literacy practices, as well as their perceptions of the use of ICTs, and recognising that individuals are members of interconnected communities, who learn through guided participation (Lave and Wenger, 1991, 1996, 2002; Rogoff, 2003), Chapter 5 provides a more detailed analysis of participant-interaction and identity construction within the online communities.

Chapter 5
Making meaning: Negotiation, participation and constructing identities in online communities of practice

In the previous chapter I established that the use of ICTs in teaching is limited in the School of Literature and Language Studies. In addition, I found that the majority of participants had minimal access to ICTs at home and previously at school, and their proficiency, when they entered the university, was minimal. Proponents of literacy as social practice and New Literacy Studies, such as Barton, Hamilton and Ivanic (2000), Street (1984, 1993, 1998, 2003), and Gee (1996, 1997, 2000), argue that literacy practices are patterned by power relationships and social institutions. This was evident in participants' feelings of marginalisation, that because of their limited electronic literacy, they did not belong to one of the dominant academic discourses of the university. In response to my first research question on the electronic (ICT) literacy practices of higher education English second and additional language speakers, I established that although access is limited, proficiency is improving, and participants perceive ICTs to play a valuable role in their futures.

Having established the broader electronic (ICT) literacy practices emanating from my data, here I proceed to examine the online class more closely, to ascertain how participants make meaning of the new online learning experience. The issue of participation and practice is important to address how participants make meaning, and addresses my second and third questions, which focus on online relationships, interaction and identities. The chapter is structured in two main sections: first, participant relationships in communities of practice, and second, participant constructions of identity.

In the first section I draw on constructivist principles, as discussed in the theoretical framework (Chapter 2), that learning is based on the premise that we construct our own understanding of the world by reflecting on our experiences, and that we generate our own rules and mental models in order to make sense of our experiences. I also draw on sociocultural theory, in which learners are not perceived as isolated entities, rather they are part of a supportive community with whom they can share and interact. 'Communities of Practice' (COPs), as discussed in the theoretical framework, emphasise the interconnectedness of people, learning, practice, participation and the social world. Therefore I examine participants' emerging online practices in relation to Lave and Wenger's (1991, 1996, 2002) and Rogoff's (2003) observations of COPs. My focus here is to establish how participants interact, and how they build and sustain online relationships, in order to answer my second question, 'What relationships do participants develop in online spaces?' I examine data elicited from semi-structured interviews conducted with participants, as well as postings made to discussion threads, personal journal entries, and field notes to ascertain the extent to which relationships are facilitated in online COPs.

Having observed carefully participants' online interactions over the course of the year, I found it impossible to make a distinction between how participants interacted online, from how they constructed their identities in general. I found that they were positioning themselves in the world, through their use of language, in multiple ways often determined by power relations, using the online medium. Thus, in the second section of this chapter, I examine the construction of participant identities, in the light of what Castells (1997, 2004) poses from a sociological perspective, that all identities are constructed, and that the social construction of identity takes place in a context marked by power relationships. In addition, I refer to Hall's (1992) view that the crisis of identity is seen as part of a wider process of change, which is dislocating the central structures and processes of modern societies, and that people increasingly make meaning, not on the basis of what they do, but on the basis of what they are, or believe they are. I also draw on Ivanic's (1998) assertion that writers portray themselves through their texts, as well as Lam's (2000) views on textual identity, or how participants position themselves through their texts. This is in response to my third question 'How do participants construct identities in online environments?' In the sections that follow, I explore communities of practice in relation to the online relationships that emerged.

Communities of practice

To recapitulate, Chapter 2 described how COPs are formed, and how the acquisition of knowledge is seen as a social process, with 'new-comers' or novices to the community participating in its practices peripherally, until they are assisted by 'old-timers' or more experienced participants, to central participation. To a certain extent, this was demonstrated in Chapter 4, where I described how participants assisted one another in attaining computer literacy. Thus, social factors, especially those that impact on how participants relate to one another, are important. Smith (1999), for instance, suggests that computer-mediated communication (CMC) contributes to more than just one-on-one relationships, and that 'CMC promotes the growth, development and maintenance of communal relationships as well' (1999: 87). These relationships form virtual communities, and when sufficient people engage in public discussions, over a substantial period of time, they form what Rheingold (1993, 2000) refers to as 'webs of personal relationships in cyberspace' (online, page 6 of 16).

A central notion of COPs is legitimate peripheral participation, which is the process through which new-comers move to attain full participation through a process of apprenticeship (or guided assistance) by more experienced participants. Lave and Wenger (1991, 1996, 2002) emphasise that participation is based on negotiation and renegotiation of meaning in the world, which implies constant interaction. Lave and Wenger (1991) add that to focus on participation implies focus on the person, which is a somewhat paradoxical notion in a community. However, any study of the sociocultural context involves focus on the person as person-in-the-world, and as a member of a sociocultural community.[1] Hence, I focus not just on the individual, but on the individual in his/her social world.

There is some debate about whether COPs could exist in online environments. Hildreth, Kimble and Wright (1998, 2000) who locate their work in organisational contexts, found that virtual communities are applicable to the educational context in terms of the core elements of communities. However, unlike my case study, their case studies in organisations focus purely on online communities, where there is no face-to-face contact. They found that while shared practices, language and tools are possible in virtual communities, an area that is not so easy to translate into virtual dimensions is the facilitation of participation. Participation, which is crucial to the evolution of a community and the creation of relationships, helps develop a sense of trust and identity, all of which define the community.[2] In my case study many of these practices and relationships were already established in the face-to-face lessons with students, since the participants had the opportunity to interact both face-to-face and online. This is also similar to Santos's ESL writing class at Aloha University, which was designed around COP principles, as described by Warschauer (2002c).[3]

The aim in this data analysis chapter is to examine the extent to which participants engage in online communities of practice. I suggest that participants interact in diverse communities simultaneously. Here I look at key elements of communities of practice, as established by Lave and Wenger (1991, 1996, 2002): relationships, peripherality and participation. I examine these issues simultaneously within the types of

1 An interesting comparison can be made here with the African philosophy of *Ubuntu* (moreso the isiZulu saying '*Umuntu ngumuntu ngabantu,*' literally meaning 'a person is a person through the otherness of other human beings'. The philosophy affirms one's humanity by recognising the humanity of others, the focus being communal identity, or shared life) (Makgoro, 1998).

2 Refer also to Carr et al. (2004) who demonstrate student participation along online communities of practice theory in an Economics class.

3 Santos (in Warschauer, 2002c) supported student learning by using computer-assisted classroom discussion, and encouraged student participation on e-mail discussion listservs. She approached her writing class as a form of apprenticeship, where she drew students into a new academic discourse community, characterised by legitimate peripheral participation principles.

communities that evolved in my online class. I have categorised the communities as overlapping sub-communities, to which I refer as:

- *communities within*, which refer to public networks and interaction created in the online class among participants, including myself as the facilitator;
- *communities beyond*, which refer to the online communication and interactions which arose outside of the online class, and which involved participants communicating online privately with one another, and excluding the facilitator;
- *global communities*, which refer to the global networks established by some of the participants who communicated with international e-pals.

Figure 22 is a diagrammatic representation of the three observable, overlapping communities within the online class:

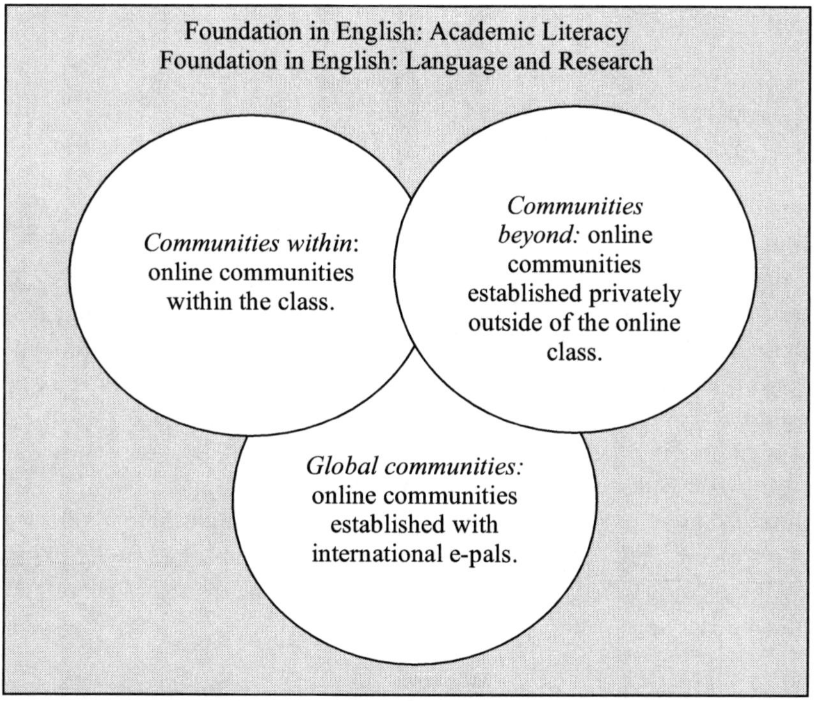

Fig. 22: Emerging communities

Not all the students participated in all three communities: thirteen participated in communities within and beyond, while four participated in global communities. I suggest that participants interact in various communities on the basis of the relationships they establish, and that these relationships determine the extent of their participation. Also the notion of 'old-timers, new-comers' is not just a physical one, because of the 'new' students who joined the class in Semester Two.[4] New Semester Two students, in some cases adapted to the online environments more readily, unlike some of the students who had been in the class from Semester One. Hence the notion 'old-timers-new comers' is not meant to be considered a physical distinction. Students who displayed characteristics of independence and initiative appeared to be more tolerant of the online environment. In the sections that follow I examine the three emerging communities.

Communities within: Public lives

In this section I explore the first community that emerged in the online environment: the interactions, relationships and networks created in the online class between participants and me, and among the participants themselves. Hildreth, Kimble and Wright (1998, 2000) are concerned with the stories and narrations that are used in a community, resulting in the transition from novice to expert. As novices' stories become accepted into the community, they become legitimate members of that community. I found that as the participants became more familiar with the online medium, having sought help from their peers or me, they became more active in the process and in the extent of their communication with us. In the section to follow I examine how participants' online relationships emerged.

4 Please refer to description of the student sample in Chapter 3.

Lally and Barrett's (1999) study of transactional distance in online environments focused on the use of CMC in a distance Masters in Education Programme. In their study they found that CMC reduced transactional distance among tutors and students, which resulted in more active participation in the online environment.

I felt that, to a certain extent, social distance had already been reduced because of the face-to-face contact we had already established. However, in order for participants not to feel threatened by the new medium, as well as to set the tone of the online class, my postings were quite conversational and informal. For instance, introductory messages at the beginning of each semester were by nature casual, and informative, in order to ensure that participants did not feel threatened by the new medium. Figures 23 and 24 are introductory notes posted at the beginning of Semesters One and Two respectively:

FROM: Leila
SUBJECT: Welcome
[Reply | Archive | Delete | Forward]

Hi All, and welcome to the Foundation 124/6 Nicenet class. This may be a new experience to most of you, but I promise, a rewarding one! The intention of the class is to help us to communicate on a more regular basis. You may participate via the 'conference' button. Notes and answers to assignments will also be posted regularly. Please feel free to contact me should you experience problems at any time, and use your class Nicenet handout as a guide until you get used to the system.

Should you continue with the course next semester (AELS 126) you may still use this virtual class.

Please drop me a note when you get this message so that I may see whether the system is working well.

Bye for now, happy chatting, Leila:-)

Fig. 23: Semester One introductory posting

FROM: Leila
SUBJECT: Greetings: Research Module
[Reply | Archive | Delete | Forward]

Hello All
Welcome back to 'old' and 'new' students. I am using the same online class so that you do not have to re-register. Hooray! This is an exciting time for us all, especially to those of you who are doing research for the first time. Remember, I am here to guide you along. Make full use of our site for the following:

Messages: messages from me and fellow students
Documents: Handouts and summaries
Conferencing: weekly discussions and opportunities for questions and debate. Every student is required to post one question or comment each week.
Links: other sites of interest – Make new friends, check out the e-pal site in China here! See your e-pals!

I also include tips on assignments and exams, so check this class regularly.

So...log on soon, students have found this site to be really valuable.

Cheers, leila :-)

Fig. 24: Semester Two introductory posting

Although I requested that students submit one question or comment per week, this did not always occur. It should be noted at this point that participants were not rewarded, for instance, with marks, for participation, and all participation was voluntary. I remember commenting on this in early journal entries as well:

> Am feeling slightly de-motivated. Students not very active. If they don't participate regularly, how far can I go in motivating them? (Teacher journal).

I found that I needed to send additional messages during the course of the early weeks to sustain the momentum of the online class component, especially when I found participation lagging.

FROM: Leila
SUBJECT: Good morning
[Reply | Archive | Delete | Forward]

Hi All Nicenetters

Welcome to all the new members who have just joined. I hope you are finding the system useful! Just a reminder, please send me a message so that I can check if your address is working.

Thus far, you will find summaries of readings and questions uploaded. Please read the summaries - they are so important!!!

Secondly, I would like you all to participate in the question and answer sessions, that is, just respond to the discussion question each week so that I can see where you are at in understanding the article. Remember you may participate as much as you like, even daily, it improves your English! But you must post a comment at least once a week so the system remains active. Now is your chance - you don't only have to respond to me, you may argue or debate whatever someone else in class has to say about a reading.

Please drop me a line and tell me what you think so far...

Have a good weekend, Leila:-)

Fig. 25: Motivating messages

The previous finding is also consistent with Nunan's (in Kahmi-Stein, 2000), where he found that the facilitator is, in the initial stages of an online class, far more active than the student-participants. This could also be attributed to student motivation. Kannan and MackNish's (2000) study of an online test-taking skills course in Singapore, for instance, further reveals that there are four stages of motivation in online environments: apprehension (because of fear of the unknown), curiosity (familiarisation because of training, assistance and peer presence), peak stage (where students find the work interesting and pleasant), and the fall stage (where students start to find the exercises too similar and they start to lose interest). I observed similar tendencies among my students. As they began to feel more comfortable with the technology, they began to participate more vigorously online, until they became distracted and, in some cases, like that of Xing and Oscar, lost interest because the postings were not updated daily.[5]

The tone of the discourse appeared to encourage participants to communicate in exchanges more freely. Lucky, one of the participants, felt that the nature of our online communication enabled him to feel comfortable with the medium. He felt that the relaxed tone of the postings and greetings gave him a sense that he was 'part of the class' (14 September 2004). In an informal conversation, Herman also expressed surprise at the sense of community. He said he felt that online communication does not have to be 'remote' (22 August 2004). This view is also consistent with Cunningham's (2000) findings on the study of the attitudes of Japanese English foreign language students towards online learning, The participants in his study found the use of ICTs non-threatening and challenging in the teaching-learning environment. The view is contrary to the feelings experienced by Czerniewicz (2001), in South Africa, however, who found her online class an isolating experience.

I also found that the tone of the messages encouraged members who were peripheral participants to respond and to start posting their own messages on the online class. Adam confirmed this view when he said that initially he only read what others had to say. Later, he too started to post messages because he said it appeared quite 'un-complicated' to do. Although Adam was a student who joined the class is the second semester, he began to participate in the class much sooner than some of the students who were in the class from the first semester, demonstrating that the 'old timer-new comer' notion is not necessarily a physical one. Adam also assisted other students when they had problems with the site.

Participants in this study narrated their stories, both online, and during interviews, of how they become part of the community. First, I will look at the contact participants had with me, as well as the kinds of communication that evolved. Thereafter I will look at the interactions they had with other participants.

5 I comment on this in Chapter 4.

Interactions with the facilitator

Participants' views on their interactions with the facilitator in the online environment were encouraging. All the participants, even those who did not participate in the online class felt that the online class provided, or had the potential to provide extended contact with the facilitator. Herman, Mabela, Leonard, Sibo, Xing, Oscar, Musa, Ernest, Blessing and Mbali felt that the use of online communication facilitated access and ease of communication. Herman said: 'Yes, it provides easy access, you don't have to always… don't disturb the lecturer, sometimes it's not consultation time'.

Students are given set times during which they may consult with lecturers. If they are not available at those times, for instance, if they have other classes, they attempt to see lecturers outside of the consultation times. Hence, Herman's comment about disturbing lecturers is appropriate. Mabela added that it was a convenient medium to use. Together with easy access, participants Farzana and Nothando also felt that it opened up learning opportunities if students had questions and lecturers were not physically available. Adam felt that writing out a message or question gave him time to formulate his message, whereas in class, he felt he sometimes could not express the question clearly. He said:

> ADAM: For sure, like sometimes I may not be able to talk to you the way I can on the computer. I have time to think about what I have to say. I can express it better than face-to-face. Sometimes I may run short of words… not know how to put it. On the computer you are alone you have time to get the words.

Although we did not know each other very well at the beginning of the semester, Adam enquired about the online class because he had heard about it from other students who were in my class in Semester One. He also sometimes came in to see me about personal problems he was experiencing during the second semester, for instance, on one occasion when he missed class for a few sessions because of a family funeral. So although he might have felt that he was better able to express himself online, this was not the only medium he used, and we did chat face-to-face during consultation sessions as well.

Precious commented that online communication is beneficial because, as new students, they often felt nervous to approach a lecturer, and that the e-mail helped relieve their nervousness. I noticed student hesitation when I recommended that they make appointments to see me about their work, or for 'one-on-one' consultations. Often, they thought they were being 'singled out to see the teacher' because they were not doing well in class. Other participants also said that the online medium helped them keep in touch and that there was less distance between the lecturer and students, which was also a finding in Lally and Barrett's (1999) study on social distance among distance Education students.

Nothando commented on the diminishing boundaries:

> Yes, there is no boundary between the class and the lecturer. You can learn all the time. But on the other hand we must also not become a nuisance. Lecturers are busy. They can't reply… only if it is necessary to our work.

In Lucky's view:

> Yes, it becomes… to become used to the lecturer. Because when I get the questions there, like the discussion questions you ask, it will make me relate it to the lecturer. And it is casual, like a class discussion, the greetings… asking how we are… sometimes lecturers don't do this… it is like business straight.

Lucky's view is that the online class presents a more collegial, collaborative environment, unlike in some classes that are more businesslike and work-focused.

Yet other participants cautioned that it was still necessary to have face-to-face contact with lecturers, and that online communication alone was unsuitable. In Hara and Kling's (1999) qualitative study of a web-based distance study course, they found that students got frustrated having only e-mail contact because the feedback was not immediate. Their students also sometimes had difficulty accessing information from the Net. Vague and ambiguous instructions from the instructor added to their frustrations. Mbali and Zinhle were of a similar view, they felt that face-to-face contact was preferable in a university context.

Therefore, certain participants felt that the online medium improved communication between facilitator and students, while others felt that face-to-face contact was still vital in the teaching-learning context. In the following section I explore the different kinds of online communication that emerged.

Emerging modes of communication

The types of student-facilitator communication ranged from work-related issues to personal requests. In addition to posting summaries of class readings, I also posted hints on writing essays and advice on writing exams. The posting on examination preparation in Semester Two was as follows:

FROM: Leila
SUBJECT: Exams!!!
Hi All
It's Friday - last day of lectures! Hooray! I'm sure you're all waiting to hear about the structure of the paper. Here goes:
1. Comprehending a text - general questions (like the reading assignment). You must have read the article very well beforehand because you can't waste time reading in the exam for the first time! Use you own words and only quote if necessary. **30 marks**
2. Proposal: you will be given a topic on which to write the proposal, based somewhat on the article. Sub headings will be given. Be sure to follow the mark scheme and make sure too that you UNDERSTAND the question! Ask yourself- what is the proposal about? What is my research question? What is my site, sample and research method? Try this with other topics when you revise and have someone check it for you. **30 marks**
3. Data analysis: Two sections: Quantitative analysis: Graphs, tables. You will be given data to analyse. **20 marks**
4. Qualitative analysis. You will be given extracts of data. You will have to analyse it qualitatively. Remember your categories and supporting evidence! **20 marks**
Take your time, and study well! Remember to check the notice board when marks are displayed in October. Please report any discrepencies to me. Make an appointment should you require any additional help.

EXAM: Arrive early. Make sure you know the venue. ...Carry enough stationery. ...Switch off your cell phones......THEN TAKE A DEEP BREATH, CLEAR YOUR MIND...BEGIN. You have been a wonderful class. I thoroughly enjoyed the time wc spent together and have delighted in seeing so many of you develop and shine! I know I set high standards, but varsity isn't for those who don't want to achieve. As E... would say 'Let's be professional!' I wish you well in all your exams and in the future! Keep in touch and go well!!

leila:-)

Fig. 26: Examination preparation

In Johnson and Huff's (2000) categorisation of student messages in computer-mediated environments, they found that the messages consisted of general housekeeping issues such as assignment extensions and due dates, as well as questions about assignments, technical problems, requests for assistance and evaluative feedback. I too found similar postings in my research, including what I call work-related issues and personal requests. I received several queries about research projects, research updates, requests, and personal messages during the course of the year:

FROM: E.........
SUBJECT: can you please help me on this
[Reply Again | Archive | Delete | Forward]

i have (been) experiencing problem in creating my own pie chart, so i was wondering if you coul help me some other time. please make to be convenient to you because i do not want to disturb your work. thank you

FROM: B.............
SUBJECT:
[Reply | Archive | Delete | Forward]

Hi. How u? Can u please tell me is it fine if u put a graph in the section Methodolgy?

Thank YoU!!!
B........

Fig. 27: Research query 1

Students also provided me with regular updates on the progress they were making on their research projects. The research component of the course excited students because it was the first time any of them were conducting field research. Their projects included language use at a local police station, language policy at the SABC,[6] naming practices, nicknames, and common themes and languages used in *kwaito*[7] and rap music.

6 SABC – South African Broadcasting Corporation

7 *Kwaito* is a genre of music that originated in the townships in South African, and is popular among the youth. It is a fusion of American hip hop, African sounds, and *tsotsitaal* (township slang).

FROM: E.........
SUBJECT: Project up date.
[Reply | Archive | Delete | Forward]

Hello Leila, I would like to thank you again for the advises you gave to us on how to keep our groups effective.My project consist of three members if you can recall,I thought it was going to be hectic since other groups have 4 members.I could not believe it when we coped very well just like other groups. D.... also encouraged us and assisted where we had problems.

Last week we were doing face to face interviews, this is one part of the research I like most.As our Topic is naming practices,we went all the way interviewing Wits students on how they feel about their names including nicknames. It was very funny and we really learned a lot.Out of 10 interviewees, can you believe that all of them had nicknames? I never expected that.

The research took some efforts and commitments from group members,as we had to make time and visit students in their residences especially at night.This is because we are about to write our exams as a result every student we found in the campus was just as busy as a bee.

At least we now done, the only thing left for us is to do presentations!

Thank you very much for reading this e-mail.

Your sincerly:
E...

Fig. 28: Research update 1

Other postings were personal requests:

FROM: O...
SUBJECT: RE: Good morning
[Reply | Archive | Delete | Forward]

I just want to thank you for helping much in our projects.you are such a caring mother.yesterday we manage to go to Jorburg central police and we met a coperating wonderfull lady who promised us that our letter will not be delayed any longer. thank you o...

Fig. 29: Research update 2

The letter referred to by O in Figure 29 was one I had to write requesting permission for the group to conduct research observations and interviews at a very busy police station in central Johannesburg. The group was investigating language use at the police station where queries were often made in a variety of mother tongues. Just before this message was posted the group was frustrated that their original letter requesting permission to conduct research was lost at the police station, and I had to intervene to assist them.

Participants also used the online medium to make appointments and for personal requests, as the following two figures show:

> **FROM:** A…
> **SUBJECT:**
> [Reply | Archive | Delete | Forward]
> hi leila it's A… just droping you a line to show you that my line is working. i also need to know how busy will we be on friday because on saturday there is unveiling @ home and if i don't leave on friday then i will leave on saturday but i'll arrive late and i would have missed the purpose

Fig.30: Student query 1

> **FROM:** M………..
> **SUBJECT:** appointment for meeting
> [Reply | Archive | Delete | Forward]
> leila, i just read your message today so i was just wodering if we could meet tomorrow at 10hoo because today i am going to attend assesment. I will further like to thank you for your undivided attention you give our class. i wish you the best of luck for the future. thank you

Fig. 31: Student query 2

The 'unveiling' referred to in Figure 30 is the unveiling of a tombstone, while M's reference to 'assesment' indicates that he had to attend a class that had probably been re-scheduled in order to accommodate an assessment task. This is not considered acceptable university practice.

Finally, the class was also used as a vehicle for personal messages, examples of which follow:

FROM: E...
SUBJECT: A GRATTITUDE
[Reply | Archive | Delete | Forward]

Hie Leila on behalf of everyone in ma class who share dis with me, I would like 2 thank u 4 all the effort u put towards our success fm the biggining till nou.thus, i wish u all the best in dis festive seasson & keep up the gud work.//**

<<// Thank you//>>

Fig. 32: Personal message 1

FROM: B...
SUBJECT:
[Reply | Archive | Delete | Forward]

Dear leila

Thank you for your support through out the whole year. I feel that Applies English helps me a lot in all my subjects, I will probally do it on next year as well.
Thank you for teaching us!
Best Wishes to you
Kindly regards
B………..

Fig. 33: Personal message 2

On the whole, the Figures reveal that students used the online medium as an alternative to face-to-face contact, and for online socialisation. In AELS we have large student numbers at first year level, and sometimes lecturers find it difficult to cope in consultation times with the number of students who have queries. I found that online requests and queries relieved me to have more consultation time with students who were experiencing more serious difficulties, such as failing grades. The personal messages and use of language reveal that students acknowledged the medium as a means of social contact and virtual intimacy. In this regard, Yates (1996: 129) makes reference to online 'imagined communities', and Moran and Hawisher (1998: 88) add that the online medium helps create the 'illusion of intimacy'. Moran and Hawisher (1998) also cite studies of 'warmth' in online communication, ranging from students who ‘chat away like old friends’ on listservs, to virtual dating and virtual sex.[8]

Online language use

In relation to literacy and language use, the written text has long been regarded as unchanging, permanent, and static in nature, while speech is considered more transient and dynamic (Horne and Heinemann, 2003). Because of its permanent nature, writing tends to be accorded higher status, which carries greater weight and authority, than speech (refer also to Derrida in Yates, 1996). Examinations of CMC show that the medium presents both oral and written linguistic features (Ong, 1982 in Murray, 2000; Yates, 1996; Crystal, 2001; Moran and Hawisher, 1998). Warschauer (2004a: 5) and Murray (2000: 402) say that CMC users employ time-reducing strategies to write the message and substitute for the lack of paralinguistic and non-verbal cues. Figure 33 that follows illustrates the linguistic strategies adopted by participants using CMC, as well as examples as they occurred in the messages posted in my study:

8 Moran and Hawisher (1998) cite studies by Deuel (1996), Selfe and Meyer (1991), Wilkens (1991), and Gelder (1991).

Linguistic strategies identified by Murray (2000) and Warschauer (2004a)	**Sample Figures**	**Example of participant strategies**
The use of abbreviations and acronyms, repeated letters and punctuation, such as 'F2F' for face-to-face, and 'Hey!!!!' for prosodic effect.	Figure 27	U (you); Thank YoU!!!
Simplified syntax, informal language.	Figure 27 Figure 32	How u? Ma (my), dis (this), 2 (to), u (you), 4 (for)
The acceptance of surface errors, such as typographical and spelling errors.	Figure 27 Figure 29 Figure 30 Figure 27 Figure 33	I have experiencing problem… …Coperating lady… Run-on sentence I was wodering… …probally…
The use of symbols to express emotional meaning, such as multiple vowels and consonants, or emoticons, such as aaaah, or ☺.	Figure 32	// * <<>> Hie
Reduced capitalisation.	Figure 28 Figure 29 Figure 30 Figure 31	For example, Figure 31 'leila, i just read your message today so i was wodering…'

Fig. 34: Emergent linguistic strategies and features used in computer-mediated communication

From the extracts provided, it is evident that the CMC messages have taken on the characteristics of speech and writing, creating a hybrid text. E, in Figure 32 for instance, uses asterisks (**) and slashes (//) in the absence of social cues. His use of punctuation creates a sense of the non-verbal. It could be that E has not yet acquired the use of emoticons, and is trying to emulate their use. Abdullah (2001) also found that participants from different countries in an online conference used such cues to position themselves as a social presence. Horne and Heinemann (2003) further discuss language use in their study of the language used in chat rooms, where participants 'seem to write as they speak, without paying much attention to spelling, punctuation, and layout' (Horne and Heinemann, 2003: 119). The messages are transient, and interactive, like speech, in the sense that they rely on feedback, although not as simultaneously as in synchronous communication modes. It is also evident from participants' casual use of discourse, such as their use of symbols, emoticons and contractions, for example '4' for four, 'dis' for this, 'gud' for good, 'ma' for my, and 'u' for you, that they are engaging in a medium that might be considered a hybrid of written and spoken language (Yates, 1996). This discussion is resumed in the section on identities later in this chapter.

One of the concerns around CMC is that writing changes in the electronic medium, and questions might be asked whether these changes are beneficial or harmful to writing. As mentioned in Chapter 4, when asked by Ancker (2002) for his views on the possibility of CMC-writing debasing language, Warschauer said he equated the possibility to conversation debasing language. His views are that teachers should use the Net to match pedagogical goals, and that the use of emoticons and other features of CMC should be considered a different register, which might be used in the classroom as language exercises. Warschauer's (2001) view, which I support, is that CMC can actually help serve as a bridge between speaking and writing, by facilitating L2 interaction 'that is linguistically complex yet informal and communicative' (Warschauer, 2001: online, page 2 of 8).

Having examined the contact established between participants and the facilitator, as well as analysed some of the postings linguistically, in the section that follows, I shift to look at the interactions between the student participants.

Interactions and contact among students: 'We are all connected. We are all together'[9]

Participants had specific views on their interactions with other student-participants. Precious' comments summed up the possibilities for student contact:

> PRECIOUS: It's also much easier because you can't get to see each one in class.
> LEILA: Is everyone communicating like this? Online?
> PRECIOUS: Ja, they do, everyone…
> LEILA: Oh... so the class helped?
> PRECIOUS: Definitely. It did. We didn't know these things before.
> LEILA: Did you learn new things from *Nicenet*?
> PRECIOUS: How to communicate with the whole class. We are all connected. We are all together.
> LEILA: Was it hard to do?
> PRECIOUS: No, not hard, just different. The instructions were very easy to follow.

Generally, the majority of the participants felt that online communication increased possibilities for contact with other students:

> LUCKY: Yes, it also increased communication with other students, because you find if we can talk about something in the Internet, you know it can make us speak about it again in class when we have a few minutes break.
> LEILA: Did you communicate with other students via the *Nicenet* class or privately?
> LUCKY: It was privately… so no one else can read it.

Lucky's interesting response about private communication will be taken up in the section *Communities beyond*, which examines interactions in which participants communicated outside of the online class. Xing cast a reminder that student-student communication is only facilitated if all students are technologically active:

> I think it helps to communicate this way. Sometimes you need to get in touch with someone, but it is only possible if every body gets more technological, right? You must check your mail regularly.

9 Precious.

Xing often expressed the need for everyone to be involved. He wanted to use technology to its fullest, but felt that other students in class were not showing enough of an interest. It was only as participants began to feel less 'technophobic' that they began to participate more actively online. Elsie is a good example of the move from peripheral to central participation. Initially, she was afraid of computers, and could not even log on with her password. Later, she began to feel more empowered as she gained skills with the assistance of others in class. She participated peripherally, and with assistance from other participants in class, including myself, she became quite active online, even initiating discussion questions, demonstrating the existence of a community of practice. She said:

> The first semester students they taught the new students and passed it on, or someone who knew… like P… taught me and we all got the ability.

Thus, participants felt a 'connection' to one another in the online class. They realised, through their interactions, that there were possibilities for communication using the online medium. The implications of these interactions for classroom communication, is elaborated on in the next section.

Further possibilities for communication: From the classroom to the virtual classroom 'It's not only a class…faces in the class'[10]

Students such as Elsie and Adam saw that online communication helped students get to know one another and form relationships:

> ELSIE: Yes, I communicated with O… the first time. It started there, and so it continued. It's a good thing to do. It makes you feel like its not only a class… faces in the class. You get to know people.
> ADAM: Even in class you can have great friendships, you get that chance to make it better. Get to know people.

Elsie continued that the environment was not stressful:

10 Elsie.

ELSIE: What I learnt new? For me, everything. All new. I think our class was united, unlike a lecture room, everyone got on. The first semester students they taught the new students and passed it on, or someone who knew... like P... taught me and we all got the ability. You feel free to put down what you feel. No tension. Like when we were doing polygamy and we had to do a presentation, and O... says there is nothing wrong with polygamy, it's our culture. I really like that. In class and on the Internet.

Elsie's interpretation of the stress-free environment is probably as a result of her feeling more comfortable and confident in the medium. Earlier in the Semester the environment definitely intimidated her.

The lack of immediate feedback was of concern to Zinhle, which was also a finding in the Hara and Kling's (1999) study cited earlier:

ZINHLE: It is good to use it for communication. But it is more easy to see the people you communicate with. You remember things and get more information. And you get answers face-to-face. Like sometimes you want to ask something and the person may take a long time to respond.
LEILA: Ja, feedback.
ZINHLE: In class they answer same time. When I answer they can also question same time face-to-face.

Therefore, a few participants, such as Mabela, felt that face-to-face communication was still beneficial to student contact:

MABELA: I normally don't like this... Personally, I don't like to e-mail students. I feel I don't have to because I see them every day. Some people send useless things on the e-mail.

Mabela is referring here to the jokes that were sent around online. He found these of little value, however, these jokes could sometimes help participants bond. Leonard and Sibo were also concerned that many students used online communication unnecessarily, and that there should be more constructive reasons for doing so:

LEONARD: Yes, it's true. It improves communication, but you must use it for a reason, not to waste time.
SIBO: This is not something I would do just for fun, only if it is necessary to keep in contact. Then there are possibilities beyond the classroom.

In relation to maintaining contact, some of the participants' messages indicate that they were beginning to see the class as a collaborative community, in which participants communicate, negotiate meaning and develop relationships. This is indicative of Warschauer's (1996a) study of electronic and face-to-face classrooms in Hawaii, which showed that students are able to collaborate and maintain contact effectively in online environments. The antithesis, however, is Davey's (2001) study, the focus of which was contact and collaboration among Japanese EFL students on web-page projects. Davey (2001) found that the students experienced difficulty maintaining contact and collaborating on the projects, like Xing and Oscar in this study. The messages that were posted in the online class are indicative of the relationships that emerged among the student-participants. Many of them were 'feel-good' messages, as the following Figure shows:

FROM: I...
SUBJECT: hi to everyone!
[Reply Again | Archive | Delete | Forward]
i just like to wish a good examination period to everyone in our class, and i hope we are all doing to well, but the only solution is to put more affort on our study....
thenk you.
I...

FROM: L...
SUBJECT: good wishes for your exams
[Reply | Archive | Delete | Forward]

ladies and gents, i am very blessed to know you. so i would to wish you all the best for your exams and future. please take care.

FROM: B...
SUBJECT: Good luck for the exams
[Reply | Archive | Delete | Forward]

Hi all!
It is wonderful to meet you guys, every minute to be with you will be the most beautiful moments in my life. Thank you very much!
Best wishes for your exams and future! I know you all can make it!
B...☺

Fig. 35: Student 'feel-good' messages

As discussed earlier in the section on *Online language use*, student interactions indicate the narrowing of the gap between speech and writing. In face-to-face tutorials, students would say 'Good luck' in wishing one another well in the examination. In online communication, the use of 'ladies and gents' (Figure 34 assumes the genre of formal speech making, while 'blessed to know you' has almost spiritual undertones, and appears to be inconsistent with the less formal tone of online communication. However, the use of inappropriate tone appears to be adopted by several participants, perhaps because of initial discomfort with the medium. B's use of 'most beautiful moments in my life' is reminiscent of the poetic, clichéd discourse of greeting-cards, and is also not compliant with normal face-to-face greetings. B also emulated my often-used greeting of 'Hi all!' and closed with a smiley, indicating his emulation of the genre of online writing, as well as his growing comfort and confidence with the online medium. Such messages further indicate that participants were beginning to feel comfortable, and were beginning to bond with one another online, even though they were using inappropriate tone.

The issue of netiquette surfaced in a minor form, when participants used the online class to discuss other lecturers. Here I had to caution participants to discuss issues, rather than individuals:

FROM: O….
SUBJECT: The lecture today
[Reply | Archive | Delete | Forward]

How was our (name removed) lecture?
I ejoyed it so much But I think it was just too fast and our lecturer hurried through out the whole thing.however it made some sence I think it was going to be much better,if we had time.

So you guys how far have you gone with your Oral presentation and what topics are you dealing with.We are dealing with Polygamy if you have some ideas on polygamy I think you should help us.If you have anything to debate about polygamy please write me.I am for polygamy bearing in mind among other things that polygamy is resistance to cutural imperialism.At least those who practice it have cutural values that they are still keeping.Although thesedays it is a total greedness of women.But I think also it is justified since males are fewer than females for example here at Wits.Say we have a comminity like this University else where. What would those un lick ones do if they have no men to love them.You know women and men need someone to give loveor vise-versa. If you have any options air them to me. thank you O…

Fig. 36: Issues around netiquette

In this instance, the students felt that a particular lecture was quite long and rushed, and they indicated that they did not enjoy it as much as other lectures. The lecturer also felt that she did not have sufficient time to cover as much as she would have liked, although, this was her own conclusion, and not one she made as a result of the online discussion. Although not an example of flaming, or online insult, I did not want the online class to evolve into sessions that were critical of individuals, rather I preferred that participants focused on content-based discussion. I also realised that such discussions were inevitable among students, and were very much part of the face-to-face class as well, so it is interesting that the statement was made public by posting it on online class.

Figure 36 also illustrates the kind of discussion participants engaged in. I refer to this extract again in the section on identities to discuss issues surrounding how this participant positions himself in relation to the theme of polygamy. Because of the dynamic nature of the different discussion forums and threads that were evolving simultaneously, as well as the fact that some of them were private discussions, it was difficult to copy all the threads hence I have only selected a few relevant interactions as illustrative examples.

The composition of the Foundation in English course encourages critical engagement with course readings. Initially participants engaged in more face-to-face discussion than online discussion. As stated earlier in this chapter, some of the participants commented that it was easier to debate issues physically and that it took too much time to debate online, and wait for an answer. Others, like Elsie, took to online discussion, however, some of the debates were private, and not open to the whole class, as is shown later in the section entitled *Communities beyond.* Discussions also showed specific patterns of turn taking. In response to the polygamy posting in Figure 36, the following extract shows some of the responses that were posted:

FROM: A....
SUBJECT: re: The lecture today
[Reply | Archive | Delete | Forward]
My grandfather had three wives. It is good for the family and according to customary law it is right. But what if the economy is bad like now? How can he provide? I cannot afford many wives or girlfriends!

FROM: B....
SUBJECT: re:The lecture today
[Reply | Archive | Delete | Forward]
Polygamy adds to HIV/AIDS – a man with many wives will spread the disease to the wives and children. In my township there are too many aids orphans. Who will look after them? We need one man-one wife.

FROM: M....
SUBJECT: Polygamy
[Reply | Archive | Delete | Forward]
I am studying to support myself when I work. I don't need a man to support me. My mother, aunties and my grandmother needed a mans support. I can do it myself. Isithembu (*Zulu word for polygamy – my addition*) is not for the modern man and woman.

FROM: O...
SUBJECT: Re: Polygamy
[Reply | Archive | Delete | Forward]
You can always say you are so independent but even you can have love.what you say you can lose the tradition?will your child know?
o...

Fig. 37: Responses to O's polygamy posting

From the previous extract it is clear that participants engaged in both face-to-face and public online discussions, similar in style to turn taking in Sinclair and Coulthard's (1975) early work on the initiation-response-feedback (IRF) pattern of conversational analysis, the only difference being a lapse in time between responses, and the absence of feedback. O, for instance, actually responded two days later to M with his feedback. However, the responses do not appear to be directed to any respondent in particular, and therefore come across as isolated stand-alone messages, rather than conversational strings.

I revisit Figure 36 in the section on identities to show how participants positioned themselves in relation to the issues being discussed. I also found that many participants lurked, or appeared to read the summaries and notes provided and ignore the discussions completely. Hence, many of the discussion topics were not well-responded to. For example, my question on multilingualism only received one response. As already stated, I found out that many responses were also being sent privately to individuals, rather than for the class to view. This is discussed in more detail in the next section.

Communities beyond: Private lives

About halfway through the online intervention, I found that not all the participants were participating in discussions regularly. My journal entry around that time reflected as such:

> Some of the students are participating in discussion. O, for instance, is contributing regularly. What about the others? What does it say about online COPs if students don't discuss issues around the readings, but only read the notes? Need to stimulate some discussion.

To alleviate my concern, I discussed the issue with some of the participants. I covered further ground during the interviews held from August to October 2004. I discovered that they were indeed participating in discussion, but doing so privately. In effect they had created their own private sub-community outside of the class community, hence the name 'communities beyond'. This gave rise to the second of my overlapping circles in Figure 22, as introduced earlier in this chapter.

Lucky, as quoted in the previous section, mentioned that he had been contributing to discussions privately. Elsie said that she too participated in private e-mail discussions with other participants quite often as she sometimes felt she was engaged in a debate with them alone, around specific issues, and that not everyone should be involved. Oscar confirmed that several participants had mailed him privately about his comments on polygamy. In Shaw and Polovina's (1999) study of how the Net is influencing teaching and learning in higher education, they found that students were often embarrassed to say if they were experiencing difficulties. I found that during interviews, some participants, for example, Lucky, Elsie, Ernest and Precious, admitted to experiencing difficulties getting started, and said that they initially contributed privately simply because they did not know how to contribute to the group discussion. At that point they were not clear that the objective of the online class was to promote class discussion and communication. They felt awkward that everyone would read what they had to say, until I explained again that this was just like verbal discussions in class. An obvious problem here was retrieving private messages, so I relied on participant feedback on these interactions.

Another type of private communication that emerged involved me as the facilitator, but also arose as a result of the kind of relationships that were established in class. On reflection, I found my role as facilitator changing as I found myself becoming more personally involved with participants to an extent that exceeded face-to-face involvement, and participants felt they could approach me more easily about personal issues. To illustrate, I present an incident that occurred during the course of the year. Because of the sensitive nature and ethical concerns around the issue I will comment on it without naming the participants, even by pseudonym. I was asked, interestingly, via e-mail, to intervene on a particular student's behalf by another student. The concern was that the student was not attending class regularly, and the fear was that he was experiencing personal difficulties, and that he would not pass at the end of the year. I found it interesting that the student who brought up the issue did so using e-mail, and felt it more comfortable to bring up a sensitive issue using the medium. I was able to trace the student under discussion by 'snail mail', as there was no telephonic contact in his village, which was in a remote area. I found that the student was ill and was also experiencing financial and other problems, and could not afford to attend class. When he returned to class after some intervention, we maintained e-mail contact, and whenever the student needed assistance, he was able to get in touch with me. Despite the work he had to catch up on, the student managed to pass and was very grateful for the intervention. To date, I have not found other researchers' studies to corroborate increased personal involvement as a result of online communication.

In conversations with Ernest, Mbali and Herman about privacy in online environments, the participants had divergent views. Ernest felt that while some participants gave their views in the face-to-face class, he was certain that those who did not talk as much in class also would not engage in discussion online. Mbali felt that this was not always the case, as some of the shy participants could be less restrained in the online environment than they were in class. Herman was of a similar opinion. He felt that the online environment gave students who did not always participate in class an equal opportunity to discuss issues. This is in keeping with Lally and Barrett's (1999) and Warschauer's (1996a) findings on the possibilities of online environments to democratise the learning environment. Because this is a qualitative study, I did not record the number of contributions made face-to-face or online in order to ascertain the extent to which the learning environment is democratised. Instead I relied on observations of the class and reports from students.

I found that there was also a divergence from findings made by Warschauer (1996a) and Lally and Barret (1999), which show that participants participate more online, than face-to-face. In my study, participants like Oscar were equally active in the face-to-face class, as well as online, while students such as Nancy and Lindiwe, who were very shy, did not participate to a great extent face-to-face, or at all in the online class. On the other hand, Herman and Ernest were more active online, while Farzana was more active face-to-face than in the online class. Four of the participants also expanded their online communication globally, by participating in the international e-pal exchange project, thus forming what I have termed 'global communities', and concluding the third of the overlapping circles presented in Figure 22 of this chapter.

Global communities

The adage 'Think globally, act locally' refers to the need for making and sustaining global connections and communicating with others outside of our communities to broaden our horizons and learning opportunities. Topper says 'Embracing multicultural, multiethnic and multiracial relationships strengthens the classroom and makes the idea of a global village real to students' (Topper, undated, online, page 2 of 4).

In this section I discuss the expansion of communities of practice into global communities. I read a request on the TESLCA-L link for student partnerships from an English teacher in China, who worked with EFL students in higher education. The students attended the Gotel Software College of the University of Electronic Science and Technology of China (UESTC) in Sichuan Province.

I discussed the possibility of intercultural exchange with my students, and having established the interest of some of the participants, I established contact with the teacher. I also requested that we maintain contact to prevent some of the problems I experienced in previous email projects (not reported on here), where participants were left to work independently, and subsequently lost contact. This was detrimental to the previous project in the sense that many students experienced problems, such as e-pals who did not respond regularly or timeously. The teacher agreed to maintain contact for the same reason. I linked the Chinese class website to the links section of my *Nicenet* class, where my students were able to access the Chinese students' introductory postings and see photographs of the students, their institution and their hometown. The teacher also asked for my students' contact details so that he could link these to the site as well. I asked them to forward their details to the teacher, and these details were posted on the e-pal page of the partner class.

Only four of the thirteen *Nicenet* participants (Herman, Oscar, Adam and Alex) maintained regular contact in the e-pal project. Others reported that they were interested in the project, but that technical problems, such as incorrect e-mail addresses, and e-pals who did not respond to their messages, were deterrents. This occurred despite the contact maintained by the teacher and myself. Because the project was voluntary and because not all the students were participating in the *Nicenet* class, I did not integrate it with an assessment task, despite what researchers such as Keogh (2001), Ho (2000), Sakar (2001), Mello (1998), and Jor and Mak (1994) advise. The reason for this was because I also could not assess students on such a project as all the Foundation students,[11] including those in other classes, had to be given the same assessment tasks.

The intention of the e-pal project was to establish the extent to which participants could engage in global communities. In the pilot study I intended for participants to send me copies of their e-mails so that I could keep track of them. However, this proved to restrict their freedom, so I allowed the participants in the final project (OLEP) to communicate privately, and rely on their views of the project, as well as some of their e-mail messages. Therefore, in this final part of my study, I decided not to have all participants send me copies of all their messages, except for Alex and Herman, who agreed to do so. For ethical reasons, I have not included e-mails from the partner-students.

In terms of maintaining contact, all four participants said that not all the e-pals responded regularly, and that some of them did not have much to write. One way perhaps, of preventing such a discrepancy in the rate of responses would be for teachers to stipulate a minimum number of contact sessions, to prevent students from feeling excluded if their e-pals do not respond. Although this sounds contrived, it is helpful towards ensuring equitable participation. Such a decision, however, depends on facilitator co-operation, and maintenance of common goals.

11 There were about 180 Foundation in English students in total in Semester One, 2004, and the number dropped slightly in Semester Two to about 140.

When asked about the content of the communication, the common topics of discussion included life in South Africa and China, university life, participants' studies, and culture. Students found that they were studying a range of courses. My students were primarily Arts students, while the Chinese students were studying Engineering. This did not appear to deter my students, who thought it was interesting to communicate with students who have different interests.

The communication was not restricted to facilitator-selected topics, but students at both universities were asked to write as extensively as they could so that they could expand their vocabulary and perhaps expand their English writing skills. Herman and Alex e-mailed me some of their messages when I asked if I could read some of the correspondence. I follow the progress of some of Herman's initial correspondence to illustrate communicative practice.

From: (Herman) <u>All headers</u>
Reply-to:
To: ……..
Subject: e-pal
Hello ………

I read in the website you are looking for a penpal. Also my English teacher Leila told us about you in China. I am happy for being apal. I am a 22 year old boy. I am from Inanda, KwaZulu.It is in a township. Before this I work in part-time work. Now I am a student. I am doing a BA. One day maybe I can be a teacher.

If you are interested you can write back and tell me about your life.
Happy for being your friend .

Sincerely, (Her-man)

Fig. 38: Herman's introductory posting

From:(Herman)
Reply-to:
To:........
Subject: hello

Hi ....

As I said, I am happy to meet you. I was surprised when you replied so quick. Now I have a new friend. What are you doing today? I had my English class today. I like to do English because we talk issues about SA and other countries. How is your English class?

My teacher says you are coming from the place pandas come? I come from a big township, but I stay here in campus in joburg now. It is a big city in south Africa.It is good to stay you can use the computers and library anytime. Tell me everything about your place and what you are doing and your culture. Do you like to be engineer? Do you like sport? Iplay soccer.
So, write agin with news. I am still learning computers so this can help me too.

Fig. 39: Herman receives a response

From: (Herman)
Reply-to:
To: ....
Subject: Hi threr

I was waiting for a letter from you. We are busy, just now we will start exams, so we are finishg assignments. Its very busy and all the lectures want the work now.

I also like music. Do you know this kwaito ?? It is cool music to listen and r/b, hiphop. I like to go to clubs, but its not so good everytime. When you come you can see my music is good.

(hh)

Fig. 40: Herman sustains contact

Herman and this particular e-pal were obviously exchanging general information about themselves. They later also exchanged cultural information about their family practices, such as naming practices, which is a topic we covered in class, and the languages they speak. Later, Herman said he explained the genre *kwaito* to his partner. Altogether, Herman says he wrote about ten times to his e-pal, and that their correspondence was of a similar nature to the above extracts. When I met Herman after the final examination in November he said that they were still in contact, but that it was not very often. Alex said that his experiences were similar.

As discussed in Chapter 1, e-pal projects have benefits for the teaching and learning of English. Reported advantages include an increase in student confidence, as well as linguistic and cultural knowledge (Ho, 2000), improved reading and writing skills (Sakar, 2001), producing a wide range of discourse structures (Lee, 2004), and writing for a 'real' audience (Jor and Mak, 1994).

Drawing on the literature, I asked participants about these reported benefits. Oscar and Adam said that they enjoyed the e-pal experience, and that they would do something like this again. Adam was not clear on how it would fit in to an English course, while Oscar thought it should be linked to other projects so that more students could gain from the experience. Both reported that they were more confident as a result of the exchanges. Adam explained:

> You can write, and someone is writing back. Like you are talking. Only you must be regular… to correspond. I can see this is a good thing. You can learn to communicate with all people… different cultures.

Herman felt that he gained most from the cultural contact, in that he would not otherwise have had an opportunity to communicate personally with someone from such a different cultural group. He said that the system '(had) possibilities'.

Alex added:

> ALEX: I had two penpals in China, they were one boy and one girl, doing some Engineering. They wanted to communicate so we are writing to each other. I learn about them, they learn about me…culture, varsity.
> LEILA: OK, wonderful, did you enjoy it?
> ALEX: For me, it was the first time I am writing to someone in China, my family say what is this? My friends say let me read. Only their [the e-pals, my insertion] English is not so good, I say I am better.

Alex spoke about the project outside class as well, and also felt that he would like to try a similar project with other students who were studying in a similar field in other countries, or at other universities. All four participants felt that the e-pal communication gave them an opportunity to improve their English because it was a 'real' situation. Adam and Oscar both felt that the interactions were like having a conversation with someone, only in writing. While the participants were not given pre- and post tests, they agreed that the e-pal exposure gave them an opportunity to use the language, and they felt that their reading and writing skills had improved, as had their confidence.

In relation to communities of practice, all the participants were able to establish relationships with partners: they discussed issues pertaining to their lives, negotiated meaning, and learnt about one another. While the one-on-one relationships do not constitute communities of practice per se, I found them to be an integral part of relationship-building, which in turn contributes to community-building. Furthermore, the partnerships established transcended classroom relationships, and show that global communication was facilitated.

Students participated peripherally, until they began to feel more confident with their e-pals, and eventually participated more centrally, thus, creating a social network that extended beyond the class. It is interesting that the four participants were the only ones who sustained contact. Those who did give up did so after participating only peripherally. Once they experienced technical problems, they did not pursue the e-pal project. However, such difficulties are a downfall in authentic tasks, and often, the teacher has little control over the development of the tasks. This is especially true if the tasks are assessed and students do not have much control over when their partners write to them.

The non-participants attributed disinterest, laziness, and lack of time in the computer laboratory as reasons why they did not pursue the contact. Not all the participants participated in all three communities, and only the four maintained contact internationally. In the following section I reflect on the extent to which participants were able to participate in communities of practice.

Conclusion on communities of practice

Thus far, it is evident that students were able to participate in diverse communities of practice in the online environment. The communities established moved beyond the confines of the conventional face-to-face class. Of the communities identified, the students participated in three types of communities: the communities within, that is, their public interactions and relationships within the Foundation in English online class, communities beyond, or the private communities established outside of the online class, and finally, global communities, where four participants communicated with international e-pals.

Participants established relationships and maintained social contact with the lecturer, with one another, and with international students, thus diminishing boundaries, and narrowing social distance. They participated peripherally, and with assistance from other students and the facilitator, they became more active participants. I further noted their use of language in the online class as displaying both the characteristics of spoken and written text.

Of particular interest in this study, is the extent to which participants constructed identities in the online environment. In the second part of this chapter, I examine the notion 'construction of identities' from the data elicited from selected discussion threads on polygamy, which is one of the course themes, their electronic literacy histories, and interviews, in response to the third question 'How do participants construct identities in online environments?'

Constructing and deconstructing identities in virtual social arenas

Identities are constructed through personality, social roles, relationships, shared values, and language use. In a computer-mediated environment, the variety of options CMC offers participants in designing their identities is an attraction (Lam, 2000). In virtual computer-mediated environments therefore, these may be manifest through participants' use of language, names and social cues such as emoticons. In his study of identity and language use in teenage blogs, Huffaker (2004), for instance describes how American teenagers constructed their identities through their disclosure of personal information, their choice of online names and avatars, and the use of emotive features. I elected to explore how participants constructed their identities on discussion threads using three categories: their use of names and nicknames, emoticons and social cues, and language use.

Names and social cues

The use of names and nicknames in computer-mediated communication makes it a social arena in which people construct multiple roles and personae (Turkle, 1995; refer also to Lam, 2000). As facilitator of the course, I referred to myself by my first name 'Leila', and would often sign off a message using only initials 'lll', sometimes with a smiley ☺. I was addressed as Leila throughout the course, both face-to-face, as well as online. Initially, all the student participants identified themselves very formally, using their given names, and using formal business correspondence style by signing off their messages 'Yours sincerely'. For instance, B signed off 'Kindly regards' (Figure 33), and E signed off 'Your sincerely' (Figure 28). Figure 41 illustrates some of the formats used:

Participants' use of names	**Facilitator's use of name**
Yours sincerely + name + surname	Leila
Your student + first name	Leila + smiley ☺
Kindly regards + first name	llll
First name + surname	
First name + smiley	
First name only	
Nickname	
Initials only	
Emoticon	
No name	

Fig. 41:Participants' use of names

After their initial posts, some of the participants adopted a less formal style by using their nicknames, evidence of their becoming more comfortable with the medium and members of the COP. Not all the participants used nicknames, but the names selected show a definite gender bias. Figure 42 that follows illustrates the nicknames used:

Male nicknames	**Female nicknames**
Dude	Number One Gal
Boss	Lucky Lady
Genius	Hottie
Clever	Beyonce
Great one	

Fig. 42: Participants' use of nicknames[12]

Bays (1998, in Lam, 2000) says that nicknames are signs of individuality, and carriers of sociological cues, such as age, gender, and interest, which affirms Turkle's (1995) view of virtual environments as social arenas. Participants tended to use stereotypical male and female nicknames, some with provocative and sexual undertones, as was seen in Bechar-Israeli's (1995)[13] study of the names used in chat rooms. The practice was only adopted when one of the students used a nickname, and this had a spill-over effect, with others following suit. Each tried to outdo the others in relation to name choice, however, it is not clear if these were the nicknames used normally by participants, or whether they were created for their online personae.

Male nicknames such as 'Dude', 'Boss' and 'Great One' indicate the tendency towards male dominance and superiority, while Clever is a nickname commonly used in the townships to indicate someone streetwise and witty. Female nicknames showed typical female stereotypes, as in 'Number One Gal' and 'Lucky Lady', and sexual undertones, as in 'Hottie'. 'Beyonce' indicates the popular female music star.

Social cues such as emoticons were not used extensively, primarily because participants had not used them before on computer. After I used a smiley, several students asked me about its use, but only a marginal

12 Nicknames revealing the identity of participants are not used here.

13 Cited in Huffaker (2004).

number of participants used emoticons, the most common being ☺, ;-) (wink), and :) (happy face). In Figure 32 referred to earlier, E used asterisks and slashes (**<<//Thank you>>//) which I interpret as his way of trying to demonstrate emotion or social presence, and the non-verbal in the absence of his knowledge of emoticons.

In relation to netspeak, although most of the participants had access to cell phones and were familiar with 'sms-talk', the use of abbreviations, contractions and acronyms were also not popular until later in the course, for example, 'I studied ovanite' (overnight), and 'C U in kls' (See you in class). The use of punctuation to convey mood and emotion was a more popular choice, such as 'So what does this mean?????' and 'Hiiiiiii!!!!!!' One participant wrote her initial messages in capital letters, but said she did this because she was lazy to change case, not because she was trying to convey any meaning in particular.

Generally, participants did not make excessive use of names, nicknames, or emoticons to construct their identity. Avatars, or graphic icons chosen to represent a real person in a virtual context, were not used at all. I suggest that this is primarily because of the novelty of the medium. When the features were used, it was to enhance the meaning of the messages. In the following section I examine how participants constructed their identities in relation to their social lives and experiences.

Identity and social lives

Rather more apparent than the use of names and emoticons, was the way in which identity was constructed in relation to the participants' roles and their sense of worth in society (Norton, 1997, 2000). As referred to in Chapter 1, Turkle (1995) said 'The Internet has become a significant social laboratory for experimenting with the constructions and reconstructions of self that characterize postmodern life' (1995: 180). Participants discussed how they felt positioned in relation to others in terms of access to technology, as well as how this positioned them in the South African context, and in relation to social issues discussed in class: polygamy, HIV/AIDs, gender, and language use.

Nothando said she felt that her ability to use technology made her a 'somebody' and a 'something', and Lucky said it gave him 'status'.

Both participants associated the ability to use technology with privilege, esteem and power, and as an entity that distinguished them from those without access. Several participants said they considered themselves fortunate, as their friends at other universities were not exposed to technology in their courses at undergraduate level. They also felt that the use of technology gave them better material, economic and career prospects. This is consistent with West's (1992) view of identity as it relates to the desire for recognition and affiliation (in Norton, 1997). Their perception of ICTs influencing their career prospects positively is also consistent with Fang and Warschauer's (2004) findings that the use of ICTs provides input that is relevant to students' lives. The desire for recognition and affiliation is inseparable from material resources in society, where those with access to such resources are accorded access to power and privilege, likewise, limited early access to ICTs left students feeling marginalised. Thus identity shifts as social and economic relations change.

Mbali related the issue of access to technology to apartheid and post-apartheid South Africa. She wrote in her electronic literacy history, and reiterated during her interview that the lack of access to material resources such as computers in post-apartheid South Africa was a perpetuation of apartheid times because it was generally white students who had ICT access at home and at the schools they attended. Thus, she positioned this particular race group as privileged, a situation which she felt was still perpetuated from apartheid to post-apartheid South Africa, where black students still lacked privilege and power.

Students also identified with the themes in the Foundation in English courses because of their strong views on issues of gender inequality, HIV/AIDS and polygamy in their communities. Thus they constructed themselves textually.[14] I analyse critically the selected texts that follow. I refer again to a posting by O:[15]

14 Please refer also to Lam's (2000) and Ivanic's (1998) work on textual identity, as discussed earlier.

15 I am grateful to Dr Carolyn McKinney for her valuable insight on the analysis of some of these postings, as well as input and comments from the Writing Group at Wits Institute for socio-economic research (WISER).

FROM: O....
SUBJECT: The lecture today
[Reply | Archive | Delete | Forward]

How was our (name removed) lecture?
I ejoyed it so much But I think it was just too fast and our lecturer hurried through out the whole thing.however it made some sence I think it was going to be much better,if we had time.

So you guys how far have you gone with your Oral presentation and what topics are you dealing with.We are dealing with Polygamy if you have some ideas on polygamy I think you should help us.If you have anything to debate about polygamy please write me.I am for polygamy bearing in mind among other things that polygamy is resistance to cutural imperialism.At least those who practice it have cutural values that they are still keeping.Although thesedays it is a total greedness of women.But I think also it is justified since males are fewer than females for example here at Wits university.Say we have a comminity like this University else where. What would those un lick ones do if they have no men to love them.You know women and men need someone to give loveor vise-versa. If you have any options air them to me. thank you O...

Fig. 43: Polygamy posting 1

The message indicates O's view on identifying with, and maintaining cultural practices and values. He perceives polygamy as 'resistance to cultural imperialism'. His use of 'at least' indicates that in his view, traditional cultural practices must be kept alive.

His comment on the 'greedness of women' is somewhat dislocated from his argument, until he refers to the number of women exceeding the number of men, which in his view also justifies polygamy. He could also be referring to women as greedy in that they do not want to share their men.[16] O constructs a particular view of masculinity as hegemonic. He also perceives relationships as heterosexual, with men playing the dominant role. He asserts that women need men and refers to these women as 'unlick' (unlucky) 'if they have no men to love them'. Somewhat ironic is that O uses high-tech Western (imperialist)

16 I am grateful to an anonymous *Perspectives in Education* reviewer for this insight.

computer-mediated communication to debate traditional values. He received several responses to this posting.

In response to the above posting, A commented that he agreed with the idea of polygamy for cultural reasons, however, not for economic reasons:

> **FROM:** A….
> **SUBJECT:** [Reply | Archive | Delete | Forward] re:The lecture today
>
> My grandfather had three wives. It is good for the family and according to customary law it is right. But what if the economy is bad like now? How can he provide? I cannot afford many wives or girlfriends!

Fig. 44: Polygamy posting 2

A constructs the traditional patriarchal view of the male as provider for the family. As a Law student it is also interesting that he makes a case to support customary law and polygamy. In referring to the poor economy, he also constructs a view of many young black South Africans who have aspirations of wealth and material possessions in a post-apartheid consumerist society. In so doing, like O, he also sees the role of the male as hegemonic provider in heterosexual relationships.

B expressed concern about polygamy for health and social reasons:

> **FROM:** B….
> **SUBJECT:** re:The lecture today
> [Reply | Archive | Delete | Forward]
> Polygamy adds to HIV/AIDS – a man with many wives will spread the disease to the wives and children. In my township there are too many aids orphans. Who will look after them? We need one man-one wife!!!!

Fig. 45: Polygamy posting 3

B's construction of gender roles engages with how women are positioned in heterosexual relationships. He positions them as powerless to negotiate sex with their partners, and the disease is 'spread' to them, placing them and often, their unborn babies, at risk. In so doing he also simultaneously positions men in a dominant position of power in their insistence on unprotected sexual relations. His social concern for the care of AIDs orphans also foregrounds the harsh reality of the dissolution of the family structure, where many AIDs orphans are being looked after by community care-givers, elderly grannies, or left to fend for themselves, hence his emotive call for the nuclear family 'We need one man-one wife!'.

O decided to respond to the thread again with the following:

FROM: O....
SUBJECT: Polygamy
[Reply | Archive | Delete | Forward]
I think polygamy works in the sense of protecting our culture.If any generations does not pass on our culture this will mean, we will be left without any history of culture.There are some after effects of polygamy especially these days.But if one does it propery it works.Today women talks of equal rights but in past women was supposed to be undermen or you will risk to be disrespected.In my country polygamy was being practised so as to have a big family.The reason of having a big family was not work in the fields and those days any one's wealth was seen on the amount of food you have in your grainery.Some families would even exchange their daughters for food.So the politics was the more food you have the more wives you get.Just like today people still have this behaviour.Modern man gets more girl friends when they have money than those without money.Women never wanted to starve even in history.If you can not look for what to eat then it means you have no one prepared to offer you love.As long as you have money these days you can have as much women as you want,although you risk HIV and AIDS and more problems.Bob Nastor Marley Said 'No women no cry' and Notorious BIG also said 'more money more problems' in their songs. I think men are still practising polygamy though in a different way or I can say they have given it a nice name to try and make it more modern.

I do not think women are being disavantaged.The problem is they do not want to take it.Even the tenth wife will not want her husband to get the eleventh wife.I think if one can afford it let him do it.
o...

Fig. 46: Polygamy posting 4

O reiterates and clarifies his position that polygamy is a cultural practice that makes sound economic sense, and should not be lost. His post, like A's in Figure 44, positions him as valuing the traditional patriarchal family structure. He constructs men as providers and protectors of women, and of women as requiring the support and protection of men. His use of 'history' and 'culture' demonstrates his view that if cultural practices are not maintained, they are lost forever. Although he acknowledges that there are 'after effects' of polygamy, he does not clarify them. His view is that if polygamy is practised 'propery' (properly), it is a successful practice, however, he also does not go on to clarify what successful practice entails. He provides a contrast between today's women who are gender-conscious, with those of the past, who would be considered disrespectful if they were not subservient, or did not abide by cultural practices ('in past women was supposed to be undermen or you will risk to be disrespected').

His argument around the need for sustenance further justifies polygamy, where he equates food with material wealth. His view is that a large family is economically sound, because large families have more food, or are able to get more food. However, he does not clarify that larger families also require more food, which off course costs more! He demonstrates the strength of his argument by saying that daughters may be exchanged for food, however, he does not provide his opinion of the practice. Interestingly, he says that the situation is still prominent today, the more money a man has, the more popular he is with females, constructing women as greedy, materialistic, and reliant on men, as he said in his earlier posting (Figure 43). He also makes reference to Bob Marley and Big who use similar themes in their music. His view is that polygamy is still practised today, but it is couched in more polite terms. Essentially, he supports polygamy in this lengthy extract, although he does not justify all his arguments sufficiently.

M, a female participant, constructed her identity strongly in terms of her views on self-reliance, empowerment and gender equality, in stark contrast to previous participants:

FROM: M....
SUBJECT: Polygamy
[Reply | Archive | Delete | Forward]
I am studying to support myself when I work. I don't need a man to support me. My mother, aunties and my grandmother needed a mans support. I can do it myself. Isithembu (*Zulu word for polygamy – my insertion*) is not for the modern man and woman.

Fig. 47: Polygamy posting 5

M's construction of gender roles positions women as strong and self-reliant, and as valuing education and career accomplishments. This is in keeping with what Hall (1990: 2) says about educated women '(they) expect and demand more from life than did the previous generations of women'. M's notions of success are redefined from the traditional roles played by women, what Hall (1990: 89) calls 'new modes of success' among modern women. M refers to her mother, aunts and grandmother as being reliant on men, and as being in positions lacking power. Her strong use of the referent 'I' supports her position: '*I* am studying to support myself... *I* don't need a man... *I* can do it myself...' (my italics). Her use of the isiZulu word '*Isithembu*' for polygamy also appears to call attention to her view on disconnecting the old and traditional from the new. In the face-to-face class discussions, M was insistent that women be more self-supporting. During class discussions on HIV/AIDS, for example, she was adamant and quite emotive that women were 'killing themselves' by not carrying condoms because of negative male perceptions of the practice (class discussion, 18 August 2004).

Finally, unlike other male students, E, a male student, equates polygamy with the abuse of women:

FROM: E
SUBJECT: Polygamy
[Reply | Archive | Delete | Forward]

Polygamy is the form of marrige where by a person get married to more than one partner.Indeed polygamy works as a result it is cultural practice. Women are emotionaly, economicaly, politicaly ...abused. Further I argue with the first response from this ISSUE, that he /she must think twice of polygamy.Firstly the ways in which it is practised, it is abusive to ayone or not?(women accept the ways in which they are treated in a polygamous mariage or not?). Secondly he or she must compare and contrat between the way, our fore fathers(refer from articles/ cases) practiced polygamy,she will see that there is a difference.IN MY OPINION I THICK IT IS ABUSSIVE TO WOMEN and as a new generation living in the developing community getting ideas from everywhere we must not practice it or be part of it (as wife).I further accept that it OUR culture (african or any...) but it is wrong.WEMUST BE AWAY OF IT. POLYGAMY IS WRONG.

Fig. 48: Polygamy posting 6

E does not justify polygamy, although it is a cultural practice ('OUR culture'), on the basis that times have changed, and that we are exposed to new global ideas. It is interesting that, as a male, he presents the woman's perspective, that women are empowered with 'choice'. He demonstrates the strength of his argument by using capitals 'IN MY OPINION I THICK IT IS ABUSSIVE TO WOMEN… WEMUST BE AWAY [AWARE] OF IT. POLYGAMY IS WRONG'. However, although he accords women with the power of choice, he does not discriminate against men who are polygamous, except for saying the practice is abusive to women, and not that they are being abused by men.

While students construct their identity in face-to-face classrooms, the analyses of their online postings indicate that they apply similar principles of identity-construction in the online medium. This discussion is sustained in my personal reflections.

Conclusion on the construction of identities

Castells says 'Identity is people's source of meaning and experience' (2004: 6). In this research project, I set out to examine how participants constructed identities in online spaces. I found that participants used language and social cues in constructing their identities, and responded to class themes in ways that illustrated how they positioned themselves in society.

In the online medium, participants positioned themselves as changing in response to the material and technological changes in society, characteristic of Hall's (1992) view of the post-modern subject. They feel a sense of dislocation, but position themselves as they do in the face-to-face class in terms of social issues such as polygamy, HIV/AIDS, and gender. This demonstrates that the online medium facilitates, supports, and promotes the construction of identities. Their constructions are also consistent with Norton's (1995, 1996, 2000) views, that identity refers to how people understand their relationships in the world, and how those relationships are constructed over space and time.

The online environment facilitated learner participation, negotiation and re-negotiation of meaning within communities of practice. The communities established moved beyond the conventional face-to-face class, with participants constructing their identities at different levels. Participants established relationships, and maintained social contact with the facilitator and with one another, thus diminishing boundaries, and narrowing social distance. They participated peripherally, and with assistance and co-operation from other students and the facilitator, became more active participants.

Part IV

Implications for teaching and learning: Towards a model of online learning

Chapter 6
Online communities of practice: From disadvantage to empowerment

In the previous chapter I explored the extent to which participants formed relationships and constructed their identities as a means of establishing the extent to which they engaged in online communities. The data demonstrates that communities of practice undeniably exist in online spaces, in fact the data indicates that students participate in diverse online communities simultaneously. However, students who appeared to be more independent, motivated, and receptive to change tended to participate more extensively in the online communities.

Given that multimedia ICT modes of delivery are emerging in South Africa's educational landscape, my work posed questions about the use of ICTs from the perspective of learners with minimal previous access and exposure to the medium. In particular, it asked the question 'To what extent do English non-mother tongue speakers in a university English classroom engage in communities of practice in online spaces?' To answer this main question, I posed sub-questions about participants' electronic literacy practices to establish an overview of their previous ICT-practice, and its influence on their current ICT-practice. Having established that COPs involve the building of relationships, interactive networks among participants, and how they construct their identities, I also asked questions concerning the relationships they develop and sustain in online COPs, and how they construct their identities in the new online medium.

The work is situated at the interface of online learning, language and literacy studies, and learning theory, and is further underpinned, from a critical perspective, by issues of power within a digital divide. I argued that students with access to, and proficiency in technology are privileged and empowered by the higher education system, and better prepared for future career and economic success. I also argued that the power struggles surrounding the use of ICTs in South Africa parallel the struggles around the use of English in the country. Thus, participants were doubly disadvantaged, being non-mother-tongue speakers of English in an environment dominated by the language, as well as having minimal previous access to ICTs, both of which are dominant discourses of the university community.

At this point I would like to provide a summary of findings and reflect on their implications for further research and teaching using technology in higher education. Then I return to the over-arching question to establish the extent to which English non-mother tongue speakers in a university English classroom engage in communities of practice in online spaces. I do not suggest that this work has all the answers on online COPs, and therefore acknowledge the limitations of the study, and make recommendations for practice and further research. I conclude by suggesting a model for online learning in English which would be appropriate for any developing country, given their current social exclusion and marginalisation.

Summarising findings and reflections on online COPs

Electronic (ICT)-literacy as social practice

Drawing on the argument that literacy is not a skill, but a social practice that is embedded in broader social goals (Barton et al., 2000; Street, 1984, 1993, 1998, 2003; Gee, 1996, 1997, 2000), the following emerged from this book thus far: the majority of participants had minimal access to ICTs at home and at their former high schools, and that their ICT-proficiency, when they entered the university, was also minimal. Access at school was limited to principals, and sometimes teachers, who were also not proficient with ICTs themselves, and if there was access in the home environment, the computer was feared and revered. However, participants noted that their former high schools were beginning to acquire ICTs through external donors. ICT access at university was considered far superior to access at home or at school, but was not considered ideal as the computer laboratories were often overcrowded, and the number of computers available was insufficient for the number of students.

Theorists argue that different literacies are associated with different domains of life, and that literacy practices are patterned by power relationships and social institutions. This became evident in participants' feelings of marginalisation within the dominant academic discourses of the university, in this case, a discourse of technological proficiency. Most experienced this as disabling to the extent that it created a divide between them and white students, whom they considered privileged by apartheid. The digital divide, which students viewed as a legacy of South Africa's apartheid past, was thus a pervasive presence, not just in the communities from which participants came, but very much so at the University. However, participants who were independent and motivated appeared to overcome these gaps and attain the ICT-skills and proficiency necessary to succeed quite rapidly.

On the whole, participants found that the Net and the online component offered diverse benefits, including access to unlimited information, ease of use, facilitation of contact, and some found a general improvement in English skills such as reading and writing. The disadvantages they reported included technophobia, lack of skills, limited access, outdated technology, poor time management and 'laziness'. The divide appeared to perpetuate feelings of inclusion-exclusion among participants. One of the most significant fears expressed by participants is that the lack of access to technology could impact negatively on their future commercial, material, and economic prospects, thus widening the divide. I consider this fear to be an obstacle that, in my experience, has already made an impact on participants' academic lives.

Online communities of practice: Relationships and participation

In COPs, the acquisition of knowledge is seen as a social process, where novices to the community participate peripherally until they are assisted by more experienced participants. This book shows that participants were able to participate in diverse communities of practice simultaneously in the online environment. The communities established transcended the boundaries of the conventional face-to-face class, and students participated in public interactions and relationships within the Foundation in English online class; in private communities established outside of the online class; and finally, in global communities, where four participants communicated with international e-pals. However, participation alone does not generate a COP. The establishment of relationships, which is intrinsic to communities, was enabled as participants assisted one another from peripheral to full participation.

Participants established and sustained relationships, reminiscent of Rheingold's comment on 'webs of personal relationships in cyberspace' (Rheingold, 2000: online, 6 of 16). They also maintained social contact with me, with one another, and with international students in China, thus diminishing boundaries, and narrowing social distance. They participated peripherally, and with assistance from other students and the facilitator, they became more active participants, by posting messages on the weekly discussion threads. This is consistent with Lave and Wenger's (1991, 1996, 2002) legitimate peripheral participation, as well as Rogoff's (2003) description of guided participation. Their messages included social messages, research queries and updates, and responses to readings.

What I also found interesting was participants' use of language. Researchers such as Ong (1982) in Murray (2000); Yates (1996); Crystal (2001); and Moran and Hawisher (1998) show that computer-mediated communication (CMC) contains both oral and written linguistic features. In addition, Warschauer (2004a) and Murray (2000) found that CMC users employ time-reducing strategies to write the messages and substitute for the lack of paralinguistic and non-verbal cues. The findings of this book are consistent with the researchers' findings on the language used in CMC. Participants used emoticons, abbreviations, and substituted numbers for words in an attempt to construct social presence, simplify their messages, and create an ambience of non-verbal communication, demonstrating that the online medium facilitates the construction of identities textually within COPs (refer also to Lam, 2000). These findings have implications for the teaching and learning of English language, and rather than being considered as weakening the English language, computer-mediated communication has emerged as a new register in the English language curriculum.

Constructing online identities

Identities might be constructed through personality, social roles, relationships, shared values, and language use. In this study, I set out to examine how participants constructed identities in the new online space. I drew on the work of Lam (2000) who argued that the attraction of CMC is the variety of options it offers participants in designing their identities. In virtual environments, therefore, identities may be constructed through participants' use of language, names and social cues, such as emoticons. Having examined their use of names, nicknames and social cues, I found these had a minimal influence on how they constructed their identities, and argued that this occurred because of the novelty of the medium. I found that participants constructed their identities more strongly in relation to how they positioned themselves in relation to sociocultural issues evident in class themes and readings, such as polygamy.

In the online medium, and characteristic of post-modern thought, participants positioned themselves as adaptive in response to the material and technological changes in their learning environment. They felt a sense of dislocation, not having used ICTs extensively before, but believed the medium accorded them status and privilege as students. Their constructions of identity are also consistent with Norton (Pierce's) (1995, 1996, 2000) views, that identity refers to how people understand their relationships in the world, and how those relationships are constructed over space and time.

The online environment facilitated learner participation, negotiation and re-negotiation of meaning within communities of practice. The communities established moved beyond the conventional face-to-face class, with participants constructing their identities in multiple layers. Participants established relationships, and created networks with the facilitator and with one another, and, in some cases, with global partners, thus diminishing boundaries, and narrowing social distance. They participated peripherally, and with assistance and co-operation from other students and the facilitator, became more active participants. This also has implications for the teaching and learning of English. From a sociocultural perspective, and recognising that the learning of English does not occur in isolation, learners acquire the language because of how they construct themselves, and because of how they interact using the language. Thus, learner-identities, relationships, and communities are valuable considerations in online communities of practice.

In this work the online environment facilitated the construction of online communities of practice to the following extent: first, participants were able to form and sustain relationships in multiple online COPs, and diminish social boundaries in the process. Second, participants were able to construct online identities in three ways. To a lesser extent, they used linguistic features such as names, nicknames and social cues, and to a greater extent, they were able to construct their identities by positioning themselves as empowered when they had access to ICTs. Using discussion threads, participants were further able to construct identities textually in relation to course themes.

Some limitations

While I have provided various responses to the questions I posed in writing this book, I acknowledge that this work is not without shortcomings or limitations, which need noting. Foremost, I did not have control over the Foundation in English curriculum. The Foundation in English course has been taught at the university since 1992, although the approach and content had been adapted over the years. As such, I could not add additional readings and tasks for my tutorial group, without influencing the work done with other tutorial groups. On the same note, I was only able to institute the online intervention with my tutorial group, and could not include other groups in the experience, as I did not have the resources to conduct the intervention with all the students, nor could other tutors be expected to cope with the task.

Second, the fact that all tutorial groups had to do the same tasks influenced what I considered one of the strongest limitations, that of assessment. The online component was not formally assessed, as assessment tasks had to be consistent across all the tutorial groups. I was thus limited by the voluntary nature of the project, in the sense that I could not motivate or encourage students to participate for reward of marks, which might have had a more positive impact on motivating them to participate.[1]

A third related limitation is the minimal participation in the e-pal project, where only four of the thirteen participants maintained e-pal contact. Because of the voluntary nature of the project, and because assessment tasks were not included, I was not able to successfully motivate more students to participate, which could have resulted in richer data in the section 'Communities beyond' (Chapter 5).

Fourth, in relation to sustaining online participation, I was informed by two participants that they lost interest in the online component because I did not update posts to the class on a daily basis. This demotivated them from participating as they logged onto the online class daily. The intention behind not updating posts daily was so as not to overwhelm less active participants. However, it had a negative impact on more active participants, which is inevitable among students with diverse proficiency levels.

Finally, in relation to specific English skills, some of the participants noted that the online component had a positive effect on their reading and writing skills. It was not my intention at the outset of this project to assess the possible improvement in English language skills. However, considering that some of the participants raised the issue of the improvement in reading and writing skills, had I included pre- and post-tests to ascertain the possible improvement in English language skills, I would have been able to assess the improvement or decline in such skills, rather than having to rely on self-report data.

1 Hodgkinson-Williams (2005: 95) cites Macdonald (2003: 377) who underscores the importance of assessment in 'ensuring online participation'.

The findings and limitations discussed thus far give rise to recommendations of the study, as well as recommendations for further research, which are discussed in the sections to follow.

Proposed recommendations

The findings of this study indicate that COPs are enabled in online environments, through the development of participant-networks, and the construction of identities. On the basis of these findings, this study recommends that online learning be considered, for the reasons provided below, as an additional or parallel mode of delivery, and to promote teacher-learner and learner-learner collaboration, networking and interaction, particularly in higher education English classrooms at university level. Thus, like O'Dowd (2000), and Kern and Warschauer (2000) I recommend that an electronic literacy approach be taken by integrating electronic literacy into English language teaching and learning in the higher education classroom.

While it is not without challenge to recommend that higher education institutions in South Africa integrate ICTs into teaching programmes merely because developed countries have done so, particular notice should be taken of South Africa and other developing countries, and their possible exclusion from global networks, should they not embrace technology timeously. As Warschauer (2002a, 2002b, 2003) argues, for developing countries in particular, technology should serve the enabling purpose of social inclusion.

I propose foremost that central units or Technology Centres be established at Universities to steer the incorporation of technology into teaching and learning at the levels of policy, practice, and curriculum. At present ICT initiatives are implemented in an *ad hoc* manner, which is inconsistent across the University studied in this book. With this in mind, the recommendations are categorised into three areas: policy and practice; curriculum design; and recommendations for facilitators and learners, all of which could be driven by the Technology Centre.

Policy and practice

While educational policies at national level recommend the use of ICTs, it is short-sighted to assume that their recommendations will be implemented successfully, unless they feed into institutional policies. The existence of sound ICT-policy and planning for technology at an institutional level would ensure a consistent university-wide approach, rather than if the integration of ICTs into teaching and learning activities were conducted in an *ad hoc* manner, as is current practice.[2] Chapter 4 explains that ICT-policy at the University of the Witwatersrand does not exist, and that the use of ICTs in teaching and learning is not preferred practice in the School of Literature and Language Studies at the University. Learners, however, are keen to embrace technology, suggesting that the role of a Technology Centre should, in part, be to drive issues such as ICT-policy and implementation.

Universities would need the technological infrastructure to cope with the demands of using ICTs in teaching and learning, as is evident from participants' comments on the limited access to technology at the University of the Witwatersrand. Commitment from University management is necessary to provide the necessary infrastructure, as well as technical support, to enhance teaching and learning. Teachers are also more likely to adopt ICTs in their teaching if they feel secure that the infrastructural framework is made available. Finally, University-wide audits of current teaching practice that incorporates the use of ICTs would provide an overview of what staff is using across the faculties. This, together with an analysis of staff, as well as students' ICT access and proficiency would provide a suitable framework for future planning.

2 Although units specialising in research and practice in multimedia have been established at certain universities, this is not standard practice at universities across South Africa.

Curriculum design

To maximise the benefits of online learning, as is discussed in Chapter 1, it is to the English language teacher's advantage to consider how ICTs can best be integrated into the English language curriculum. My suggestion is certainly not that the integration of ICTs be adopted merely because teaching staff feel pressurised into doing so. Teachers need to be made aware of the benefits of online learning from University teaching-support services to reflect on ways in which ICTs can best be integrated into the curriculum. This is not to suggest that all face-to-face teaching be replaced with online strategies, or that this occurs only in the English classroom. Input should be made to promote a blended model of face-to-face and online practices, with due concern for what is best for the curriculum, facilitators and learners. This would require careful planning as well as teacher-development in ICT skills, practices and pedagogies, all of which could be supervised by Technology Centres.

Facilitators and learners

Kurek (2002) argues 'New conditions pose new challenges and call for new skills, yet it needs to be stressed that computers can never substitute teachers. On the contrary, they can offer them new opportunities for better language instruction' (Kurek, 2002: 26). While computers cannot replace good teachers, where ICTs are used, it is inevitable that teachers will need professional and technological development and support. Berge (1995), for example, categorises the conditions necessary for successful online facilitation as pedagogical, social, managerial, and technical conditions.

In relation to pedagogy, facilitators should use questions that focus discussions on critical concepts, principles and skills. On a social level, facilitators should maintain an appropriate environment to promote learning, human relationships and group cohesiveness. The managerial role involves managing the online learning experience effectively by setting objectives, managing online materials and discussion, and making decisions where necessary. With regard to technical expertise, while not every teacher can be expected to be a technical expert, it is the responsibility of the facilitator to ensure that students feel comfortable with the medium, for instance, by providing them with user-friendly handouts. This is particularly true for students who have had minimal previous access to ICTs. Teachers need to provide students with the support necessary for successful online interaction so that students do not feel overwhelmed by the tasks they are required to complete. Thus I recommend that the facilitator adopt a community of practice approach that encourages participants to collaborate, communicate, and construct identities.

Teachers too would benefit from working in communities of practice. To allay anxieties about the integration of ICTs into teaching and learning, the development of teacher networks and ICT interest groups, would be a positive experience. Teachers could communicate through special interest networks or listservs about common concerns, as also recommended by Kahmi-Stein (2000) and Murphy (2000).

The following suggestions refer specifically to facilitators who are new to integrating ICTs in the classroom:

- Teachers who would like to start implementing ICTs in the classroom should start at a manageable scale, for example, by referring to Internet sites as reference material during lessons;
- Students should be encouraged to use technology to complete tasks, for example, by asking them to access websites to complete assignments;
- Students should also be taught to evaluate websites critically, so that they can make informed choices of available material; and
- teachers and teacher-trainees should be encouraged to develop their own skills as new technology is introduced, and filter these skills to students.[3]

For teachers new to teaching online, the following points are recommended for successful online web course facilitation:

- Students should be given clear instructions about joining and participating in online classes;
- Students should be made aware of netiquette, or acceptable online behaviour;

3 Refer also to the University of Chattanooga website www.utc.edu/Teaching-Resource-Center/5things.html.

- Material should be organised logically so as not to confuse students;
- General housekeeping should be done regularly so that messages appear in the correct threads, if not, they should be moved. It is confusing to students to have to read messages that are posted to incorrect threads; and
- Teachers should only commit according to the time they have available. Students cannot be expected to participate if the teacher does not have time to respond to all participants.[4]

It is inevitable that with the increasing introduction of ICTs to schools[5] in South Africa by donor agencies, learners entering universities will shortly do so with improved computer literacy skills, provided that teachers are trained as well. Thus it is inevitable that teacher education departments at universities and colleges offer courses in ICTs and electronic literacy to pre-service teacher-trainees, as well as to in-service teachers already in the education system. Until then, universities should attempt to bridge inequities that marginalise students from under-resourced environments and ensure that all students have access to computer literacy training, rather than in the *ad hoc* manner with which it is currently approached.

Where does this road lead? Implications for further research

Because the use of online interventions is fairly uncharted territory in South Africa, the research possibilities are unlimited, and studies of online learning in the English classroom undertaken internationally can certainly be duplicated in the context of developing countries. Of particular interest is the use of online interventions for social inclusion, to bridge the digital divide, and the related power issues involved.

Van der Merwe (2005), in her study of the evaluation of *WebCT* at the University of Stellenbosch in South Africa, recommends the

4 Refer also to Kessler (2001).

5 This is discussed in Chapter 4.

need for research into classroom practice. Although not in response to her recommendation for further research, this book points to the need to address classroom practice as a gap created by the sporadic implementation of ICT-based teaching in South Africa. Bearing in mind that this small-scale study into online communities of practice is not generalisable to the larger student bodies in South Africa and other developing countries, I propose further research into online classrooms, with specific focus on communities of practice, networking among participants, and the identities they construct.

I believe that this work has unlocked possibilities for research in the areas of online environments, online participants, and to an extent, language use. Further research into what constitutes a successful teaching-learning online environment would be of benefit to all teachers, teacher-trainers, teacher-trainees, and course designers, as would studies of who are successful online teachers and learners. In the former instance, research might be conducted into web courses that are considered effective in relation to learner success and achievement. In the latter instance, specific teacher- and learner-characteristics and attributes would require careful examination. In relation to language studies, in particular, as demonstrated in the section on limitations, I would be interested in the possible improvement in English language skills, as a result of using online interventions in the English classroom. I would also be interested in studies that investigate the use of other online interventions in the English language classroom, as well as how these online interventions are assessed. Finally, with the increasing introduction of ICTs into schools from donor agencies and organisations, I would recommend long term case studies of how teachers, learners and schools are being prepared for the integration of ICTs into curricula, and how ICTs are being used, especially as a means of social inclusion. Drawing on the recommendations made in this book, as well as the suggestions for further research, the final section proposes a model of ICTs and learning in a developing context.

Towards a model of ICTs and learning

To the extent that this book recommends the integration of ICTs into policy and the curriculum, it also has further implications for learning. While recommendations derived from research conducted elsewhere have generally been made for the use of ICTs in North American and British contexts, I believe that a model that takes into consideration the South African sociocultural context might be beneficial for online teaching and learning. Such a model might include the following characteristics:

- a community of practice approach to teaching and learning online;
- an examination of ICT-literacy as social practice; and
- the creation of an environment which enables learners to make meaning by constructing their identities and positioning themselves in relation to the use of ICTs.

In relation to the first characteristic, Vygotsky (1978) suggests that individuals learn through interacting and negotiating meaning with other individuals and more knowledgeable peers in social situations. Similarly, Lave and Wenger (1991, 1996, 2002) suggest that the establishment of relationships is intrinsic to communities of practice. Thus communities of practice are enabled as participants assist one another from peripheral to full participation. In the South African context, a framework for online learning designed around community of practice principles (including participation, interaction, the development and sustaining of relationships, mentorship and assistance, and the negotiation of meaning) is appropriate, especially in the light of the African humanist philosophy of *Ubuntu*, as referred to in Chapter 5.[6]

Second, drawing on the work of Gee (1996, 1997, 2000), Street (1984, 1993, 1998, 2003), Barton, Hamilton and Ivanic (2000), Lankshear and Knobel (1997, 2004) and Knobel and Lankshear (2002), literacy as social practice theory demonstrates the value of considering learners' social practices with ICTs as a lens through which to view

6 *Ubuntu* refers to mutual reliance on other people, and communal identity.

their use of technology in the classroom. The majority of participants studied in this book came from disadvantaged, under-resourced backgrounds, with little previous access to computers and the Internet. Social practice theory therefore highlights the influence of learners' home and school encounters with ICTs, which impacts on their ICT-practices at university.

Third, identities, as described in the work of Hall (1992), Lam (2000), and Norton (Pierce) (1995, 1997, 2000) may be constructed through personality, social roles, relationships, shared values, and language use. Thus, how learners construct and position themselves in relation to ICTs and sociocultural issues discussed in the online space are significant to consider in relation to how they make meaning in any online learning environment.

Although this research on an online intervention demonstrates that successful communities of practice are enabled in online environments, through participant networking, and the construction of identities, I cannot claim to have authoritative solutions to all the questions and dilemmas raised in the course of this work. Technology should, in fact, enhance the curriculum, not dictate it. As Warschauer (2000a) says 'Technology itself does not *determine* human behavior, such as how we teach. However, it does create possibilities for new forms of behavior and of education' (2000a, 1 of 6). The research reported on in this book demonstrates that online COPs represent a shift from the dominant role of the teacher, to enabling learners to take greater responsibility for their learning, thus creating a more democratic, inclusive teaching-learning environment. Furthermore, my research shows that using a framework of technology for social inclusion empowers participants, who otherwise feel marginalised and disempowered, not only by introducing technology into under-resourced contexts, but by exploring issues such as networking and identity, which are fundamental to online communication and communities of practice.

Appendix
Character sketch of the participants

ADAM is under 20 years old. He is from Giyani and speaks Tsonga as his home language. He is a BA student. He is independent, and prefers to work on his own, rather than in a group.

ALEX is a 21-year old male from KwaZulu Natal. His home language is isiZulu. He is an LLB student who works very hard. He is a determined young man and generally does very well in his written work.

BLESSING, a 20-year old male from Gauteng, was born in KwaZulu Natal, but left the province while he was still at school because of the violence in the province at the time. He is an LLB student who applies what we do in class to his other courses, and generally does quite well.

ELSIE is a 20–25 year old female who is doing LLB. She is from the North West and is Tswana speaking. She is friendly, outgoing, and enjoys class discussions. She has many friends in class. Elsie often 'popped in' to visit or to consult in my office, sometimes bringing along friends from other classes.

ERNEST is under 20. He is from Mpumalanga, and is Tswana speaking. Although he was interested in Law, he changed to Social Work, which he felt was his calling. He is a mature young man who conducts himself very professionally. He is also considered a role model by teachers and learners at his former high school, and is sometimes called upon to address and motivate learners.

FARZANA is a 19-year old Iranian by birth. She arrived in South Africa to pursue her studies. Although she was born in Iran, she also spent a few years in Zambia with her family. She speaks English quite fluently, and is enthusiastic about the English class. Her home language is Persian. Conversations with her reveal that she is settling in very well and would like to pursue English as a possible career choice.

HERMAN is a first year student, aged between 20 and 25. He is originally from KwaZulu Natal, and speaks isiZulu as his home language. He has spent some time working since completing matric. He worked at odd jobs, including gardening, before making his way to university. He is mature and focused and knows what he wants to do with his life. He sometimes feels that he has lost his head start, which makes him more determined to succeed. He tends to be quiet in class, but asks questions and consults when necessary.

LEONARD is Mabela's close friend. He is under 20 years old, and is from a Sepedi background. Of the two friends, Leonard is the quieter.

LINDIWE is an under-20 female. She is from Mpumalanga and is Tswana speaking. She is doing a BA. She is very shy, but opens up when we speak in my office. She has been in my class from the beginning of the year. She is not a very strong student, but is trying very hard, and her marks have improved during the course of the year.

LUCKY is a very confident 20-year old male. He is a Dramatic Arts student, and always participates in class discussions. He is Tsonga speaking. He speaks confidently. His written work, which was weak at the beginning of the year, improved steadily during the course of the year. He is particularly interested in script-writing.

MABELA joined my class in the second semester. He is 20–25 years old, and very talkative. He often asks questions in class. He is from Pietersberg, and his home language is Sepedi. He is very good friends with Leonard, but they are sometimes disruptive in class.

MBALI is 21 years old. She is from Limpopo. She speaks Tswana. She is doing a BA degree and hopes to work in Psychology. She speaks her mind and is an ardent defender of women's rights. She often asks questions in class.

MUSA is a 20–25 year old male from KwaZulu Natal. He is Tswana speaking. He is a friendly student who is doing an LLB. He joined my class in the second semester. He studied previously at Vista University.

NATALIE is a 20-year old Portuguese speaking female. She was born in South Africa, but moved to Maputo as a child. She was taught basic English at school, but Portuguese was the medium of instruction. She had to make a difficult choice to come to South Africa to study, while her family remained in Maputo. She hopes to improve her English.

NOTHANDO is an under-20 year old female who is also doing an LLB. She is from the Northern Province and is Tsonga speaking. She is an enthusiastic student, who is eager to learn more. She sometimes feels lonely being far from home.

OSCAR is a 26–30 year old Visual Arts student from Zimbabwe. He obtained an Art qualification in Zimbabwe at what he refers to as a 'lower level', and came to South Africa to study further following political struggles in which he was involved in Zimbabwe. He has exhibited his art and is known for his rock art, which he paints onto fabric. He has also exhibited for former US President Clinton, and says he has had a piece of art on display in the White House. He also has clients in Europe. Oscar is extremely talkative in class, and always offers an opinion. He gets on very well with everyone in class, and his spoken and written English appear to be improving. At the beginning of the year he wanted to discontinue English, but said he is glad he eventually did not do so. In the first semester he would carry his *mbira* (African thumb piano) to class, which he played for us. Toward the end of the first semester he started to carry around a digital camera, and then a laptop, on which he also listened to music. He often e-mailed photographs to students in class.

PRECIOUS is an 18-year old female who was born in South Africa. She speaks siSwati at home. She is very hard working and tends to score good marks in all her assignments. She is quiet and serious in class.

SIBONELO is 20–25 years old. He is from Limpopo and speaks Sepedi at home. He says he is from a very disadvantaged background. He is an LLB student who often quotes from the South African Constitution to support his arguments.

XING is a 20–25 year old male who is from Shanghai, China. He studied briefly at the University of Shanghai before coming to study B. Comm in South Africa, where he hopes to improve his English. He has been in South Africa for two years. His home language is Mandarin. He does not participate much in class, and refers to his digital dictionary when he needs to use a particular English word in class.

ZINHLE is a 20-year old male from Gauteng. He is Xhosa speaking. He joined my class in the second semester, and is very quiet in class, sometimes appearing disinterested.

Bibliography

Abdullah, M.H. (2001) 'Social Presence in Online Conferences: What makes people real?' Paper presented at the 2nd Malaysia International Conference on Languages, Literatures and Cultures. 17–19 April 2001. Kuala Lampur, Malaysia.

African Virtual University. http://www.avu.org Last accessed 31 December 2005.

Albrektson, R.J. (1995) 'Mentored online seminar: a model for graduate level distance learning', *T.H.E. Journal*, October Issue, pp.1–6. http://www.thejournal.com/Magazine/vault/A1175.cfm Last accessed 30 December 2005.

Aldrich, R. (2001) 'Situated Learning'. http://hale.pepperdine.edu/~rsaldric/situated.html Last accessed 30 December 2005.

Alexiades, J., Gipson, S. and Morey-Nase, G. (2001) 'Deconstructing "the classroom": Situating learning with the help of the World Wide Web', Teaching and Learning Forum. Proceedings of the 10th Annual Teaching Learning Forum, 7–9 February 2001. Perth: Curtin University of Technology. http://lsn.curtin.edu.au/tlf/tlf2001/alexiades.html Last accessed 30 December 2005.

Ally, M. (2004) 'Foundations of educational theory for online learning', in Anderson, T. and Elloumi, F. (eds), *Theory and Practice of Online Learning*, Canada: Athabasca University. http://cde.athabascau.ca/online_book/ Last accessed 31 December 2005.

Ancker, P. A. (2002) 'The challenge and opportunity of technology: an interview with Mark Warschauer', *English Teaching Forum*, October issue, pp.2–8.

Appleton, K. (1996) 'Using learning theory to guide reflection in school', *Asia-Pacific Journal of Teacher Education*, vol.24, no.2, pp.147–58.

Aronson, J. (1994) 'Pragmatic view of thematic analysis', *The Qualitative Report*, vol.2, no.1. http://www.nova.edu/ssss/QR/BackIssues/QR2-1/aronson.html Last accessed 31 December 2005.

Asmal, K. (2000) Address at the National Association of Distance Education Awards Ceremony for Courseware Development, South African College of Teacher Education. Groenkloof, Pretoria.

Barab, S. (2000) 'Communities of practice', University of Indiana http://inkido.Indiana.edu/research/vrcamp.html Last accessed 26 November 2001.

Barton, D. and Hamilton, M. (2000) 'Literacy Practices', in Barton, D., Hamilton, M. and Ivanic, R. (eds), *Situated Literacies: Reading and Writing in Context*, London, New York: Routledge.

Barton, D., Hamilton, M. and Ivanic, R. (2000) (eds), *Situated Literacies: Reading and Writing in Context*, London, New York: Routledge.

Barton, D. and Tusting, K. (2005) (eds), *Beyond Communities of Practice: language Power and Social Context: Learning in Doing: Social, Cognitive and Computational Perspectives*, Cambridge: Cambridge University Press.

Belisle, R. (1996) 'E-mail activities in the English second language class', *The Internet TESL Journal*, vol.2, no.12. http://iteslj.org/Articles/Belisle-Email.html Last accessed 31 December 2005.

Berge, Z.L. (1995) 'Facilitating computer conferencing: recommendations from the field', *Educational Technology*, vol.35, no.1, pp.22–30.

Bickmore-Brand, J. (1996) 'Bickmore-Brand's literacy and learning principles', *Stepping Out: Literacy and Learning Strategies*. EDWA.

Birkets, S. (1994) *The Gutenberg Elegies: The Fate of Reading in an Electronic Age*, Boston: Faber and Faber.

Bless, C. and Higson-Smith, C. (1995) *Fundamentals of Social Research Methods: An African Perspective*, 2nd edn, Cape Town: Juta and Co. Ltd.

Bolter, J.D. (1991) *Writing Space: The Computer, Hypertext, and the History of Writing*, Hillsdale, NJ: Lawerence Erlbaum Associates.

Bordonaro, K. (2003) 'Perceptions of technology and manifestations of language learner autonomy', *CALL-EJ Online*, vol.5, no.1. www.clec.ritsumei.ac.jp/english/callejonline/8-1/bordonaro.html Last accessed 31 December 2005.

Bourdieu, P. (1991) *Language and Symbolic Power*, Cambridge: Polity Press.

Brice-Heath, S. (1983) *Ways with Words: Language, Life, and Work in Communities and Classrooms*, Cambridge: Cambridge University Press.

Brown, I. (1999) 'Internet Treasure Hunts: a treasure of an activity for students learning English', *The Internet TESL Journal*, vol.5, no.3 http://iteslj.org/Lessons/Brown-TreasureHunts.html Last accessed 31 December 2005.

Brown, J. and Duguid, P. (2000) *The Social Life of Information*, Harvard: Harvard Business School Press.

Brush, T.A. and Uden, L. (2000) 'Using Computer-Mediated Communications to enhance instructional design class: a case study', *International Journal of Instructional Media*, vol.27, no.2, pp.157–63.

Burgstahler, S. (1997) 'Teaching On The Net: What's The Difference?' *T.H.E Journal*, April Issue, pp.1–6. http://www.Thejournal.Com/Magazine/Vault/A1365.Cfm Last accessed 20 November 2001.

Candy, P. (1991) *Self-direction for Lifelong Learning*, San Francisco: Jossey-Bass.

Carr, T., Cox, G., Eden, A. and Hanslo, M. (2004) 'From peripheral to full participation in a blended trade bargaining simulation', *British Journal of Educational Technology*, vol.35, no.2, pp.197–211.

Castells, M. (1996) *The Information Age: Economy, Society and Culture. Volume 1: The Rise of the Network Society*, Malden, MA: Blackwell Publishing Inc.

—— (2004) *The Information Age: Economy, Society and Culture. Volume 2: The Power of Identity*, Malden, MA; Oxford, UK; Victoria, Australia: Blackwell Publishing Ltd.

Chapman, J. (1996) 'A new agenda for a new society', in Leithwood. K. (ed.) *International Handbook of Educational Leadership and Administration*, Dordrecht: Kluwer.

Chick, K. (1998) 'The relationship between English and Zulu in KwaZulu Natal', in Extra, G. and Martens, J. (eds) *Multilingualism in a Multicultural Context*, Tilburg University Press: Amsterdam.

Chisholm, L. (2003) 'The use of information communication technologies in curricula', proposal submitted in terms of the Southern African Development Community Education Policy Support Initiative (SADC EPSI). Available http://www.sadceducation.com/documents/ict.doc Last accessed 14 May 2004.

Chisholm, L., Dhunpath, R. and Paterson, A. (2004) 'The use of ICTs in the curriculum in Botswana, Namibia and Seychelles', report presented to SACHES: Commissioned by Southern African Development Community Education Policy Support Initiative (SADC EPSI).

Clark, R.E (2001) 'A summary of disagreements with the "mere vehicles" argument', in Clark, R.E. (ed.) *Learning with media: Arguments, analysis and evidence*, Greenwich, CT: Information Age Publishing Inc.

—— (1983) 'Reconsidering research on learning from media', *Review of Educational Research*, vol.53, no.4, pp.445–59.

—— (1994) 'Media will never influence learning', *Educational Technology Research and Development*, vol.42, no.2, pp.21–30.

Clarke, P. and Cronje, J.C. (1998) 'Teaching "Teaching" on the Internet', in Le Roux, A. (ed.) *Media for the New Millenium: Looking into the Future*, Pretoria: Educational Media Institute of the South African Association for Research and Development in Higher Education.

Cohen, L., Manion, L., Morrison, K. (2000) *Research Methods in Education*, 5th edn, London: Routledge Falmer.

Colburn, A. (2000). 'Constructivism: Science Education's "Grand Unifying Theory"', Eric Clearing House September/October 2000, vol.74, no.1, pp.9–12.

Colorado State University (1997–2004) 'Writing at CSU: Case Studies' http://writing.colostate.edu/references/research/casestudy/pop2c.cfm Last accessed 30 July 2004.

Cope, B. and Kalantzis, M. (1993) *The Powers of Literacy: A Genre Approach to Teaching Writing*, London: Falmer Press.

Cronje, J. (1997) 'Interactive Internet: using the Internet to facilitate co-operative distance learning', *South African Journal of Higher Education*, vol.11, no.2, pp.14–156. Also available http://hagar.up.ac.za/catts/abc/rbo96.html Last accessed 31 December 2005.

—— (2000) 'Paradigms lost – towards integrating instructivism and constructivism', IT Forum paper 48. http://it.coe.uga.edu/itforum/paper48/paper48.htm Last accessed 31 December 2005.

Cronje, M. and Murdoch, N. (2001) 'Experience of lecturers using WebCT from a technology adoption perspective', paper presented at the Third Annual

Conference on World Wide Web Applications. Rand Afrikaans University. September 2001.

Crystal, D. (1997) *English as a Global Language*, Cambridge: Cambridge University Press.

—— (2001) *Language and the Internet*, Cambridge: Cambridge University Press.

Cummins, J. (2000) 'Academic language learning, transformative pedagogy, and information technology: towards a critical balance', *TESOL Quarterly*, vol.34, no.3, pp.537–48.

Cunningham, K. (2000) 'Integrating CALL into the writing curriculum', *Internet TESL Journal*, vol.6, no.5. http://iteslj.org/Articles/Cunningham-CALLWriting/ Last accessed 5 March 2002.

Czerniewicz, L. (2001) 'Reflections on learning online-the hype and the reality', *South African Journal of Higher Education*, vol.15, no.3, pp.17–23.

—— (2004) 'Cape of Storms or Cape of Good Hope? Educational technology in a changing environment', *British Journal of Educational Technology*, vol.35. no.2, pp.145–58.

Czerniewicz, L. and Brown, C. (2005) 'Access to ICTs for teaching and learning: From single artefact to inter-related resources', *International Journal of Education and Development: using Information and Communication Technology*, vol.1, issue 2, pp.42–56.

Czerniewicz, L. and Carr, T. (2005) 'Growing communities of practice among educational technology researchers and practitioners in development-oriented contexts: linking local and global debates', *International Journal of Education and Development: using Information and Communication Technology*, vol.1, issue 2, pp.3–24.

Danet, B. (2001) *Cyberplay: Communicating Online*, Oxford: Berg.

Davey, I. (2001) 'The use of collaborative Web-page design projects for teaching EFL, with a focus on Japanese university students', *CALL-EJ Online*, vol.3, no.1. http://www.clec.ritsumei.ac.jp/english/callejonline/6-1/davey.html Last accessed 31 December 2005.

De Pourbaix, R. (2000) 'Emergent Literacy Practices in an Electronic Community', in Barton, D., Hamilton, M. and Ivanic, R. (eds) *Situated Literacies: Reading and Writing in Context*, London, New York: Routledge.

Denzin, N.K. and Lincoln, Y.S. (eds) (1998) *The Landscape of Qualitative Research: theories and issues*, California: Sage Publications.

Derewianka, B. (1993) 'Text and beyond: Literacy in the world of information technology', extract from Literacy for the New Millenium. Conference Papers from the Australian Reading Association. 1st International Conference, July 1993.

Derry, S. (1992) 'Beyond Symbolic Processing: Expanding horizons in educational psychology', *Journal of Educational Psychology*, vol.84, pp.413–18.

Downes, S. (2000). 'Giving control to students: But will they pick up the ball and run?' in Herrmann, A. and Kulski, M.M. (eds) *Flexible Futures in Tertiary*

Teaching, Proceedings of the 9th Annual Teaching Learning Forum, 2–5 February 2000. Perth: Curtin University of Technology.

Doyle, T.M. and Song, G. (2005) 'Writing and identity in adult non-credit bearing level classes', proceedings of the CATESOL State Conference, 2005.

Dreyer, C. (1995) 'Identifying ESL learning problems in multilingual classrooms at university', *Journal for Language Teaching*, vol.9, part 1, pp.285–96.

Du Pre, R. (2002) 'Coping with changes in higher education in South Africa' http://www.face.stir.ac.uk/Paper101-RoyduPre_000htm Last accessed 14 October 2003.

Duncan, B. and Leander, K.M. (2001) 'Constructing maps for the new promised land: learning, community and the Internet' http://lrs.ed.uiuc.edu/students/k-leand/tlp/aera_abs_internet.html Last accessed 31 December 2005.

Durban Institute of Technology website www.dit.ac.za Last accessed 31 December 2005.

Fang, X. and Warschauer, M. (2004) 'Technology and curricular reform in China: A case study', *TESOL Quarterly*, vol.38, no.2, pp.301–23.

Feenberg, A. (1991) *Critical Theory of Technology*, New York: Oxford University Press.

GautengOnline Project, www.gautengonline.com Last accessed 31 December 2005.

Gee, J.P. (1996) *Social Linguistics and Literacies: Ideology in Discourses* 2nd edn, London: The Falmer Press, Taylor Francis Inc.

—— (1997) 'Foreword: A Discourse approach to language and literacy', in Lankshear, C. (ed.) *Changing Literacies*, Buckingham, Philadelphia: Open University Press.

—— (2000) 'The New Literacy Studies', in Barton, D., Hamilton, M. and Ivanic, R. (eds), *Situated Literacies: Reading and Writing in Context*, London, New York: Routledge.

Goodfellow, R. (2004) 'Online literacies and learning: operational, cultural and critical dimensions', *Language and Education*, vol.18, no.5, pp.379–99.

Gordin, D.N., Gomez, L.M., Pea, R.D. and Fishman, B.J. (1996) 'Using the World Wide Web to build Learning Communities in K-12', *Journal of Computer Mediated Communication*, vol.2, no.3, http://www.ascusc.org/jcmc/vol2/issue3/gordin.html Last accessed 26 November 2001.

Graddol, D. (1997) *The Future of English*, London: The British Council.

Granville, S. and Dison, L. (2005) 'Thinking about thinking: Integrating self-reflection into an academic literacy course', *Journal of English for Academic Purposes*, vol.4, pp.99–118.

Greenfield, R. (2003) 'Collaborative e-mail exchange for teaching secondary ESL: a case study in Hong Kong', *Language Learning and Technology*, vol.7, no.1, pp.46–70.

Greyling, F. and Pete, M. (2001) 'Making the gears work- a dual perspective on the management and implementation of e-learning at South African Technikons',

Paper presented at the 3rd Annual Conference on World Wide Web Applications, September 2001, Rand Afrikaans University.

Gunton, T. (1993) *Dictionary of Information Technology*, London: Penguin.

Hall, M.C. (1990) *Women and Identity: Value Choices in a Changing World*, New York, Washington, Philedelphia, London: Hemisphere Publishing Corporation.

Hall, S. (1992) 'The question of cultural identity', in Hall, S., Held, D. and McGrew, T. (eds) *Modernity and its Futures*, Cambridge: Polity Press in association with Blackwell Publishers and the Open University.

Hara, N. and Kling, R. (1999) 'Students' frustrations with a web-based distance education course', *First Monday*, vol.4, no.12, http://firstmonday.org/issues/issue4_12/hara/index.html Last accessed 31 December 2005.

Harasim, L., Hilz, L. and Turoff, M. (1994) *A Field Guide to Teaching and Learning Online*, Massachusetts: MIT Press.

Harris, S. (2005) 'PCs more hindrance than help', *The Star*, 23 March 2005.

Hartshorne, K.B. (1987) 'Language policy in African education in South Africa, 1910 – 1985, with particular reference to the issue of medium of instruction', in Young, D. (ed.) *Bridging the Gap: Essays in Honour of L.W. Lanham*, UK: Maskew Miller Longman.

Hedegaard, M. (1990) 'The zone of proximal development as basis for instruction', in Moll, L.C. (ed.) *Vygotsky and Education: Instructional Implications and Applications of Sociohistorical Psychology*, New York, NY: Cambridge University Press.

Herring, S. (1996) *Computer-mediated Communication: Linguistic, Social and Cross-Cultural Perspectives*, Amsterdam: John Benjamins.

Hildreth P., Kimble C. and Wright P. (2000) 'Communities of practice in the distributed international environment', *The Journal of Knowledge Management*, MCB University Press, vol.4, no.1, pp.27–37. Also available http://uk.arxiv.org/ftp/cs/papers/0101/0101012.pdf Last accessed 24 December 2005.

Ho, C.M.L. (2000) 'Developing intercultural awareness and writing skills through e-mail exchange', *Internet TESL Journal*, vol.6, no.12, http://iteslj.org/Articles/Ho-Email.html Last accessed 31 December 2005.

Hodgkinson-Williams, C. and Mostert, M. (2005) 'Online debating to encourage student participation in online learning environments: a qualitative case study at a South African university', *International Journal of Education and Development: using Information and Communication Technology*, vol.1, issue 2, pp.94–104.

Horne, F. and Heinemann, G. (2003) *English in Perspective*, Cape Town: Oxford University Press.

Huff, C. and King, R. (1988) 'An experiment in electronic collaboration', in Goodchild, J.D. (ed.) *Interacting by Computer: Effects on Small Group Style and Structure*, American Psychological Association: Atlanta.

Huffaker, D. (2004) *Gender similarities and differences in online identity and language use among teenage bloggers.* Unpublished Masters thesis, Georgetown University.

Hymes, D. (1971) 'Sociolinguistics and the ethnography of speaking', in Ardener, E. (ed.) *Social Anthropology and Language*, London: Tavistock, pp.47–93.

ICT Empowerment Charter (2005) 'Draft Black Economic Empowerment Charter for the ICT Sector', ICT Steering Committee www.ictcharter.org.za/ Last accessed 31 December 2005.

Internet World Statistics. Available on http://www.internetworldstats.com/af/za.htm Last accessed 20 April 2007.

Ivanic, R. (1998) *Writing and Identity*, Amsterdam: John Benjamins Publishing.

Janesick, V.J. (1998) 'The dance of qualitative research design: metaphor, methodolatory, and meaning', in Denzin, N.K and Lincoln, S.L. (eds) *Strategies of Qualitative Enquiry*, Thousand Oaks, California: Sage.

Janks, H. (2004) 'The access paradox', *English in Australia*, Issue 139, pp.33–42.

Jaramillo, J.A. (1996) 'Vygotsky's Sociocultural theory and contributions to the development of constructivist curricula', *Education*, vol.117, no.1, pp.133–40.

Jarvis, H. (2003) 'A framework for investigating the practice of CALL' Paper presented at the 21st World Congress of the World Federation of Modern Language Associations, 2–5 July 2003, Rand Afrikaans University, South Africa.

—— (2004) 'Investigating the classroom applications of computers on EFL courses at Higher Education Institutions in UK', *Journal of English for Academic Purposes*, vol.3, pp.111–37.

Johnson, M.M. and Huff, M.T. (2000) 'Students' use of computer-mediated communication in a distance education course', *Research on Social Work Practice*, vol.10, no.4, pp.1–11.

Jones, J. (2001) 'CALL and the teacher's role in promoting learner autonomy', *CALL-EJ Online*, vol.3, no.1, www.clec.ritsumei.ac.jp/english/callejonline/6-1/jones.html Last accessed 31 December 2005.

Jor, G.C.K. and Mak, L. (1994) 'International e-mail projects in ESL curriculum: what works, what doesn't?' Proceedings of the Tel-Ed Conference, 1994.

Kahmi-Steyn, L.D. (2000) 'Looking into the future of TESOL teacher education: Web-based bulletin board discussions in a methods course', *TESOL Quarterly*, vol.34, no.3, pp.423–55.

Kajee, L. (2000) *Language in the workplace: an investigation into language policy and training and development at ESKOM, with specific reference to departmental practice*, Unpublished Masters dissertation. University of Natal: Durban.

—— (2001) 'Language policy and practice: observations of an interventionist strategy at ML Sultan Technikon', *South African Journal of Higher Education*, vol.15, no.3, pp.39–45.

—— (2002) 'Online in South Africa: Tears and Joys', Proceedings of the International Conference on Information Technology and Universities of Asia (ITUA 2002). Bangkok, Thailand, pp.219–33.

—— (2003) 'A Case Study in South Africa: Going online in under-resourced ESL classes', *Academic Exchange Quarterly*, Spring Issue, pp.102–7. http://www.rapidintellect.com/AEQweb/spri03.htm Last accessed 31 December 2005.

—— (2005a) 'Sites of struggle, sites of opportunity: constructions of identity, relationships and participation in online communities of practices', *Perspectives in Education*, vol.23, no.4, pp.39–53.

—— (2005b) 'Technology for social inclusion: telling virtual stories.' Proceedings of the Second International Reading Matrix Online Conference on Second and Foreign Language Teaching and Research, Long Beach, California, 16–18 September 2005, pp.103–25. http://www.readingmatrix.com/conference/pp/proceedings2005/kajee.pdf Last accessed 31 December 2005.

Kamwangamalu, N.M. (2000) 'Language policy and mother-tongue education in South Africa: the case study for a market-oriented approach', Georgetown University Round Table on Languages and Linguistics 2000, pp.119–34.

Kamwangamalu, N.M. (2003) 'Globalisation of English, and language maintenance and shift in South Africa', *International Journal of the Sociology of Language*, vol.164, pp.65–81.

Kannan, J. and MackNish, C. (2000) 'Issues affecting online ESL learning: A Singapore case study', *Internet TESL Journal*, vol.6, no.2, http://iteslj.org/Articles/Kannan-OnlineESL.html Last accessed 31 December 2005.

Karyan, S. and Crowe, J. (1997) 'Student perceptions of electronic discussion groups', *T.H.E. Journal*, April Issue, pp.1–4, http://www.Thejournal.Com/Magazine/Vault/A1367.Cfm Last accessed 18 September 2003.

Kearsley, G. (1998) 'A guide to online education' http://home.sprynet.com/~gkearsley/cyber.htm Last accessed 21 November 2001.

Keats, D.W., Collins, J. and Peterson, Y. (2001) 'The Internet as an outreach tool: the UWC case', *South African Journal of Higher Education*, vol.15, no.2, pp.185–93.

Kennard, W.E. (2001) 'Equality in the Information Age', in Compaine, B.M. (ed.) *The Digital Divide: facing a crisis or creating a myth?* Massachusetts: MIT Press.

Kern, R. and Warschauer, M. (2000) 'Theory and practice of networked-based language teaching', in Warschauer, M. and Kern, R. (eds) *Networked-based language teaching: concepts and practice*, New York: Cambridge University Press.

Kessler, G. (2001) 'Online course management', *The Ohio TESOL Newsletter*, vol.25, no.2, pp.11–15.

Knobel, M. and Lankshear, C. (2002) 'Critical cyberliteracies: What young people can teach us about reading and writing the world', Keynote address at the National Council of English Teachers' Assembly for Research Mid-Winter

Conference, New York, www.geocities.com/c.lankshear/cyberliteracies.html?200522 Last accessed 31 December 2005.

Knowles, M. (1975) *Self-directed Learning: A Guide for Learners and Teachers*, New York: Association Press.

Knowles, M. (1980) *The Modern Practice of Adult Education: From Pedagogy to Andragogy*, Chicago: Follett.

Koszalka, T.A. (2001). 'Effects of computer-mediated communications on teachers' attitudes towards using web resources in the classroom', *Journal of Industrial Psychology*, vol.28, no.2, pp.1–11.

Krashen, S. (1981) *Second Language Acquisition and Second Language Learning*, Oxford: Pergamon.

Kurek, M. (2002) 'The Internet in ESL College Education: A proposal for the Internet-enhanced college course', *Teaching English with Technology: A Journal for Teachers of English*, vol.2, no.5, http://www.iatefl.org.pl/call/j_article11.htm Last accessed 31 December 2005.

Lally, V. and Barret, E. (1999) 'Building a learning community online: towards socioacademic interaction', *Research Papers in Education*, vol.14, no.2, pp.147–63.

Lam, W.S.E. (2000) 'L2 literacy and the design of the self: a case study of a teenager's writing on the Internet', *TESOL Quarterly*, vol.34, no.3, pp.457–82.

Lam, Y. (2000) 'Technophilia versus Technophobia: a preliminary look at why second-language teachers do or do not use technology in their classrooms', *Canadian Modern Language Review*, vol.56, no.3, http://www.unb.ca/slec/Publications/Lam.html Last accessed 31 December 2005.

Langston, M.D. and Batson, T. (1990) 'The social shifts invited by working collaboratively on computer networks: The ENFI project', in Handa, C. (ed.) *Computers and Community: Teaching Composition in the Twenty-first Century.* Portsmith: Boynton/Cook.

Language in Education Policy (1997) Department of Education, Pretoria.

Language Policy of the University of the Witwatersrand (2003) www.wits.ac.za/depts/wcs/policy/languagepolicy.pdf Last accessed 31 December 2005.

Lanham, R.A. (1993) *The Electronic Word: Democracy, Technology and the Arts*, Chicago: University of Chicago Press.

Lankshear, C. and Knobel, M. (1997) 'Different worlds? Technology-mediated classroom learning and students'social practices with new technologies in home and community settings', in Lankshear, C. (ed.) *Changing Literacies*, Buckingham, Philadelphia: Open University Press.

Lankshear, C. (ed.) (1997) *Changing Literacies*, Buckingham, Philadelphia: Open University Press.

Lankshear, C. and Knobel, M. (2004) '"New" Literacies: Research and Social Practice', Plenary address at the Annual meeting of the National Reading Conference, www.geocities.com/c.lankshear/nrc.html?200522 Last accessed 31 December 2005.

—— (1997) 'Literacies, texts and difference in the electronic age', in Lankshear, C. (ed.) *Changing Literacies*, Buckingham, Philadelphia: Open University Press.

Lave, J. and Wenger, E. (1996) 'Practice, person, social world' in Daniels, H. (ed.) *An Introduction to Vygotsky*, London and New York: Routledge.

—— (1991) *Situated Learning: Legitimate Peripheral participation*, Cambridge: Cambridge University Press.

—— (2002) 'Legitimate peripheral participation in communities of practice', in Lea, M.R. and Nicolls, K. (eds) *Distributed learning: social and cultural approaches to practice*, London: Routledge-Falmer.

Lazenby, K. (1996) 'How to achieve mobility in South African higher education', *South African Journal of Higher Education*, vol.10, no.2, pp.30–8.

Lee, K.W. (2000) 'English teachers' barriers to the use of computer-assisted language learning', *The Internet TESL Journal*, vol.6, no.12, http://iteslj.org/Articles/Lee-CALLbarriers.html Last accessed 31 December 2005.

Lee, L. (2004) 'Learners' perspectives on networked collaborative interaction with native speakers of Spanish in the US', *Language Learning and Technology*, vol.8, no.1, pp.83–100.

Lelliott, A.; Pendlebury, S. and Enslin, P. (2000) 'Promises of access and inclusion: online education in Africa', *Journal of Philosophy of Education*, vol.34, no.1, pp.41–52.

Leloup, J.W. and Ponterio, R. (2000) 'Enhancing authentic language learning experiences through Internet technology', *ERIC Digest* http://www.cal.org/resources/digest/0002enhancing.html Last accessed 31 December 2005.

Lemmer, E.M. (1996) 'Selected linguistic realities in South African schools: problems and prospects', *Educare*, vol.24, no.2, pp.82–96.

Liao Chao, C. (1999) 'E-mailing to improve English foreign learners' reading and writing abilities: Taiwan experience', *The Internet TESL Journal*, http://iteslj.org/Articles/Liao-Emailing.html Accessed 31 December 2005.

Lundall, P. and Howell, C. (2000) 'Computers in schools: A national survey of Information Communication Technology in South African schools', Education Policy Unit, University of the Western Cape.

Mak, L. (1995a) 'The WWW as a resource for language education', Language Centre, Hong Kong University of Science and Technology, http://home.ust.hk/~lclindam/apweb96/linda.htm Last accessed 31 December 2005.

—— (1995b) 'Language learning of a new kind', Language Centre, Hong Kong University of Science and Technology, http://www.hkwebsym.org.hk/95/newLearn.html Last accessed 17 June 2003.

Makgoro, J.M. (1998) 'Ubuntu and the Law in South Africa' http://epf.ecoport.org/appendix3.html Last accessed 26 December 2005.

Marcos, K. (1994) 'Internet for Language Teachers', *ERIC Digest*, ERIC Clearinghouse on Languages and Linguistics www.cal.org/resources/digest/marcos01.html Last accessed 31 December 2005.

Martin, K. (2000) 'Learning Theories, Processes and Models: Issues of Teaching and Learning', The University of Western Australia, http://www.csd.uwa.edu.au/newsletter/issue0100/processes.html Last accessed 31 December 2005.

Matsuda, P.K., Canagarajah, S., Harklau, L., Hyland, K. and Warschauer, M. (2003) 'Changing currents in second language writing research: a colloquium', *Journal of Second Language Writing*, vol.12, pp.151–79.

Mbeki, T. (2002) 'State of the Nation Address' www.info.gov.za/speeches/son/ Last accessed 30 December 2005.

—— (2003) 'State of the Nation Address' www.info.gov/speeches/son Last accessed 30 December 2005.

—— (2004) 'State of the Nation Address' www.info.gov/speeches/son Last accessed 30 December 2005.

—— (2005) 'State of the Nation Address' www.info.gov/speeches/son Last accessed 30 December 2005.

McGuire, T., Kiesler, S. and Siegel, J. (1987) 'Group and computer mediated discussion effects in risk decision making', *Journal of Personality and Social Psychology*, vol.52, no.5, pp.917–30.

Mello, V. (1998) 'Report on a penpal project and tips for penpal-project success', *Internet TESL Journal*, vol.4, no.1, http://iteslj.org/Techniques/Mello-Penpal.html Last accessed 31 December 2005.

Meraka Institute, African Advanced Institute for Information and Communication Technology, www.meraka.org.za Last accessed 30 December 2005.

Meskill, C. and Mossop, J. (2000) 'Electronic texts in ESOL classrooms', *TESOL Quarterly*, vol.34, no.3, pp.261–77.

Moll, L.C. (ed.) (1990) *Vygotsky and Education: Instructional Implications and Applications of Sociohistorical Psychology*, New York, NY: Cambridge University Press.

Moote, S. (2002) 'Evaluation considerations for online ESL courses', *Internet TESL Journal*, vol.8, no.3 http://iteslj.org/Articles/Moote-Evaluation.html Last accessed 31 December 2005.

Moran, C. and Hawisher, G.E. (1998) 'The rhetorics and languages of electronic mail', in Snyder, I. (ed.) *Page to Screen: Taking Literacy into the Electronic age*, London, New York, Canada: Routledge.

Muianga, X.J. (2005) 'Blended online and face-to-face learning: a pilot project in the faculty of Education, Eduardo Mondlane University', *International Journal of Education and Development: using Information and Communication Technology*, vol.1, issue 2, pp.130–44.

Murphy, E. (2000) *Strangers in a strange land: teachers' beliefs about teaching and learning French as a second or foreign language in online learning environments*, Unpublished PhD thesis, Faculty of Science Education, University Laval, Quebec, www.ucs.mun.ca/~emurphy/strangers/toc.html Last accessed 31 December 2005.

Murray, D.E. (2000) 'Protean communication: the language of computer-mediated communication', *TESOL Quarterly*, vol.34, no.3, pp.397–421.

Norton, B. (1997) 'Language, identity, and the ownership of English', *TESOL Quarterly*, vol.31, no.3, pp.409–29.

—— (2000) *Identity and Language Learning: Gender, ethnicity and educational change*, London, New York: Longman.

Norton-Pierce, B. (1995) 'Social identity, investment, and language learning', *TESOL Quarterly*, vol.29, pp.9–31.

Nunan, D. (1992) *Research Methods in Language Learning*, Cambridge: Cambridge University Press.

O'Dowd, R. (2001) 'In search of a truly global network: the opportunities and challenges of on-line intercultural communication', *CALL-EJ Online*, vol.3, no.1, www.clec.ritsumei.ac.jp/english/callejonline/6-1/o_dowd.html Last ac–cessed 31 December 2005.

O'Dowd, R. (2004) *Network-based language teaching and the development of intercultural communicative competence*, Unpublished PhD thesis, University of Essen, Germany.

Odendaal, A. (2001) 'The development of interactive online learning for distance education: a South African case study', paper presented at the Third Annual Conference on World Wide Web Applications, September 2001, Rand Afrikaans University.

Pathak, A. (2001) 'Teacher-made activities for a computer-based ESL/EFL class', *The Internet TESL Journal*, vol.7, no.7, http://iteslj.org/Lessons/Pathak-ComputerClass.html Last accessed 31 December 2005.

Pereira, L. (1996) 'Stepping out with the constructivists', *Australian Science Teachers' Journal*, vol.42, no.2, pp.26–8.

Peyton, J.K. (1990) 'Technological innovation meets institution: birth of creativity or murder of a great idea?' *Computers and Composition*, no.7, pp.15–32.

Piaget, J. (1977) *Equilibration of Cognitive Structures*, New York: Viking Press.

Pickard, V. (2002) 'Internet Listening', Paper presented at the CALLAsia/ITUA Conference, April 2002, Bangkok, Thailand.

Raven, F. (2005) 'Technology for social inclusion: An Interview with Mark Warschauer', EDC Centre for Media and Community, http://www.digitaldivide.net/articles/view.php?ArticleID=102 Last accessed 31 December 2005.

Reeves, T.C. (1998) 'The impact of media and technology in schools: a research report prepared for the Bertelsman Foundation', University of Georgia, http://www.athensacademy.org/instruct/media_tech/reeves0.html Last accessed 31 December 2005.

Rheingold, H. (1993, 2000) *The Virtual Community*, Reading, MA: Addison-Wesley, MIT.

Riddle, E. (1999) 'Lev Vygotsky's social development theory', available on http://chd.gse.gmu.edu/immersion/knowledgebase/theorists/constructivism/vygotsky.htm Last accessed 31 December 2005.

Rogoff, B. (2003) *The Cultural Nature of Human Development*, New York: Oxford University Press.

Roszak, T. (1994) *The cult of information: a neo-Luddite treatise on high-tech, artificial intelligence, and the true art of thinking*, Berkeley, CA: University of California Press.

Sakar, A. (2001) 'The cross-cultural effects of electronic mail exchange on the Turkey University students of English as a foreign language (EFL)', *CALL-EJ Online*, vol.3, no.1, http://www.clec.ritsumei.ac.jp/english/callejonline/6-1/sakar.html Last accessed 31 December 2005.

Sanders, M. and Ayayee, E. (1997) 'Engaging learners in computer-aided learning: Putting the horse before the cart', proceedings of the Fourteenth Annual Convention of the Association for Computers in Learning in Tertiary Education, pp.528–37. 8–10 December 1997, Curtin University of Technology, Perth, Australia.

Schneiderman, B. (1997) 'Foreword', in Debski, R., Gassin, J. and Smith, M. (eds) *Language learning through social computing*, Melbourne: Applied Linguistics Association of Australia.

Schutz, R. (2002) 'Vygotsky and language acquisition' http://www.sk.com.br/sk-vygot.html Last accessed 31 December 2005.

Scotellaro, G. (2002) 'Radio broadcasting: a macro task for ESL and foreign language students', Paper presented at the CALLAsia/ITUA Conference, April 2002, Bangkok, Thailand.

Setati, M., Adler, J., Reed,Y. and Bapoo, A. (2002) 'Incomplete journeys: code-switching and other language practices in Mathematics, Science and English language classrooms in South Africa', *Multilingual Matters: Language and Education*, vol.16, no.2, pp.128–49.

Shaw, S. and Polovina, S. (1999) 'Practical experiences of, and lessons learnt from, internet technologies in higher education', *Educational Technology and Society*, vol.2, no.3 http://ifets.ieee.org/periodical/vol_3_99/stephen_shaw.pdf Last accessed 31 December 2005.

Silva, P. (1997) 'South African English: oppressor or liberator?' http://www.ru.ac.za/affiliates/dsae/MAVEN.HTML Last accessed 14 October 2003.

Sinclair, J.M. and Coulthard, R.M. (1975) *Towards an analysis of discourse: The English used by teachers and pupils*, London: Oxford University Press.

Singhal, M. (1997) 'The Internet and foreign language education: benefits and challenges', *Internet TESL Journal*, vol.3, no.6, http://iteslj.org/Articles/Singhal-Internet.html Last acessed 31 December 2005.

Skinner, B.F. (1953) *Science and Human Behavior*, New York: Simon and Schuster.

Smith, M.J. (1999) 'Strands in the Web: Community-building strategies in online fanzines', *Journal of Popular Culture*, vol.33, no.2, pp.87–99.

South Africa (1994) *White Paper on Education and Training, Government Gazette No 16312*, Cape Town: Parliament of the Republic of South Africa.
South Africa (1996) *Green Paper on Higher Education Transformation*, Government Printers: Pretoria.
South Africa (1996) *The Constitution of the Republic of South Africa, Act No.108*, Government Printers: Pretoria.
South Africa (1997) *Higher Education Act 101 of 1997*, Pretoria.
South Africa (2001) *National Plan for Higher Education*, Pretoria.
South Africa (2004) *Draft White Paper on e-Education*, Pretoria.
South African Development Community (SADC) e-readiness Review and Strategy, available on www.schoolnetafrica.net/fileadmin/resources/SADC_report.htm Last accessed November 2005.
South African Institute of Distance Education (SAIDE) (1997) *The Green Paper on Higher Education: An Open Learning Perspective.*
South African Institute of Distance Education (SAIDE) (2000a) *ICTs and South African Higher Education.*
South African Institute of Distance Education (SAIDE) (2000b) *Lessons in the application of educational technology in South Africa*
South African Institute of Distance Education (SAIDE) (2003) *Computers in schools.*
Spurrett, D. (2005) 'Computer-supported development of critical reasoning skills', *International Journal of Education and Development: using Information and Communication Technology*, vol.1, issue 2, pp.57–69.
Statistics South Africa, 2001 Census. Available on http://www.statssa.gov.za Accessed 20 April 2007.
Stevens, V. (1989) 'A direction for CALL: from behaviorism to humanistic courseware', in Pennington, M. (ed.) *Teaching Languages with Computers*, La Jolla, CA: Athelson.
Stockley, D. (2005) 'What is e-learning?' http://derekstockley.com.au/elearning-definition.html Last accessed 31 December 2005.
Street, B. (1984) *Literacy in Theory and Practice*, Cambridge: Cambridge University Press.
—— (1998) 'New literacies in theory and practice: what are the implications for language in education?' *Linguistics and Education*, vol.10, no.1, pp.1–24.
—— (2003) 'The implications of the "New Literacy Studies" for literacy education', in Goodman, S., Lillis, T., Maybin, J. and Mercer, N. (eds) *Language, Literacy and Education: A Reader*, London: Trentham Books, Open University Press.
—— (ed.) (1993) *Cross-cultural Approaches to Literacy*, Cambridge: Cambridge University Press.
Tella, S. (1991) 'Introducing international communications networks and electronic mail into foreign language classrooms: A case study in Finnish senior secondary schools', Helsinki: Department of Teacher Education, University of Helsinki, http://www.helsinki.fi/~tella/95.pdf Last accessed 31 December 2005.

Thutong Portal, Department of Education, www.thutong.org.za Last accessed 30 December 2005.
Tillyer, A. (1993). 'Discourse analysis of student e-mail writing', *CAELL Journal*, vol.4, no.3, pp.20–5.
Titlestad, P.J.H. (1998) 'Some thoughts on English in South Africa at the present time: English at the turn of the millennium', proceedings of the English Academy of South Africa Conference, Johannesburg College of Education.
Tobin, K. (1990) 'Social constructivist perspectives on the reform of science education', *Australian Science Teachers Journal*, vol.36, pp.29–35.
Topper, A. (undated) Global connections. LETSNet, Michigan State University College of Education and Ameritech, http://commtechlab.msu.edu/sites/letsnet/noframes/bigideas/b3/b3theor.html Last accessed 31 December 2005.
Tudge, J. (1990) 'Vygotsky, the zone of proximal development and peer collaboration: implications for classroom practice', in Moll, L.C. (ed.) *Vygotsky and Education: Instructional Implications and Applications of Sociohistorical Psychology*, New York, NY: Cambridge University Press.
Turkington, T. and Frank, R. (2005) 'DITonline: a journalistic experiment in blended, collaborative teaching and learning', *International Journal of Education and Development: using Information and Communication Technology*, vol.1, issue 2, pp.145–55.
Turkle, S. (1995) *Life on the Screen: Identity in the Age of the Internet*, New York: Simon and Schuster.
Underwood, J.H. (1984) *Linguistics, Computers, and the Language Teacher: A Communicative Approach*, Massachusetts: Newbury House.
University of the Witwatersrand website, www.wits.ac.za Last accessed 31 December 2005.
Van Buren-Schele, C. and Odendaal, A. (2001) 'Challenges facing developing countries in the design and delivery of online courses', paper presented at the 3rd Annual Conference on World Wide Web Applications. Rand Afrikaans University, South Africa.
Van der Merwe, A.D. (2004) *Evaluating the integration of ICTs into teaching and learning activities at a South African higher education institution*, unpublished PhD thesis, University of Stellenbosch.
Van Lier, L. (1996) *Interaction in the language curriculum: Awareness, Autonomy and Authenticity*, USA: Longman.
Von Glasersfeld, E. (1989) 'Cognition, construction of knowledge, and teaching', *Synthese*, vol.80, no.1, pp.121–40.
Vygotsky, L.S. (1978) *Mind in Society*, Cambridge, MA: Harvard University Press.
Walker, R. (1985) *Doing Research: A Handbook for Teachers*, Routledge: London.
Wall Street Journal. *Edupage*, 4 February 2002.
Warschauer, M. (1995) *E-mail for English Teaching*, Alexandria, VA: TESOL Publications.

—— (1996a) 'Comparing face-to-face and electronic discussion in the second language classroom', *CALICO Journal*, vol.13, no.2, pp.7–26.
—— (1996b) 'Computer-assisted language learning: an introduction', in Fotos, S. (ed.) *Multimedia Language Teaching*, Tokyo: Logos International.
—— (1997a) 'Computer-mediated collaborative learning: theory and practice', *Modern Language Journal*, vol.81, no.3, pp.470–81. www.gse.uci.edu/markw/cmcl.html Last accessed 3 May 2002.
—— (1997b) 'A sociocultural approach to literacy and its significance for CALL', in Murphy-Judy, K. and Sanders, R. (eds) *Nexus: The Convergence of Research and Teaching through New Information Technologies*, Durham: University of North Carolina.
—— (1999a) *Electronic Literacies: Language, Culture and Power in Online Education*, Mahwah, NJ: Lawrence Erlbaum Associates.
—— (1999b) 'Milleniumism and Media: language, literacy and technology in the 21st century', Keynote address delivered at the World Congress of Applied Linguistics (AILA), Tokyo, August 1999.
—— (2000a) 'The death of cyberspace and the rebirth of CALL', Plenary speech at the 21st Century IATEFL and ESADE Conference, 2 July 2000, Barcelona, Spain.
—— (2000b) 'The changing global economy and the future of English teaching' http://www.gse.uci.edu/markw/global.html Last accessed 3 May 2002.
—— (2000c) 'Online learning in second language classrooms: an ethnographic study', in Warschauer, M. and Kern, R. (eds) *Network-based Language Teaching: Concepts and Practice*, New York: Cambridge University Press.
—— (2000d) 'Language, identity and the Internet', in Kolko, B., Nakamura, L. and Rodman, G. (eds) *Race in Cyberspace*, New York: Routledge.
—— (2001) 'Online Communication', in Carter, R. and Nunan, D. (eds) *The Cambridge Guide to Teaching English to Speakers of other Languages*, pp.207–12, Cambridge: Cambridge University Press.
—— (2002a) 'Reconceptualising the digital divide', *First Monday*, vol.7, no.7, http://www.firstmonday.dk/issues/issue7_7/warschauer/ Last accessed 31 December 2005.
—— (2002b) 'Dissecting the "digital divide": A case study in Egypt', *The Information Society*, vol.19, pp.297–304.
—— (2002c) 'Networking into academic discourse', *Journal of English for Academic Purposes* , vol.1, pp.45–58.
—— (2003a) 'Demystifying the digital divide', *Scientific American, Inc.*, August Issue, pp.42–7.
—— (2003b) *Technology and Social Inclusion: Rethinking the Digital Divide*, Cambridge, Massachusetts: MIT Press.
—— (2004a) 'Technology and writing', in Davison, C. and Cummins, J. (eds) *Handbook of English Language Teaching*, Dordrecht, Netherlands: Kluwer.

—— (2004b) 'The rhetoric and reality of aid: Promoting educational technology in Egypt', *Globalisation, Societies, and Education*, vol.2, no.3, pp.1–30.

—— (2005, in press) 'Networking the Nile: Technology and professional development in Egypt', in Inman, J. and Hewett, B. (eds) *Technology and English Studies: Innovative professional paths*, Mahwah, NJ: Lawrence Erlbaum.

Warschauer, M. and Healey, D. (1998) 'Computers and language learning: An overview', in *Language Teaching*, Mahwah, NJ: Erlbaum Associates, Inc.

Warschauer, M., Turbee, L. and Roberts, B. (1996) 'Computer learning networks and student empowerment', *System*, vol.14, no.1, pp.1–14.

Weedon, C. (1987) *Feminist Practice and Poststructuralist Theory*, Oxford, Cambridge: Blackwell.

Wenger, E. (1998) *Communities of Practice: Learning, Meaning and Identity*, Cambridge: Cambridge University Press.

—— (2000) *Communities of Practice: Learning, Meaning and Identity* http://www.infed.org/biblio/communities_of_practice.htm Last accessed 31 December 2005.

Wertsch, J.V. (1990) 'The voice of rationality in a sociocultural approach to mind', in Moll, L.C. (ed.) *Vygotsky and Education: Instructional Implications and Applications of Sociohistorical Psychology*, New York, NY: Cambridge University Press.

Yager, R.E. and Lutz, M.V. (1994) 'Integrated Science: the importance of "how" versus "what"', *School Science and Mathematics*, vol.94, no.7, pp.338–47.

Yates, S. (1996) 'English in cyberspace', in Goodman, S. and Graddol, D. (eds) *Redesigning English: new texts, new identities*, USA, Canada: Routledge.

Yates, S.J. (1996) 'Oral and written linguistic aspects of computer conferencing: A corpus-based study', in Herring, S.C. (ed.) *Computer-mediated Communication: Linguistic, Social and Cross-cultural Perspectives*, Amsterdam: John Benjamins.

Yin, R.K. (1994) *Case Study Research: Design and Methods.* 2nd edn, London: Sage Publications.

Zafeiriou, G., Nunes, J. and Ford, N. (2001) 'Using students' perceptions of participation in collaborative learning activities in the design of online learning environments', *Education for Information*, vol.19, no.2, pp.1–20.

Index